The Criollo in the Mirror

Celebration and Identity, 1521-1821

100 años GRUPO SALINAS

MUSEO FRANZ MAYER
ARTES DECORATIVAS Y DISEÑO

THE HISPANIC SOCIETY OF AMERICA

The Criollo *in the* Mirror

Celebration and Identity, 1521-1821

Collections of Ricardo B. Salinas Pliego/Fomento Cultural Grupo Salinas
The Hispanic Society of America
Museo Franz Mayer

Fomento Cultural
Grupo Salinas

I

Si merecí Calíope
tu acento]
de divino furor mi
mente inspira,]
y en acorde compás
da a mi instrumento,]
que de marfil canoro,
a trompa aspira.]

Tu dictamen: atienda
a mi concento]
cuanto con luces
de sus rayos gira]
ardiente Febo sin
temer fracaso]
del chino oriente,
al mexicano ocaso.]

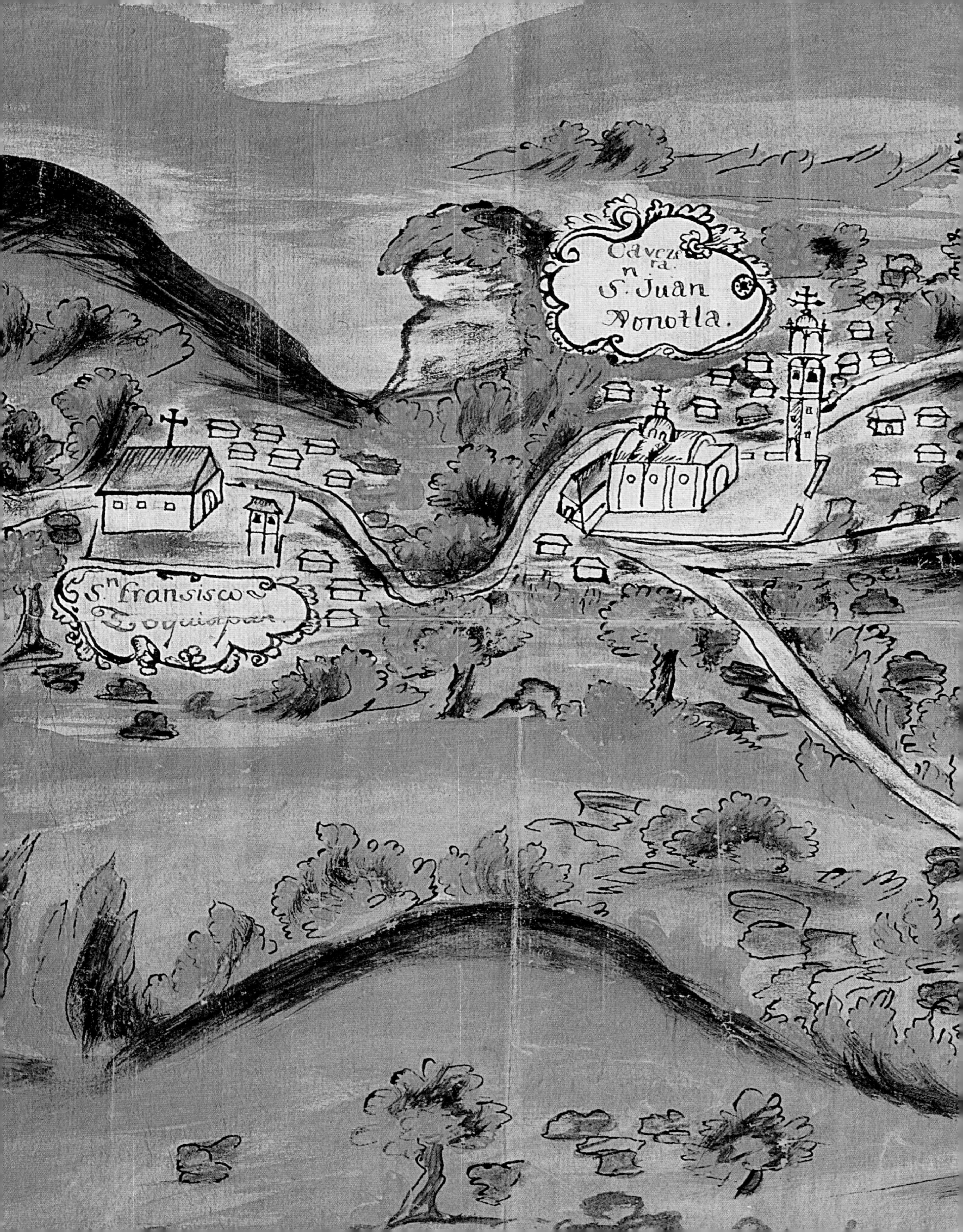
Cavezera
S.n Juan
Nonotla.
S.n Fransisco

Cavezera
Sn. Martin
Tuzamapan
Sn. Andres
Tetelilla
Sn tiago
Oleccatlan

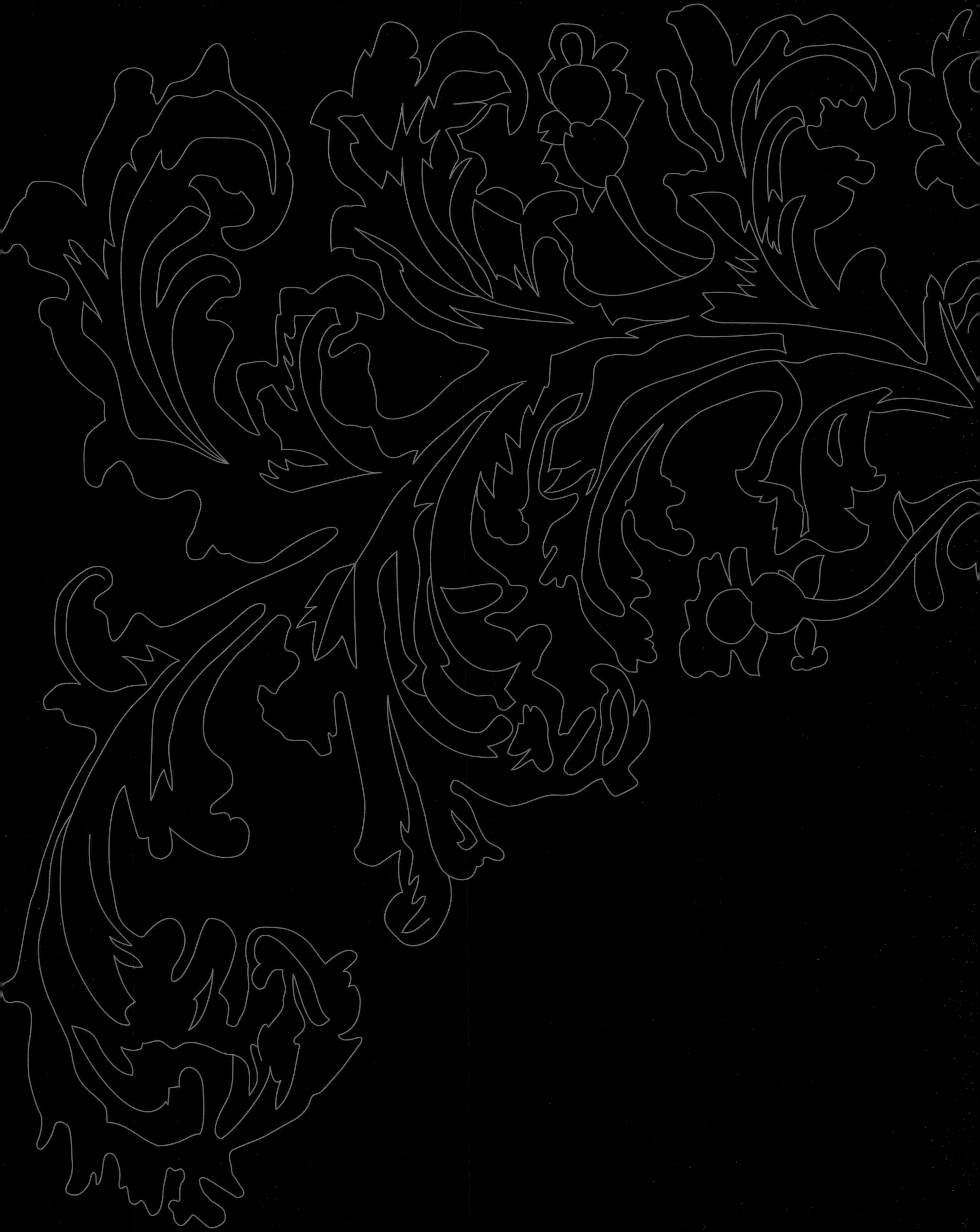

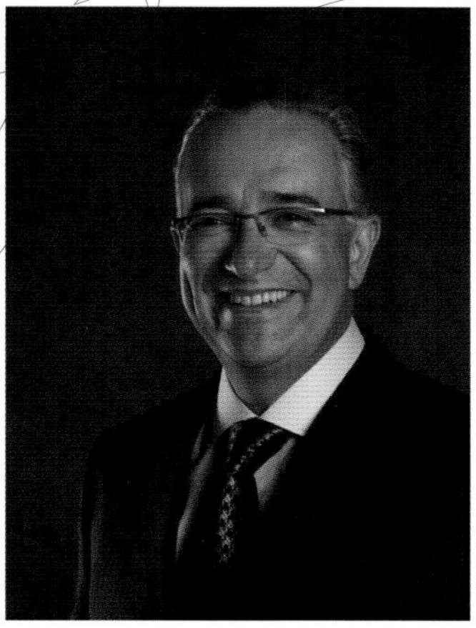

At first glance it might seem that a collector pursues, tracks down and obtains the various pieces in his collection only for himself, for the mere pleasure of owning them and creating an intimate, private universe with them. But the truth is that, in addition to this undeniable desire to build his own beautiful world, inside every collector is a noble impulse: sharing with others the collection he has built up slowly and with great effort. In fact, only when others—a relative, a friend or, even better, many and very different viewers—contemplate the pieces gathered with such care, does a collection fulfill its real task: preserving for others the works of the past, contributing to keeping alive the collective memory, essential to uniting peoples, and promoting smoother coexistence among their citizens.

That is the spirit—to preserve the past and share it to enrich our present—that motivates the collection we created and continue to expand in Fomento Cultural Grupo Salinas. That same spirit breathes in this important historical exhibition: *The Criollo in the Mirror*, an exciting documentary and iconographic journey into the past of all Mexicans, the birth of our nation, and the source of our national identity. As part of the celebrations for the Bicentennial of Independence and the Centennial of the Mexican Revolution, Fomento Cultural Grupo Salinas, The Hispanic Society of America, and the Museo Franz Mayer have decided to bring together their collections to provide an original, fresh perspective of our country, in an initiative that also had the by no means lesser merit of strengthening cultural ties between Mexico and the United States.

Through *The Criollo in the Mirror*, Fomento Cultural Grupo Salinas reaffirms its commitment to spreading knowledge and encouraging reflections that allow us to understand where we came from and where we are going. Of course, it is already clear that we can not fully imagine the latter without first looking deeply into the former.

It is a matter of pride and satisfaction for Grupo Salinas, through Fomento Cultural Grupo Salinas, that it has been the driving force behind the conceptualization and organization of this project, exhibition and book of *The Criollo in the Mirror*. It illustrates our passion and commitment to and for Mexico. This is a collective effort of great value that we are thankful for and share with all those who helped make it possible.

Ricardo B. Salinas Pliego
President and Founder Grupo Salinas

There was no doubt about it: at Fomento Cultural Grupo Salinas we were always aware of the symbolic importance of the year 2010 and the many historic achievements that, fortunately, we Mexicans continue to celebrate. In fact, since our foundation in 2001, we have been celebrating, through publications, exhibitions, contests, and many other events, the most vibrant part of our country: its art, craft, culture, its people.

The questions before us were: How could we join the celebrations for the Bicentennial of Independence and the Centennial of the Revolution? How could we provide a significant and lasting contribution to Mexican society at this very special time? We can say with pride that we decided to participate in the bicentennial commemorations in an original way: joining forces with The Hispanic Society of America and the Museo Franz Mayer for an exhibition that makes visible that invisible but absolutely essential part of each one of us: our national identity.

To make this possible, we went beyond the timeframe of the bicentennial to include a rich heritage that began to emerge from the time of the encounter between Europeans and the inhabitants of the Americas in the 16th century. In other words: we chose as our axis the figure of the criollo, the child of Spaniards settled in the Americas, the synthesis of the best of both worlds, the origin of a new temperament and the pioneer of Mexican independence and identity.

Both the exhibition *The Criollo in the Mirror* and the book the reader is holding are the result of extensive efforts that bear fruit today, allowing us enjoy the splendor of a constellation of objects, documents, and art works preserved in three wonderful collections: that of The Hispanic Society of America, a distinguished American institution founded in 1904; that of the Museo Franz Mayer, the exhibition venue; and that of Ricardo B. Salinas Pliego/Fomento Cultural Grupo Salinas.

This felicitous institutional collaboration is a privilege and the homage we pay to the richness and diversity that make us who we are as Mexicans.

Mercedes García Ocejo
Executive Director Fomento Cultural Grupo Salinas

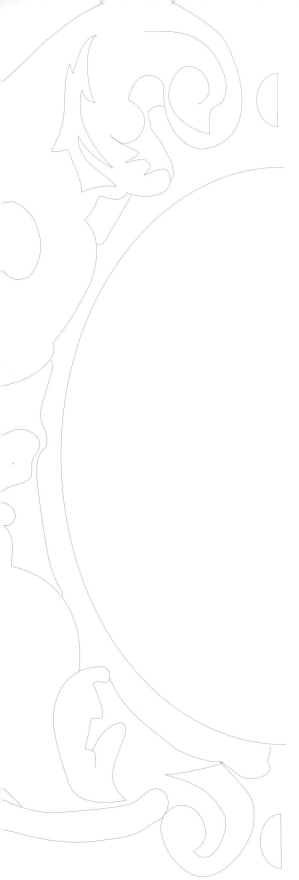

ĐMESTIZO, YĐINDIA
PRODUCE COYOTE

The Hispanic Society of America is renowned for its vast Spanish art collections, which include important works by El Greco, Velázquez, Zurbarán, Murillo, Goya, Sorolla, and Zuloaga; it is equally famous for its library of rare books and manuscripts. Among its gems are first editions of great works of Spanish literature, like *Tirant lo Blanc*, *La celestina*, *El lazarillo de Tormes*, *Don Quijote*, to mention just a few. Less well known are its exceptional collections of Mexican paintings, arts and crafts, maps, manuscripts, and rare books, dating from the viceregal era. It is with enormous pleasure that we take the opportunity of showing for the first time in Mexico an exhibition based on the rich Mexican collections of The Hispanic Society of America to celebrate the Bicentennial of the Mexican Independence. This all-time first was further enhanced by being presented next to the splendid collections of the Museo Franz Mayer and with the sponsorship of the Fomento Cultural Grupo Salinas.

The Criollo in the Mirror exhibition brought together 124 of the best Mexican colonial works from the collections of the museum and the library of The Hispanic Society of America. Many of them had never been published or exhibited before. Most of them came to The Hispanic Society of America thanks to the enlightened vision of its founder, Archer Milton Huntington (1870-1955), who devoted his life and fortune to establishing a library and a museum of Hispanic culture. Founded in 1904 by this erudite philanthropist, after many efforts over many years, the Hispanic Society of America fulfilled his desire: creating a museum free to the public and a research library for the promotion of the study of the arts and cultures of the Iberian Peninsula and Latin America. For more than a century, The Hispanic Society of America has contributed in a fundamental way to the dissemination of Hispanic culture, not only in the United States of America, but all around the world, supporting important exhibitions and hundreds of publications.

For making this groundbreaking exhibition in Mexico possible, we wish to convey our sincere thanks to Ricardo B. Salinas Pliego, President and Founder of Grupo Salinas, and to Mercedes García Ocejo, Executive Director of Fomento Cultural Grupo Salinas. We would also like to particularly thank the Museo Franz Mayer; Miguel Escobedo Fulda, President of its Patronato; and Héctor Rivero Borrell, its Director, for their resolute support of The Hispanic Society of America in carrying out this wonderful exposition. We also congratulate all the people who worked to prepare the exhibit and the catalogue, especially the exhibition's co-curator, historian Salvador Rueda Smithers, Director of the Museo Nacional de Historia Castillo de Chapultepec.

Mitchell A. Codding
Executive Director The Hispanic Society of America

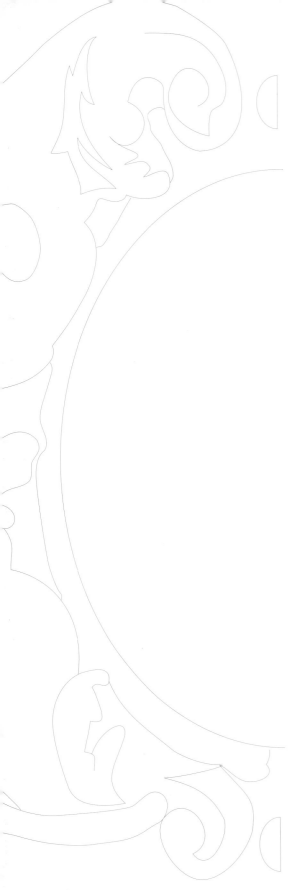

A

F
BATALLA D. SEMPUALA
A. Acude Cortes con la Caballeria

A result of Archer Milton Huntington's spirit as a collector and bibliophile, The Hispanic Society of America was established in 1904 as a library but also as a museum to encourage the study of Spanish and Portuguese art, literature, and history. It is definitely the owner of the largest number of Hispanic books and manuscripts outside the Iberian Peninsula. Although this merit has been broadly acknowledged, it is worth underlining not only the way in which it strives to preserve and study its various collections, but also to increase and disseminate them. Not long ago, the Museo Nacional de Arte showed selected paintings from The Hispanic Society of America collection, making it possible for a large number of visitors to enjoy an important and significant exhibition of Spanish art. Therefore, on this occasion, we are pleased to join efforts with The Hispanic Society of America, in partnership with Fomento Cultural Grupo Salinas, to present the exhibition *The Criollo in the Mirror* to the visitors to the Museo Franz Mayer. It brings together an interesting collection of books, documents, maps, and objets d'art from our viceregal period, many of which had never been displayed before in Mexico.

It is important to emphasize that, although the collections of The Hispanic Society of America were the foundation for this exhibition, they were complemented with pieces from the collections of Ricardo B. Salinas Pliego and the Museo Franz Mayer. And while some are key to our permanent exhibit, this inter-institutional alliance made it possible to show them outside their usual contexts, and thus to offer different interpretations, which will certainly prove to be original and new.

On behalf of the Patronato and the Museo Franz Mayer, I wish to express my deep gratitude for the trust and support of The Hispanic Society of America and Fomento Cultural Grupo Salinas, institutions and collections with which we are pleased to have shared this cultural adventure, especially in 2010, a year of enormous significance for our history. I hope that *The Criollo in the Mirror* has fostered knowledge about our past, and, particularly, allowed us to reflect about the accomplishments of New Spain that gave rise to the building and birth of Mexico as a nation.

Miguel S. Escobedo
President of the Patronato Museo Franz Mayer

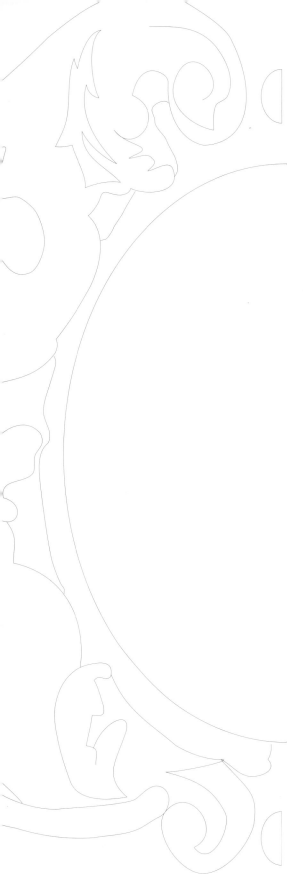

Fomento Cultural Grupo Salinas would especially like to thank Héctor Rivero Borrell, Director of Museo Franz Mayer and his Patronato, for having presented the exhibition *The Criollo in the Mirror. Celebration and identity, 1521-1821*, from october 14 to december 12, 2010. The exhibition integrated for objects, art works, maps, books and historical documents from the collections of Ricardo B. Salinas Pliego / Fomento Cultural Grupo Salinas, The Hispanic Society of America and the Museo Franz Mayer, was a contribution of Grupo Salinas to the celebrations for the Bicentennial of Independence and the Centennial of the Mexican Revolution. We would like to thank all the mentioned institutions and their people for this exhibition.

Conceptualization, Proyect and General Direction
Mercedes García Ocejo

Editorial Coordination
Miguel Fernández Félix / Bernardo Esquinca

Editorial Process
Emma Hernández Tena / Antonieta Cruz

Works Comments
Sara Gabriela Baz Sánchez

Design
Antonieta Cruz

Translation
Jaime Soler Frost / Pablo Soler Frost

Style Correction
Jenny Jiménez Herrada

Photographs
The Hispanic Society of America, pages 33, 34, 46, 77, 95, 96, 106, 107, 108, 109, 113, 114, 117, 120, 122, 134, 135, 136, 142, 149, 155, 162, 175, 176, 178, 193, 203, 207, 206, 210, 219, 220
David Eisenberg, page 9
Francisco Kochen, pages 30, 40, 42-43, 48, 50, 53, 55, 58, 61, 63, 64, 67, 70-71, 72, 75, 84-85, 86, 88-89, 92-93, 105, 111, 129, 130-131, 146-147, 153, 161, 164-165, 169, 172-173, 194, 197, 200, 204, 212, 213
Museo Franz Mayer, pages 45, 83, 133, 139, 141, 150, 166, 181, 182, 191, 199, 209, 215
Michel Zabé, Cover detail and page 26

Aknowledgments
Heather Dashner / Rafael Lemus Falcón / Roberto Mayer

Periférico Sur 4121. Col. Fuentes del Pedregal. México, D.F. 14141
Telephone(55) 1720 1313
www.gruposalinas.com
www.fomentoculturalgruposalinas.com.mx
fomentocultural@gruposalinas.com.mx
@fcgruposalinas
Fomento Cultural Grupo Salinas

First edition, 2011

ISBN: 978-607-9076-02-3

II

Oiga del septentrión
la armoniosa]
sonante lira mi
armonioso canto]
correspondiendo a su
atención gloriosa]
del clima austral el
estrellado manto.]

Alto desvelo pompa
generosa]
del cielo gloria, del
Leteo espanto]
que con voz de metal
canta Talía]
o nazca niño el sol, o
muera el día.

Introduction
The visible and invisible universe

Salvador Rueda Smithers

In a text of 1813, Father Servando Teresa de Mier defined his ideal of complete independence of New Spain. The statement foreshadowed a Magna Carta for Spanish America. The former Criollo Dominican friar argued, as he had done two decades earlier with a different thesis, that the old West Indian laws were sufficient support for the inhabitants of the north of the empire in the new world to govern themselves—they were capable of that and more—without accepting legal or theological justification of the subjection to the metropolis. Mier, like many of his contemporaries, already imagined the future face of the Mexican nation. And its root pointed to the image that New Spaniards had built for themselves over generations. They had arrived to the conclusion of a lengthy process of reflection, the pursuit of a glimpse of a particular way of being and believing, to look at themselves as if in a mirror and to define those reflections.

It is known that Servando Teresa de Mier was not alone in thinking on the separation of Spain, although he was quite original in his arguments. Since 1808, other Criollos sought the recognition of their right to political autonomy; others more struggled later for independence. At that time, the word Criollo was twofold: the most common meant a vassal of the King born in America, and the exclusive one of being the American child of mainland Spaniards. The first was a natural character of all subjects; the second, an adjective that highlighted the family lineage and the separation of the Indians and castes. By the early 19th century, the word Criollo designated the American in general. Geography established the status: birthplace distinguished the Criollos from their counterparts, the *Gachupines* or Spaniards. They lived, in short, the last chapter of colonial dependence, and the beginning of Mexico's life as a sovereign nation.

But the idea of outlining the very being of the Criollo was a long story: for three centuries the ontological uniqueness of the Spanish kingdoms in America had been thoroughly analyzed through the sometimes not very rigorous introspective view, and for the two following centuries Mexico and the Mexican continued to be debated as an

In New Spain and, particularly, in the Criollo taste, mirrors played an essential role: its brightness and the reflection of light and color were evident in altars, furniture and of course on the walls of houses and temples. This large mirror with engraved, cast and gilded silver frame has an ornamental work characteristic of the 18th century, based on the interlocking of acanthus leaves, valances and *rocaille*, elements that can also be seen in the stone decoration of the facades of some buildings, the ornamental work of altarpieces and household and liturgical use furniture. [CAT. 10]

intellectual consideration. Nearly five centuries of existence of a concern that has focused on the outline of the own profile, first as a humanist and messianic explanation planted by the chroniclers facing the uniqueness of the new territories of the empire of the Catholic monarch; in parallel, the threat of rebellion by Martín Cortés and the first Criollos discontent of political segregation. Shortly after, as the construction of a pride that spoke against the alleged inferiority of the non-European, and later, in time of Father Mier and other insurgents—as Morelos in Cuautla, or Iturbide in Iguala—to claim the rights to self-government.

This process was long-termed. The essays in this book, by authors who argue with neat historiographical support their views, address some of its most important facets. The texts of Alfonso Alfaro, Sara Gabriela Baz, Mitchell A. Codding, Manuel Ramos, Antonio Rubial and myself, trace the possible readings of a modern interpretation of the old way of being and imagined have been. The reflection of the Criollo began as a foreign inspection: the American novelty goes back to the second decade of the 16th century, with clear Erasmian influence; American uniqueness was a Spanish theme, years before the conquest of the indigenous civilizations of the mainland. It begun as geographical wonder, then it was ontological. The Aristotelian wonder—seed of philosophical curiosity—discovered and identified the differences in the cosmos that was America. This mechanism built by Spanish thinkers at the time of Emperor Charles V was inherited by New Spain Criollos—from Sigüenza y Góngora and his contemporaries, scientists and theologians—, who unfolded as national pride the findings of the visible and invisible universe of the New Spaniards; the third impulse, our heritage, would be the construction and discussion of nationalism and belonged to Mexicans. A common denominator is noticeable in this line: the original intention was already far from parochialism; New Spain was more than a remote province of the possessions of the Crown. The essays presented here show the attempted explanation of New Spain (and Mexico) as part of the huge catalog of things in the world. It was not regionalist vanity—that would be the modern political and historiographical idealization—, but rather the search for its place in Creation.

It is then possible to venture a definition: more than a legally established racial profiling in the viceregal estate society, Criollo refers to a philosophical concept, that of a way of being, the one that draw the uniqueness of American nature. Its sphere is cultural history, history of ideas and customs, rather than history of West Indian law.

Criollos were the extraordinary first American blossoming of Western civilization. They began the day after the Conquest, and extended over the three centuries of existence of New Spain. They were a way to understand a world that was discovered every day, to order it, to typify it. They were also a way of looking at themselves, to explain their differences from Europeans. Their most visible legacy unfolded in the Latin American nationalist pride of the 19th and 20th centuries. They were, in particular, the roots of the cultural genealogy of the Mexican.

The Criollo being was a dynamic construction. His changes were built over generations. A common characteristic unveils his profile: he was the mixture of pride for his land, for the nature that made America different from the rest of the universe, for the faith being touched by divinity for a higher destiny. To do this he devised an original and effective intellectual tool: history. He turned back toward the indigenous past. He imagined Moctezuma as a refined and brutal emperor, joyous of golden and feathered ornaments, a resident of tall and complex buildings, surrounded by court protocols and devoted to a bloody religion. The Criollo accepted pagan times as his own and thought them remote; to use them, he Christianized them. He also put together the story of his own history: the wonder of the apparition of the Virgin of Guadalupe would mark a sacred distance; shortly after the arrival of the conquistadores, the land known as New Spain was designated as a promise for the new chosen people, the American. These two strands of history would nurture the pride for an antiquity that became the seeds of legitimacy.

The rest was provided by Nature. It was God's gift: a vast horizon of unknown lands and riches only suspected, which was offered to the senses without losing Christian virtue. An inventory of treasures and rarities grew year after year. The almost infinite silver veins discovered along the geography traced the paths between the confines and cities, between the shores of the world and urban centers. Nearby, *haciendas*, ranches and missions, small towns and Indian villages advanced a new own world. Odors and flavors of chocolate and chili peppers, *atoles*, *tamales* and "bread of the land"; *pulques* derived from generous agaves; brightly colored fruits and flowers; silver, tortoise shells and different woods in the personal ornaments of rich families and their household goods, on the altars of the mendicant orders and cathedrals. Cornucopias that came from the corners of the world, from the East via the Nao of China and its uncertain security; others by the much more regular *caminos reales de tierra adentro* (the inland royal roads to the northern provinces) and districts of the South Sea.

Thus, the text of Alfonso Alfaro, "Criollo taste and the Mestizo nation," sheds light on one of the driving forces of the eccentricity of thought and ethos of New Spaniards. He points out a filiation that seemed to bring closer the people of the Kingdom of New Spain to the Spanish regional multiculturalism—a closeness that did not broke, in the first decades of the 17th century, the existence of indigenous civilizations that unfolded its colonial being. The basis of this line of descent would be in the practice of the Counter-Reformation and its political, legal, cultural and religious effects on the way of thinking of Spanish Catholicism. But in New Spain, in the 17th and 18th centuries, religious and lay disciples of the Jesuits—arrived from around the world the previous century—showed their love for the American homeland. Alfaro begins his essay with an invitation to wonder. The multicultural and ethnic existence of New Spaniards, plural but not integrated, barely foreshadowed a nation whose people recognized each other as equal; and the cohesive element is what we now call *métissage*—more, perhaps, as synonymous with cultural

Map of Mexico and adjacent countries to the north and east, design according to the large map of New Spain by Mr. A. Humboldt. Since the publication of the Geographic political tables of the Kingdom of the New Spain made by Alexander von Humboldt during his visit to America, between 1799 and 1804, many of these maps were made according to the German scientific, who had worked on the materials given by scientifics and spaniard learned. The Revillagigedo Viceroy asked for a census between 1790 and 1791 on which the Humboldt investigations about the New Spain are based. At the end of his investigation Humboldt pointed that the lands of New Spain were rich in resources and that the social inequalities were huge in the Viceroyalty. All this was the basis of the Insurgent uprising in 1810. [CAT. 110]

mix, than in its racial connotation. It is also in the same sense that the reading of the word "Criollo" is intended: not as a strange pride in being "white child of whites" (absurd from the point of view of anthropology and history, but certainly the origin of numerous misunderstandings and violence), but as the face of a Western culture that developed historically in North America, in the Kingdom of New Spain. And this outcome was not accidental, but the product of a secular effort that is not over yet; Alfaro accounts for the constant political and social attempt to make less flagrant the distinctive features of the various ethnic groups from around the world that inhabited and reproduced the biology and cultures in this part of the continent since the 1530s. Vocabularies that reveal mentalities, values and tastes, attitudes and gestures that begin as regional and sectorial peculiarities, that little by little have been coming together, claiming for spaces, adapting, forgetting, recreating, until forming into a huge underground stream that is transmitted from generation to generation, migrating and transmigrating with its enigmatic rules and its geographies without borders. Alfaro ventures in that boundless world map to identify the genealogical principle of the common signs of New Spain mentalities; and he does so with a particular compass: that of the production and reproduction of conducts and ethical values, of sensibilities and aesthetic forms that shaped the complex building of shared cultural references, from Baroque paradise to the survival of regalist political strategies of neo-classicism against the spreading of American histories. This context explains, as the texts by Alfaro, Baz and Rubial reveal, the expulsion of the Jesuits and the tearing of Criollo values, which a generation later would plant the desire for autonomy and independence. The first effect of Criollo political inexperience was the inability to put together an effective diplomacy facing the hostilities of the empires that sought to rebuild world colonial geopolitics. Alfaro offers a disturbing proposal to understand our cultural history: the Mestizo response of the Criollos, which is the core of Mexican imaginary.

In another horizon, Manuel Ramos summed up the picture of the social and historical phenomenon of Western cultural transposition in America. His essay "The Criollo sentiment" is an accurate and punctual line of some of the most recognizable references to this way of thinking and being that precedes nationalistic pride. From the outset, he seeks to define its historical complexity and to update its vocabularies for an interested but not expert reader from the point of Edmundo O'Gorman of Criollism as ontological sign: not "as a mere racial or roots category but as a 'sentiment' of identity, of appropriation of the conquered, peopled and racial mixed places, a pride of having a country that could be favorably compared with the very best in the world." The subordinate political role of the Criollos in the imperial bureaucracy was the limitation that served as catalyst for separation: "being displaced by Spaniards, Criollos began, since the 16th century, to search for their own values, identifying themselves with the country where they were born." For this reason, the generation of some signs was decisive in the enormous symbolic production; in the context of the huge list of saints, martyrs and blessed of the Spanish Christian cosmogony, stood out the special fervor for the Virgin of Guadalupe, a sign of distinction whose spatial, temporal and cultural expansion has been sufficiently highlighted—as Ramos points out—by several scholars. It is worth adding that the symbolic Guadalupan range touches lay, religious and even skeptical persons, from the mid-16th century to the present day, from the epidemics that ravaged the Baroque world to the insurgent banners, the imperial medals, the Zapatista and Cristero flags.

The Criollo microcosm also gave shades to its reflections. The essay by Sara Gabriela Baz deals with devotions and identities: the body and its uses in a history that we would now barely recognize as the one of our ancestors, but which surely marks certainty references regarding the origin of "the Mexican."

The viceregal world was complex, affectionate to ornaments, fervent, but also brutal. Texts of "vain rhetoric craft" abounded—as Borges would qualify the 16th and 17th centuries—consumed by students and grammarians of the Pontifical University and the Jesuit colleges before going to sleep and be forgotten in the monastic libraries. The descriptive prose was also tested, less famous at the time but now of invaluable historiographical value. One example, among a dozen, is the account of Sigüenza of the violent and carnavalesque mutiny in Mexico City, subverter of hierarchies and scene of destructive celebration. Other examples are the diaries and intimate notes of Robles and Güijo, who portrayed at a distance the society in which they lived. These texts are now polished surface that reflects the New Spaniard and his silently dominant Criollo origin of Mexicanity. The authoritarian rulers and hierarchs, festivals and parades, processions and devotions, permissible behaviors and violations on the banks of the social order, crimes and punishments—always extreme—, join the voices that rose as rumors in Christian prayers, the shouts of squares and markets, in scents of flowers, food, human and animal fluids, to fresh air as well as to rottenness, those that made the Viceroys Bucareli and Revillagigedo to put the capital city in order, to seek to reduce the miasma and clean up the cities, to introduce drains and worry about public health, or which concerned father San Miguel, who modernized Valladolid, garden of the Viceroyalty and cradle of the Criollo insurgency.

In the world of scholars and identity builders stands out Carlos de Sigüenza y Góngora, cosmographer, historian, chronicler... and a sort of mythographer, as Mitchell Codding well stated in his essay on the intelligent and famous 17th century Criollo. His universe were documents—most of them lost, as the historians Burrus, Leonard and Trabulse, among many others, showed years ago—; he also moved between sundials, clocks, sextants and other devices that were measuring instruments for cartographers, cosmographers and engineers, builders and architects, globes and allegorical figures that served the curiosity of minds prone to mathematical precision for the greater glory of God. Codding leads the reader through the areas of symbolic structures, ranging from the articulation of pre-Hispanic past with Baroque emblems, to the micro-historical chronicles and scientific studies and inquisitions on Guadalupan subjects.

Antonio Rubial explains one way of Criollo reflection: the role of religious orders in the construction of signs and symbols of identity. In his essay explains that the friars were the spreading vehicles of Western culture. While at first the monks on the list were European, the Criollos soon began to occupy places even in the confines of the mainland. The administrative geography of the Church made the cultural diaspora possible: Christian schools were the focus of expansion of ideas and institutions. The cities of Mexico, Puebla, Oaxaca, Valladolid, Guadalajara, Guanajuato, Guatemala, Zacatecas and San Luis Potosí, and the nearby agricultural villages, haciendas, ranches and Indian towns, homogenized concepts and customs, markets and rents, even without achieving social integration. The thaumaturgical power of miraculous images is highlighted by Baz and Rubial while opening the outline of a map of the apparitions. Of course, that of the Virgin of

The complex and diverse society of New Spain had many social spaces, portrayed in paintings and engravings that appeared in various publications, as in *Origin, customs and present state of Mexicans and Filipinos* by Joaquín Antonio Basarás. [CAT. 112]

HISPANIA VICTRIX.

PRIMERA Y SEGVNDA PARTE

de la historia general de las **Indias** cõ todo el descubrimiento, y cosas notables que han acaescido dende que se ganaron hasta el año de 1551. Con la conquista de Mexico, y dela nueua España.

En Medina del Campo por Guillermo de Millis. 1553.

Guadalupe would have the greatest historical significance. The "rhetoric exaltation of space," as it has been effectively described, unfolded in the invention of historical accounts of the Conquest, evangelization, exemplary lives, along with the search for explanations of the land in the remote Indian past... Universalist vision. In the list of chroniclers of orders who also delved into regional events, the Criollo history of New Spain (Motolinía in the 16th century) and later of Mexico (Clavijero in the 18th century) began disjointed; the 19th century would bring the texts together—during the construction of nationalism.

Two centuries ago this history closed its Criollo chapter. It ended with the political and ontological life of New Spain, to open into Mexico's history and follow the deep currents of the routine, repeated daily habits and customs, in the peculiar areas of taste, popular religious rituals, domestic languages, cuisines that blend smells and colors... To commemorate this history that wears seven-league boots—to steal the phrase to Fernand Braudel—has been the concern that brought together, in a kind of historiographical allegory, the Museo Franz Mayer, The Hispanic Society of America and Fomento Cultural Grupo Salinas in an intellectual adventure far from simplistic and apologetic vocabularies. Names and surnames are abundantly inscribed in this important project in order to look at the imagery and mythography of the Criollo. Stand out, I must say, those of Ricardo Salinas Pliego, collector and driving force of these reflections; of Mercedes García Ocejo, of Fomento Cultural Grupo Salinas, who created and promoted the project for the exhibition and the publication of the book that is now a landmark in the memory of this commemorative year of the foundations of Mexico; of Héctor Rivero Borrell and Mitchell A. Codding, directors of the Museo Franz Mayer and The Hispanic Society of America, respectively, whose collections enabled to peer the look of *The Criollo in the Mirror*, a project that falls within the current of cultural history. It is, as every history of course, an approximation: to look at the reflection of a colorful genealogy. Ours.

Francisco López de Gómara (1511-1566) was the chronicler responsible on writing the great account of the events of the Conquest of Mexico. Commissioned by the King, López de Gómara was never in America, nor did he take part in the facts related, however, he was someone close to Cortés. His view of things led to soldiers like Bernal Díaz del Castillo to undertake the task of writing their own version of the Conquest, discrediting the statement by the royal chronicler, who did not witness what he asserted. [CAT. 100]

III

Rompa mi voz al
diáfano elemento]
los líquidos obstáculos,
y errante]
encomiendo a sus alas
el concento,]
que aspira heroico a
persistir diamante.]

Plausible empresa,
soberano intento,]
que al eco del clarín
siempre triunfante]
de la fama veloz
monstruo de pluma,]
sonará por el polvo
y por la espuma.

266.
112.
y de varios particulares de Estudios
Colegios de Niñas
Mugeres y 6 Carceles.
Academia de las tres Nobles Artes de Pintura, Escultura, y Arquitectura
pesado mediocre y ligero de diversas Canterias, variedad de Maderas.
Un Comercio libre que atrae á su centro quanto produce
Historiadores, y sabios Ingenios, por gozar de su Clima
Indios por la Erbia demais, no pasando á segundo dia,

Criollo eccentricity

Revisiting the roots of Mexican being, 1563-1813

Salvador Rueda Smithers

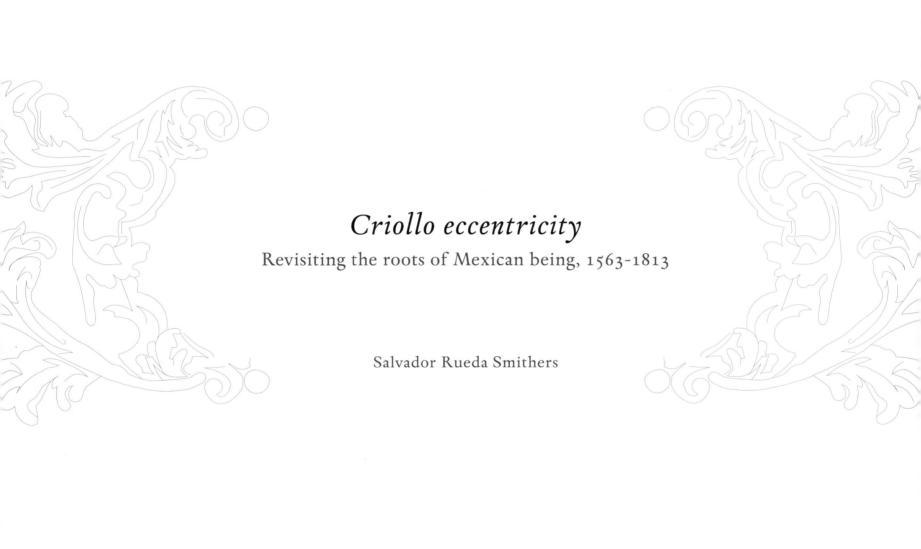

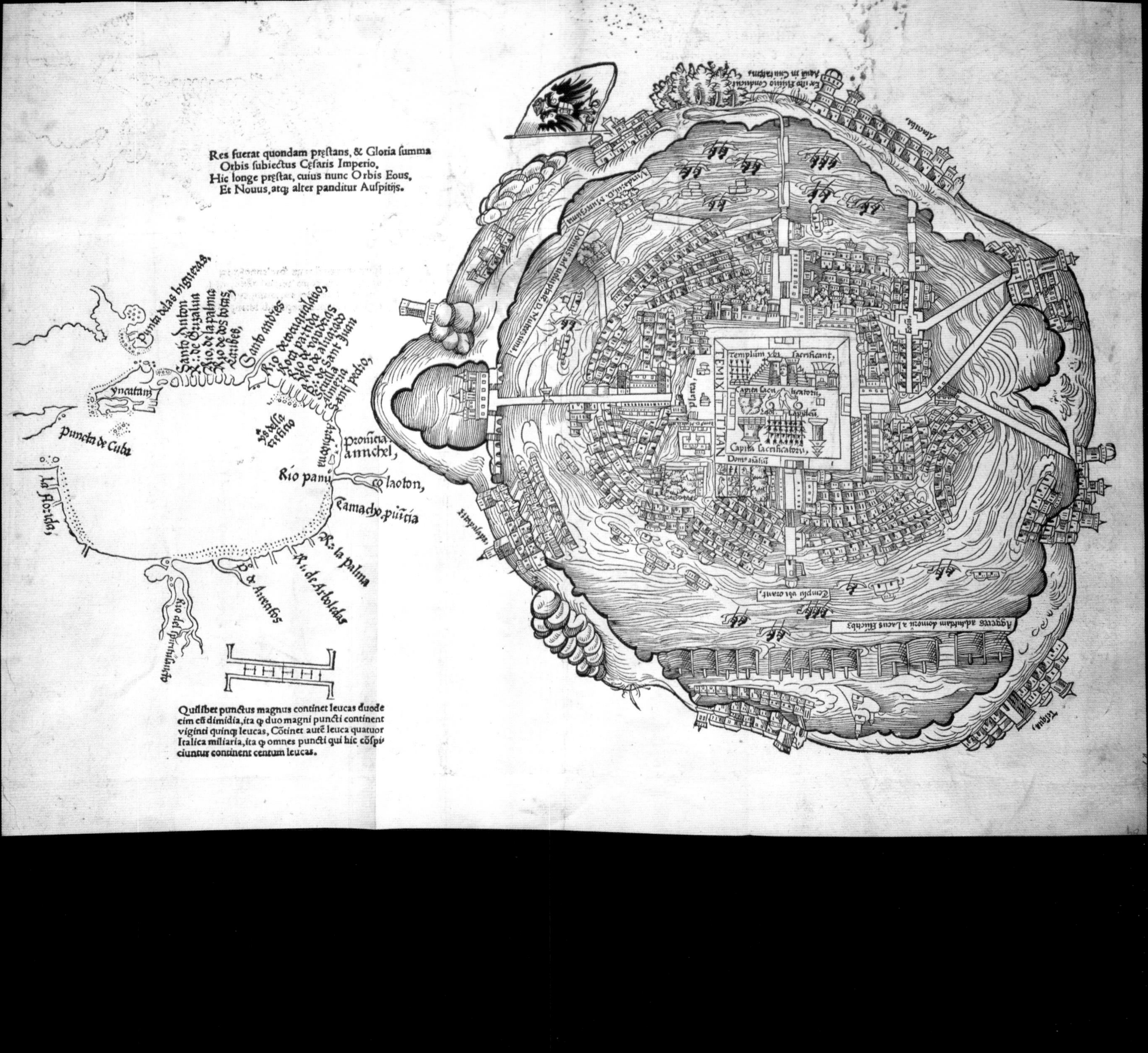
Res fuerat quondam prestans, & Gloria summa
Orbis subiectus Cesaris Imperio.
Hic longe prestat, cuius nunc Orbis Eous,
Et Nouus, atq; alter panditur Auspitijs.
Quilibet punctus magnus continet leucas duodecim cũ dimidia, ita q duo magni puncti continent viginti quinq; leucas, Cõtinet autẽ leuca quatuor Italica miliaria, ita q omnes puncti qui hic cõspiciuntur continent centum leucas.
Templum vbi sacrificant
TEMIXTITAN
Capita sacrificatorum
Dom' aialiu
Puncta de Cuba
La Florida
Yucatan
Rio panu
Tamacho puicia
R. la palma
R. de Arboledas

Map of Tenochtitlán, in Praeclara Ferdinãndi. Cortesii de noua maris ocenai hyspania narratio. (Second letter. Latin translation by Petrus Savorgnanus). Hernán Cortés wrote a series of letters to Emperor Charles V to account for the progress of his venture in West Indies and to stress the wealth of the cities and resources of the territories won for the Spanish Crown. Cortés' second letter is dated in Segura de la Frontera, and it describes the killing that ended the siege of Tenochtitlán.*

¡Archaeology of world's forms

On August 13, 1521, St. Hippolytus Day, Hernán Cortés consummated the venture of conquering Moctezuma's city. In his cartas de relación (letters of account), the Captain General explained to the Emperor Charles V the details of his efforts to take possession of the vast territory controlled by the Mexica on behalf of the Christian ruler. Not without admiration, in the second and third letters (published in 1524, although perhaps written around October 20, 1520[1]), Cortés proposed an urban diagram, "figure of the city of Temixtitan," and its organization amid the lake. Incidentally, in another letter, signed by his soldiers the same date, suggested that the conquest of the amazing city would change the history of the Spanish empire.[2] One of his first decisions was to establish the capital of the new kingdom on the island of Tenochtitlán, seat of the defeated. He was not ruthless: among the charges he had to face, during the juicio de residencia (a sort of impeachment trial) against him that followed a few years later, he had to answer the charge of not destroying the vestiges of ancient idolatry: "don Fernando said that [...] they better had not burnt them, and he was very angry because he wanted those houses of idols to remain as memory."[3]

Less than a decade did the dream of golden cornucopia that Cortés wanted to see in the world of Moctezuma last. Discreetly disenchanted, if we consider the energy he invested in subsequent ventures, since 1524 the Captain General and Marqués del Valle sought other sources of wealth. He organized and led expeditions trying to find impossible veins of gold and shorter routes to the East, which had indeed proven to be a lush territory. Other men of valor, a character that was a sign of the times, also blazed trails through unknown paths. All also mapped and began to outline the coastlines and landforms on the continent that escaped sight, towards the northern *terra ignota*. Not without inaccuracies, of course: geographical science would much later discover that California was not an island but a peninsula, or to fill the vast gaps beyond the inland provinces...

The dream was over, but no the daydreams, due to, for instance, the influence of Spanish folk legends or reading the improbable adventures of Preste Juan on treasures and blessings. The enormous extensions of the South Sea (the Pacific Ocean) course to India, the route to the Strait of Anian, the territory of the amazons and their queen Califia, the spring of eternal youth, the golden cities, among other ports in the confines of the world, populated the geography that during their New Spain years ventured with varying fortunes the conqueror of Mexico and the *adelantados* and explorers who wanted to emulate him.

Nevertheless, before the middle of the 16th century maps already contradicted much of the medieval statements. The world and its shapes were no longer fabulous; their descriptions were very different from the ones that filled Columbus fantasies. More pragmatic, and with the experience of staying in the Caribbean islands, Cortés sensed credible treasures, not heaven on earth. The followers were also not out of their depth: mostly— in spite of men such as friar Marcos de Niza, inventor of golden cities among infidel

PP. 42-43: This work was published in Cologne in 1572. It is an atlas, developed by Georg Braun and illustrated with Franz Hogenberg's engravings, that renders the major cities around the world. The views of the city, presented as "bird's eye views" were intended to record it, but also to be collected and to seduce the eye with their grandeur. Unlike the *theatros*, the *civitates* omitted information concerning pretty details and numbers, giving priority to the image. [CAT. 105]

Mexico.
MEXICO, REGIA
ET CELEBRIS
HISPANIAE NO-
VAE CIVITAS.
Cum Priuilegio.

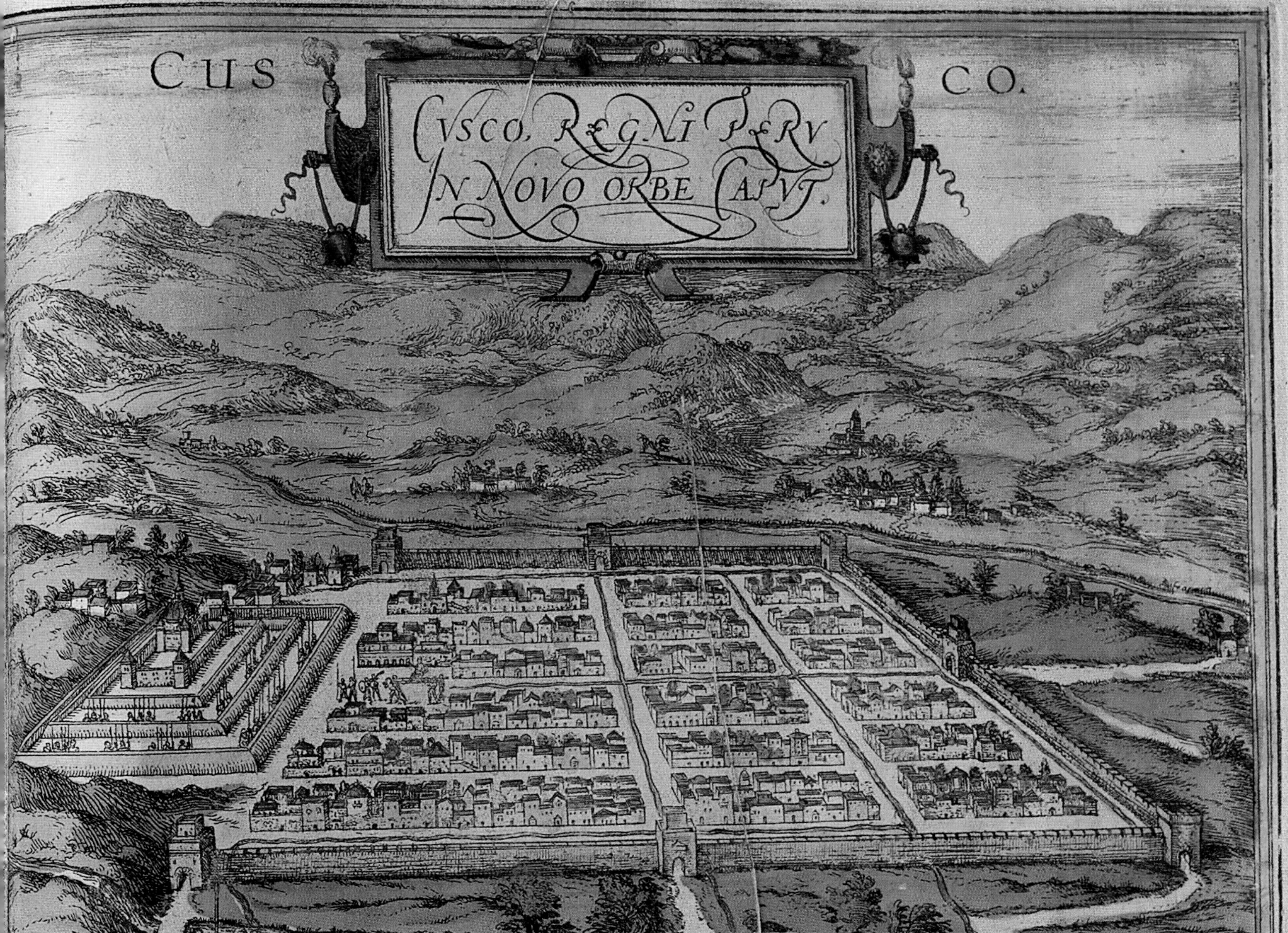
CUS
CO.
CVSCO, REGNI PERV
IN NOVO ORBE CAPVT.

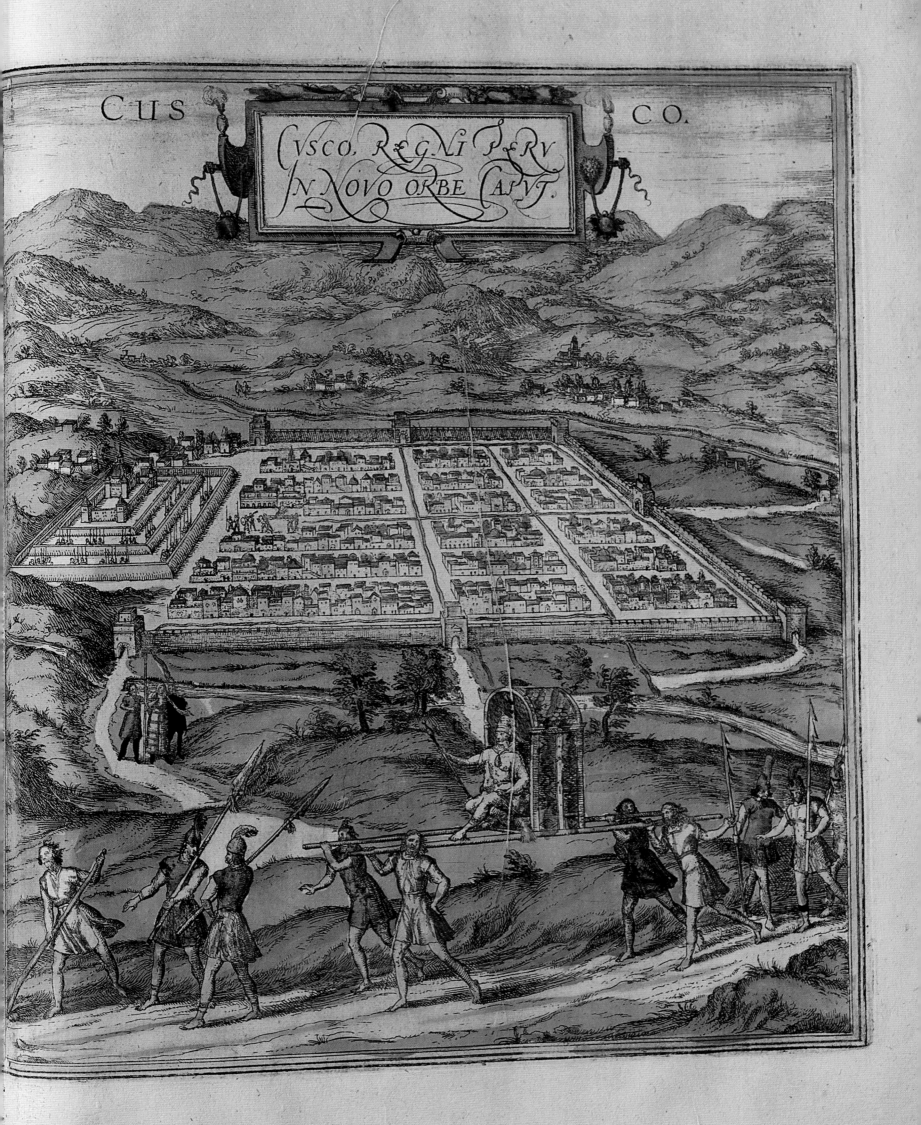

Indians—they followed orders and instructions for observing nature and founding towns and cities that took advantage of geography. They measured, drew, decreed the livable points of the new kingdom and identified routes by land and sea courses with an eye to the East Indies; it was not long before the return route to New Spain was traced: the Manila galleon and its convoys were the bridge for the first globalization.

Although from time to time they got in the way the image of a siren, or the solemn but falsely sworn news of *El Dorado*— that lost province of the Spanish Empire—, Cortés and his contemporaries were men of the Renaissance. Their power, in the Mexico City he refounded, was grounded in a political reality that shed light on what was done and thought, on loyalties and diplomatic formalities.

The imperial dream: to organize space

The Europeans who ventured in New Spain sought their fortune; they knew they would spend most of their lives in the territory that now was opening for them, and therefore the cultural transfer of their customs and ways of being settled in the image of the world they built for themselves. The news arrived to Spain and spread as promise of wellbeing for a very needy population; the social phenomenon marked the beginning of a colonization that nourished New Spain demography with steadily secular rhythms. This population would hardly return to Europe after a marine adventure that had been expensive, risky and full of fatalities;[4] they were the seed of the Criollos without nobility between the 17th and 19th centuries, the inhabitants who would later reproduce in castes or in "American Spaniards" of the New Spain Kingdom, that rooted American ideals and fervors. They were the ones who rescued the stories and myths of the original indigenous dwellers; they Christianized and regionalized agricultural products as well as dishes, words, legends, devotions, customs and tastes, and unfolded them into traditions of national identity. These Criollos inventors of American patriotism would be, finally, other ancient Mexicans.

Over the years, Criollos populated cities, *haciendas*, ranches and mining towns. But their dominant presence was achieved through the generational round. At first, their habitat was small: despite the size of the population or the extent of their settlements, the inhabitants of New Spain copied the already known ideals. Let us start with the most original creation of European civilization: the cities as an expression of dawning Renaissance. Lets us venture a modern definition, used to understand the anthropological and historical phenomenon: "Cities are a combination of many things: memories, desires, signs of a language; they are places of exchange, as all economic history books explain, but these trade-offs are not only of goods, but also of words, desires, memories."[5] This idea of the living space had a face: a Spanish one, the one who won the war of Reconquest against the Moors in Granada, the same year that Columbus made his first trip, which would have so unexpected results for history. It was his children who projected the first

Female portrait typologies varied slightly over the three centuries of Spanish domination. However, it is easy to recognize the particularities of 18th century fashion in this work, in which the sitter appears in a dress lavishly ornate with lace and brocade, and the clock that hangs from her waist, wich denotes modernity. [CAT. 51]

PLANO IGNOGRAPHICO DE LA
hecho en el año de 1776. por D. Ignacio
for de tierras, aguas, y minas por S.
FRENTE DEL Rl. PALACIO.
NOBILISSIMA CIUDAD DE MEXICO
Castera Mro. de Architectura, y Agrimen-
M. y aumentado en el de 1778.

Tace map of the noblest city of Mexico made in the year 1776 by Don Ignacio Castera, Master of Architecture and Surveyor of land, water and mines for His Majesty, and increased in 1778. Ignacio de Castera was surveyor and master builder of Mexico City. The plans he drew were the result of policy, urban, social and administrative changes that the cities, especially the major ones, began to experience as a result of the enlightened reform process brought to New Spain Graphical representations of territories and cities obey, following the reforms, to a new attitude that should reflect reality accurately, in order to achieve a better management and control thereof.

cities on the mainland, forty years later. In the Renaissance manner of Alberti, the first Viceroy Antonio de Mendoza thought of founding model-cities; his contemporaries, Vasco de Quiroga and friar Juan de Zumárraga, projected spaces for desired Christian societies close to biblical perfection, as Quiroga stated before the Council of Indies: "in the upright way, like in the Primitive Church." The best minds of that generation that founded the New Spain conceived "the city as a living space, ruled by a rational order, which was, simultaneously, geometry and beauty, justice and peaceful coexistence."[6] Guillermo Tovar y de Teresa explained the movement of this hopeful European urbanism to American mainland.[7] A harmonious planning, ordered under the seemingly simple rules of geometry and beauty. Quadrangles—checkerboards—that were blocks of houses and gardens, monasteries, temples and stores. Scattered in the geography and initially separated by distances that were measured in days, New Spain cities wanted to be an example of the best and most modern Christian ethics and humanism reason as the glorification of God.

Perhaps that is why during these founding decades the cities repeated the same schemes, with similar weaknesses and strengths. It is worth mentioning a common feature in the new cities: they did not fear war, that old ghost that, on the contrary, haunted the pragmatic politicians of Europe. Tovar y de Teresa wrote that in early New Spain the Albertian ideal was sought not only in the urban grids and its aesthetic principles, but in the very foundation of a humanism thought to be near the end of times, a true utopia: "His urban concept, for example, was against fortifications, towers and city walls, being the opposite pole of the medieval concept of the city. Architecture and urban planning were to Alberti a problem of harmony, correspondence and agreement of parts to the whole. The harmony between number, placement and finish produce beauty; in that sense, the city is a big house and a small town."[8]

But the conquistadores and first settlers thought subtly different: the Spanish architectural tradition and the fear of an Indian or black slave revolt—there were early examples of both, violently fought by the same Viceroy Antonio de Mendoza: Mixtón's rebellion on the borders of Nueva Galicia and the threat of a black uprising in the capital of the Kingdom—provoked the construction of crenellated buildings, with large fortified towers, watchtowers and thick walls. The pattern, as Tovar y de Teresa explains, may have a possible historical basis—and we should add that also an effective one—: Santa Fe de Granada, the Roman *castrum* emblem and Renaissance ideal, outlined possible cities on the promising horizon overseas. Open trace cities in the modern way were then planned or founded following the checkerboard lines: the cities for Spaniards of Valladolid, Puebla, Querétaro, Guadalajara, Antequera.[9] A generation later, under Philip II, the looming specter of another type of insurgency would appear, which ultimately would take the cities and the Kingdom; it would not be the Indians or the black slaves, but the first Criollos who would seriously question the political stability of New Spain. Tovar y de Teresa

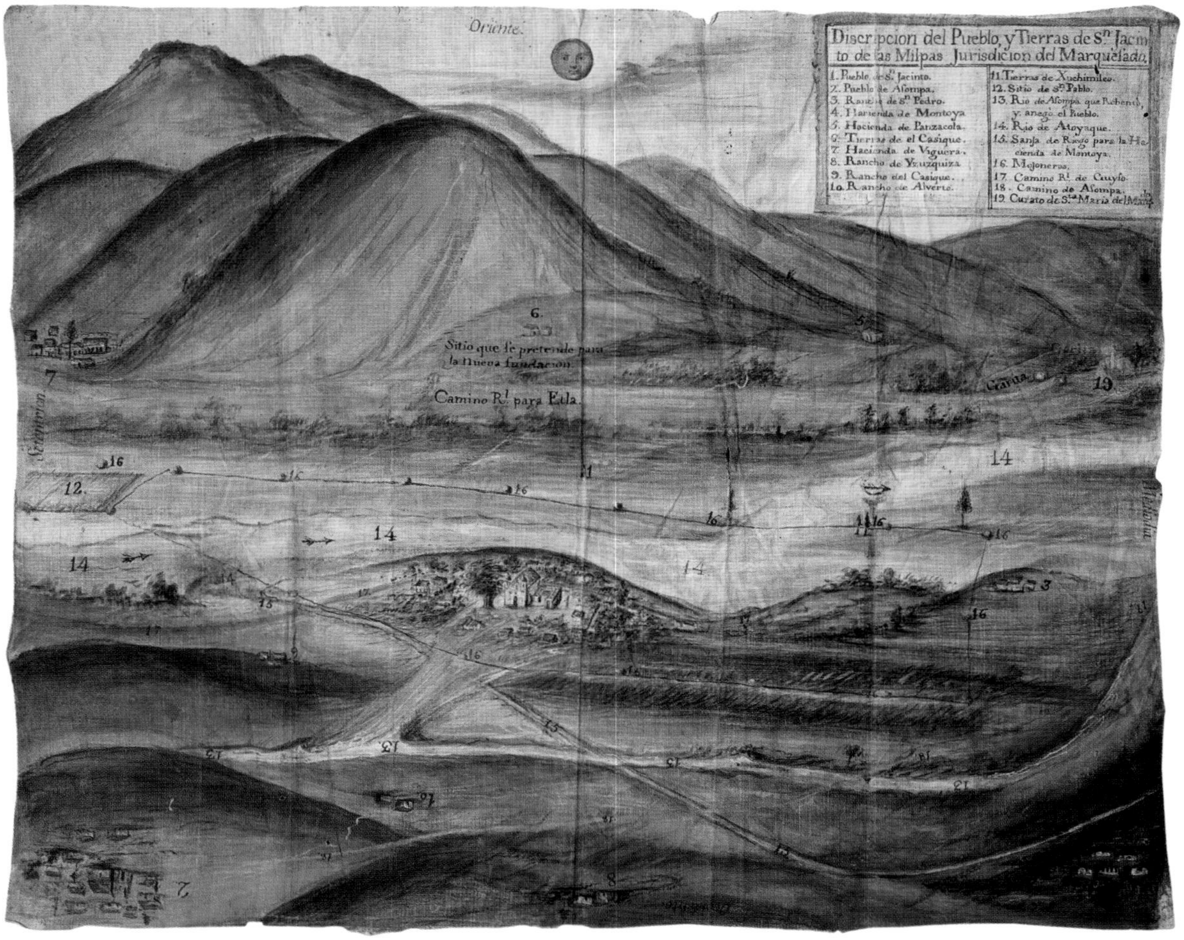

points out a significant aspect, the generational cycle: "One year after the death of Quiroga broke out the conspiracy of the Marquis del Valle de Oaxaca. Faced with the threat of losing their rights, children and grandchildren of the conquerors and *encomenderos* attempted to proclaim the son of the conquistador as king of New Spain. They were executed in public squares and their houses salted for example."[10]

Awareness of one's own

Octavio Paz said, not without reason, that Criollos were born the day after the conquest was completed. And they kept the laws of biology, yet it took decades for them to mature. The first generation, according to the rules of the time round, would express their ideas under Philip II, son of the Emperor. The historical development of the civilization that arose in Spanish America from the late 15th century started by readjusting the spaces. The *adelantados* and the expeditions' captains conceived other worldviews, other places, different from those they had lived; were those they had dreamed. With those dreams the New World was invented.

Description of the village and lands of San Jacinto de las Milpas, jurisdiction of the Marquessate of Oaxaca. Indian villages were founded after the establishment of so-called "heads of doctrine," namely, Indian densely populated settlements that were to be evangelized by the friars of the mendicant orders. However, the Spanish Crown wanted these settlements to have an orthogonal urban trace and a housing system that allowed the Indians to get used to the urban lifestyle characteristic of Europe. [CAT. 31]

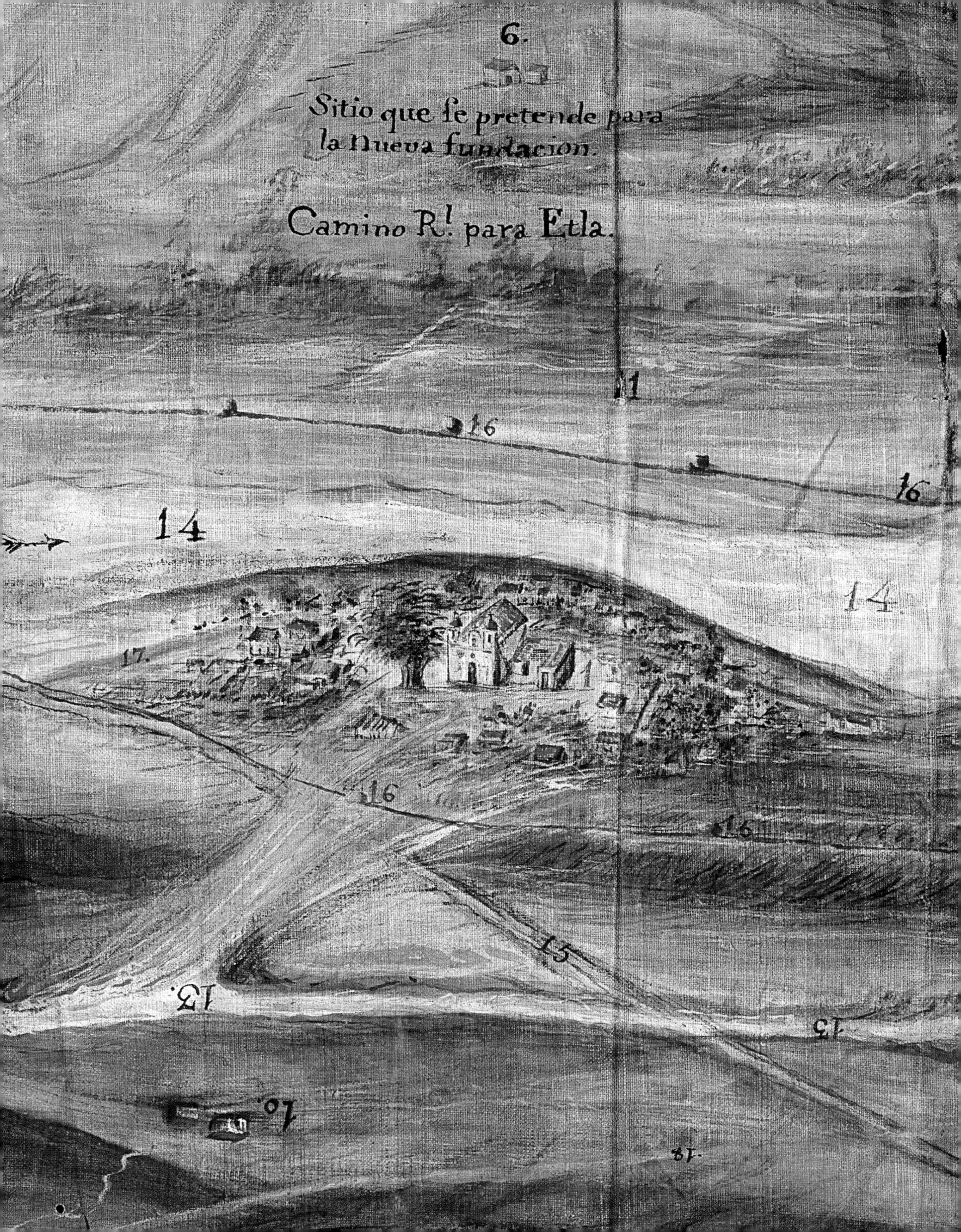
6.
Sitio que ſe pretende para
la Nueva fundacion.
Camino Rl. para Etla.
11
16
16
14
14
17.
16
16
15
13.
13
10.
18.

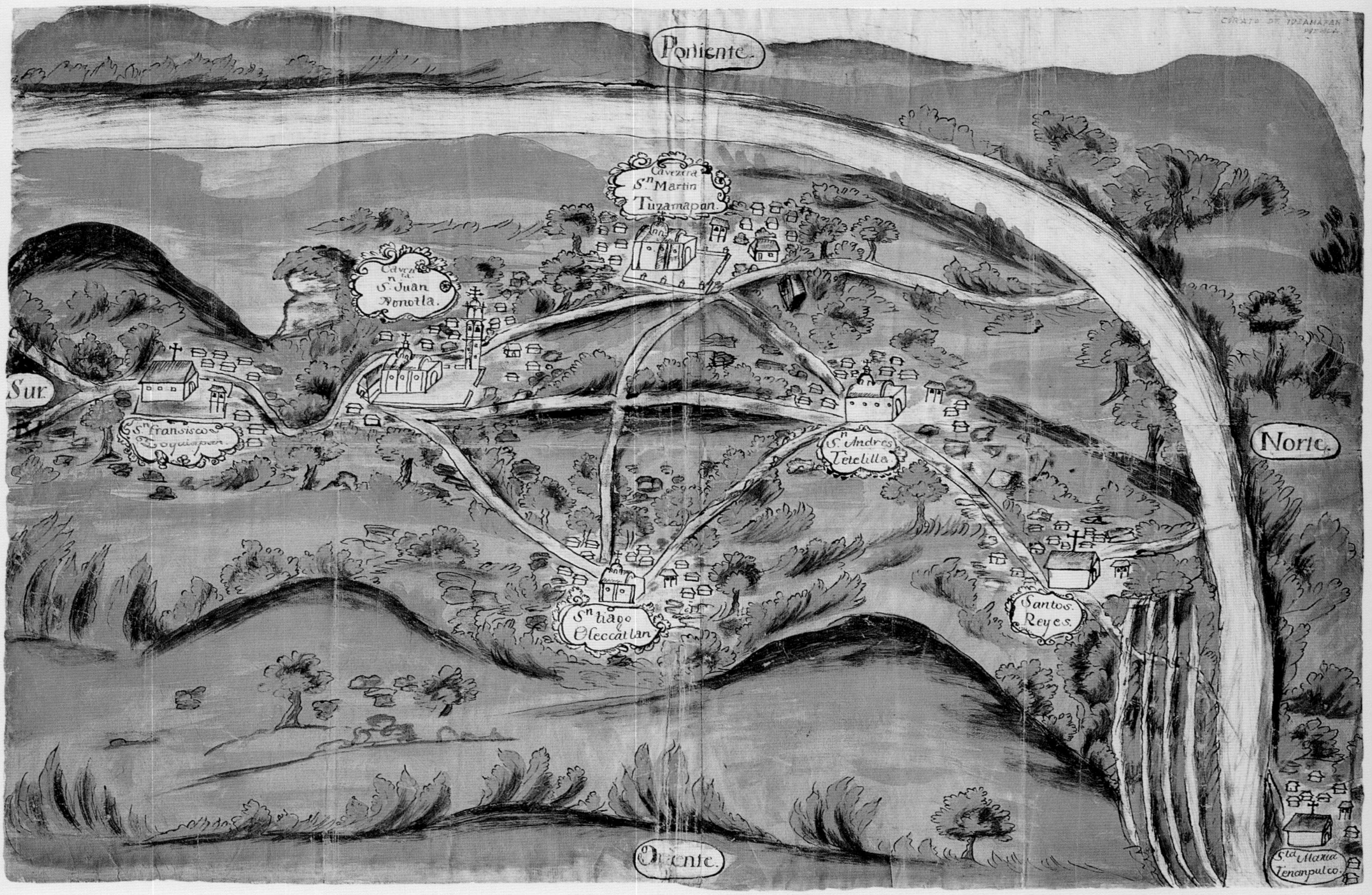

Villages of San Martín Tuzamapan, San Juan Nonotla and surroundings. Puebla. Indian villages were founded after the establishment of so-called "heads of doctrine," namely, Indian densely populated settlements that were to be evangelized by the friars of the mendicant orders. At the beginning of colonization, the Spanish authorities considered it necessary to separate the native population from the one newly arrived in the American territories, so that the Indians were not contaminated with the vices characteristic of the Spaniards. [CAT. 48]

Soon the Spanish rulers imagined forms of potential disaster: European-style cities, a Christian invention imbued with humanism, suffered from a weakness. They were not afraid of neophytes—unlikely Indian rebels who would want to return to pagan times—nor of the barbarian Chichimecas—who, from the mountains of Nueva Galicia, would attempt to restore their world. The weakness was intrinsic. The Criollos, the sons of the conquerors, explorers and early settlers in the mainland, who saw themselves as vassals of the king in an empire that was just being founded. The Criollo cities, planned following the utopias, cities that were open to the horizon for the greater glory of God, were not designed for their defense. Some buildings could serve as fortresses, but the city was around them; forts were made to defend its inhabitants, the Spaniards... to defend them from their own children. The warning came very soon, in the time of Luis de Velasco, the second Viceroy of New Spain. It would not be the first threat of violence, but certainly the most insidious: the Chichimeca War had already begun—which in the end lasted almost four centuries, until the 20th century—; the black slaves revolt had also ended in a bloody way. This warning came from within, between Europeans and their children. The division would begin, leading to rude and insulting conflicts: Criollos against Peninsulares (mainland Spaniards). Also began a political history that, at its base, grew with the uncertainty principle.

A decision by the King on the *encomiendas* would be the beginning of the unveiling of the struggle. It involved the sons of Hernán Cortés—the Martín Cortés half-brothers, although mainly the one who sustained the privilege of Marqués del Valle—, and also the Ávila brothers. The repression was ruthless; the judges razed implacably accusers and accused. They ended up paying a terrible fate themselves for the threat of separation of the inhabitants of the American lands from Spain.

One of the judges, Muñoz, gentleman of the bedchamber of Philip II, recommended in writing to the King the urban reconsideration of Mexico City. In the absence of defenses, in the manner of the Renaissance ideal cities, Muñoz proposed its construction; not against the Indians, or by fear of the traditional enemies of Spain, English and French who now became "Lutherans," but against the children of Spaniards, the Criollos. The ancient Tenochtitlán—as demonstrated by Guillermo Tovar y de Teresa—was rebuilt on the humanistic ideals of Alberti according to the reading code of Viceroy Antonio de Mendoza. It was designed as a place to renew the holy agreement that held the balance of the universe; it was wished to be a humanist seat. But history, or rather the human condition through time, would prove that Muñoz was not so misguided: three centuries later, a Criollo threatened to take Mexico City at all costs: Miguel Hidalgo and his insurgents menaced the capital of the viceroyalty at the start of a civil war involving the Criollo imaginary on their own homeland and political rights. Muñoz's proposal could have been revolutionary: the ability to predict the behavior of the "other" is the foundation of the exercise of power—Max Weber wrote. But his fate was less fortunate: his letter was added

1
2
3
Z
V
Q
P
T
11
F
6
22

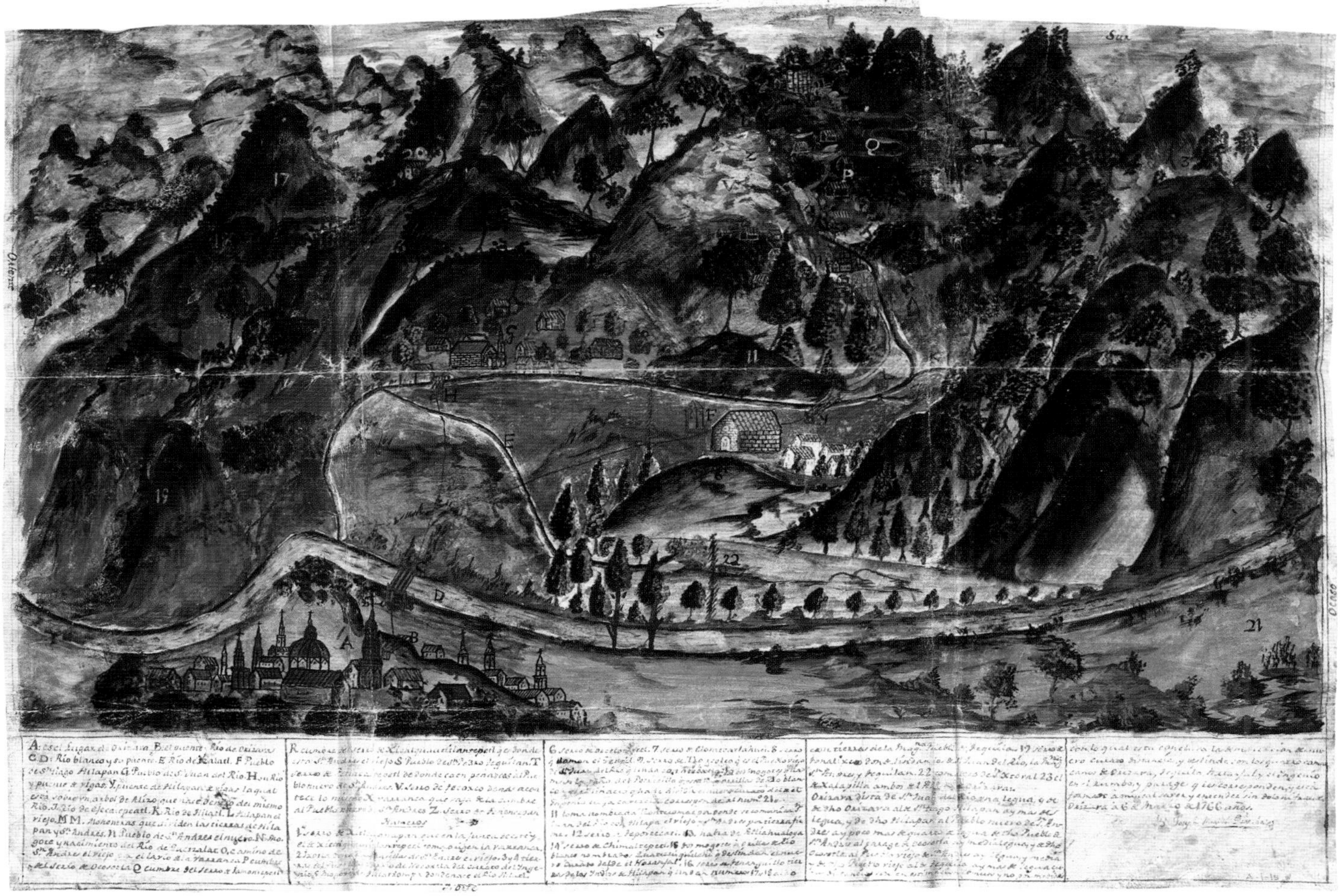

to the oblivion of history, and the conflict between Criollos and mainland Spaniards was sometimes solved casuistically, sometimes Solomonically: in the first case, the mutiny of 1692—by Indians and castes, spurred by some Criollos and Spaniards—, that became known for the destruction of part of the Viceregal Palace, unleashed the power of the State against the identified culprits; in the second case, as in the constant disturbances between Friars of both sides each time they had to change the prior of the monasteries, it was decided to alternate between Criollos and Peninsulares, a measure that persisted until the decline of the mendicant orders during the late 18th and early 19th centuries.

The Criollo heart

At the core of geography the heaviness of history imposes itself. Human activity made the Criollo city stand out as the country's capital, raised to sign of power over the past five centuries, heart of trade and investment, ruler of economy, crossroad and bridge between

Plan of the jurisdiction of the parish of Orizaba. The organization of the jurisdictions, from the standpoint of the secular clergy, responded basically to the needs of administration of the titles collected in the territories and their population density. Each diocese was divided into parishes, more or less important depending on the number of people assigned to the care of a priest. Orizaba comprised several neighborhoods and it was a city of great economic importance. [CAT. 74]

north and south, between the Gulf of Mexico (gateway for ships and news from Spain) and the west. The nature of the big capital city was ancient. And its remote history, based on the myth of a promised land announced by a golden eagle perched on a nopal cactus, was adapted and appropriated by the conquerors that repopulated it, and by their descendants. According to historian Jorge González Angulo, part of its strength comes from a political decision made just after the Conquest. Hernán Cortés established the political center of New Spain in the same site of the ancient city of Tenochtitlán, overlapping the Spanish buildings on the demolished Indian temples. His action meant to maintain the old grandeur and history of its prodigious origin. The Christian idea of predestination arranged the founding words of the dead gods to the plan of the one God of Christianity. The sign of the eagle on the nopal cactus was Christianized, but it was not the only symbol of American identity: Criollo mentality added another portentous apparition, seed of a differentiating emblem that would unfold on national symbol: the Virgin of Guadalupe.[11] Although the eagle on the nopal cactus identified the Mexica group (Tenochtitlán and Tlatelolco) until well into the 16th century, the symbol was adopted by New Spain heraldry and adorned the central fountain of the Plaza Mayor of Mexico. Throughout the colonial period it was used in public buildings, documents, stamps, maps, clothing and banners of viceregal government officials and even in the Metropolitan Cathedral. Thus we find many images (especially paintings) of the Virgen de Guadalupe accompanied by the eagle of the ancient Tenochtitlán, making it the most authentic representation of the Kingdom of New Spain. The historian Enrique Florescano states that this was the symbol of Mexico itself, linking the territory formerly occupied by the Mexica with the people miraculously designated for the Marian apparition.[12] This symbol gradually consolidated as an element of identity between different sectors of the population until covering the entire geography of New Spain. It was no coincidence, then, that the insurgent forces incorporated it into their struggle as a sign of American patriots against viceregal misrule and for the deposed king, Ferdinand VII.

The coordinates of territory

Strict obedience to ecclesiastic dogma that inspired the Counter-Reformation, even with the extreme severity and relentless surveillance of the Holy Office of Inquisition, did not lead the New Spaniards to the apathy born of fear. It is true that a timorous air seemed to be breathed from the last third of the 16th century to the mid-17th century, but fear never invaded the spirits, at least not the best and most firm ones. In fact, the multiplied festive tone of living religion and classical literature reinterpreted by Renaissance codes was the other face of Counter-Reformation, which would have the profile that foreshadowed the identity of New Spain Criollo and later of Mexican culture. The watchful eyes of various scholars—like Manuel Toussaint, Irving Leonard, Octavio Paz, Guillermo Tovar y

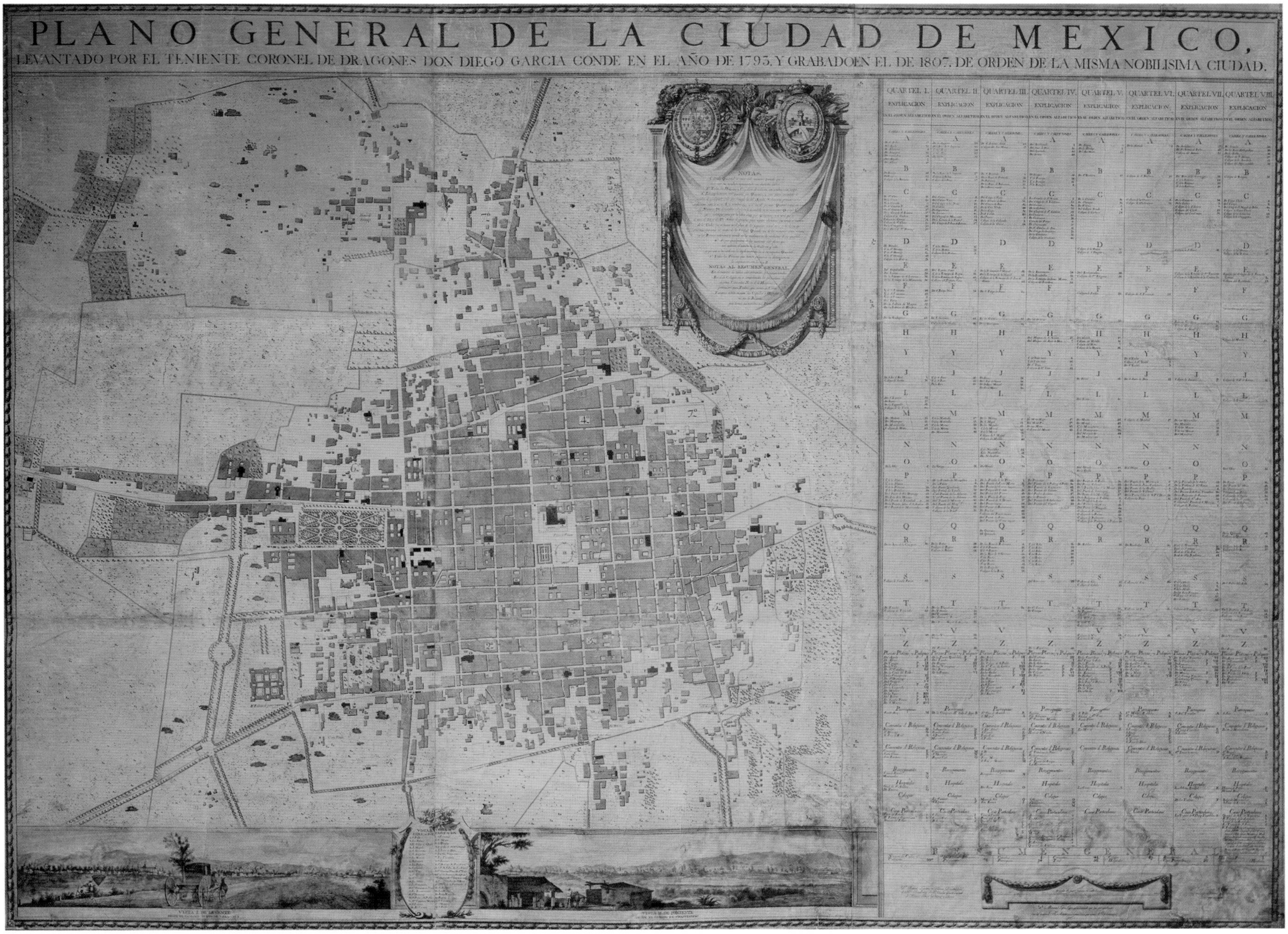

General map of Mexico City, made by Lieutenant Colonel of Dragoons Don Diego García Conde in the year 1793 and engraved in 1807, depicting the order of the same noblest City. This map, engraved by José Joaquín Fabregat, depicts, by virtue of its great detail, how the buildings were arranged in Mexico City in the late 18th century. Diego García Conde lived between 1760 and 1822. New Spain was not his homeland, since he was born in Barcelona and came to Mexico to serve the Crown as Dragoons captain. For his part, Fabregat was one of the Valencian artists who came to join the faculty of the Academy of San Carlos. [CAT. 113]

7º
4º
1º
5º
3º
2º

America displayed according to the system of Hasius. (Dedicated to His Excellency Conde de Povolide, gentleman of the bedchamber of Infante Don Antonio de Portugal). Johannes Hasius was professor of mathematics at the University of Wittenberg. Hasius distinguished himself as a cartographer and published several collections of maps from around the world during the early 18th century. The royal cartographers and cosmographers were in charge of copying the principal maps of those times and the Hasius' map was known in the Hispanic Monarchy. [CAT. 145]

de Teresa, Mitchell Codding, Sonia Lombardo, Guadalupe de la Torre and Jaime Cuadriello, among a long list—reveal that literature, painting, architecture and urbanism of the 17th century and early 18th century tied their fates more closely than it has been thought: calligraphy as pleasure and technique, wordplay as literary and visual figure, metaphor and emblem as principle and form of communication, ornaments overelaborated with fantasies as formal architectural vocabulary and the prosperity of the cities defined the rich New Spain Baroque.

It is possible that the inhabitants of the Criollo cities, constantly involved in natural disasters, typical of the rude American geography, a land still strange and fascinating despite living there for almost three centuries, never doubted the certainty of their origin as part of the divine plan, rooting history to the local past, to the ancient times of the American people, while proud of the genealogy of their Spanish family lineages. Thus, their surnames and nobility were based on being Old Christians and on their (real and imagined) special services to the Crown beyond the obligations of vassalage. Of all these shared ideas, elements of a vast culture that was just spreading, it was the acceptance of the collective past what was inherited by birth in New Spain, a past granted by the land along with its own history. From the late 17th century it would reveal itself as the engine of the Criollo sentiment. In 1808, following the Napoleonic invasion of Spain and the disappearance of royal power with the imprisonment of Ferdinand VII, the political legitimacy of the Kingdom of New Spain was discussed and fought: Criollo independence arguments would be based on Castilian law in times of Emperor Charles V. It clearly pointed out that the power could return to the city councils, its original source. Criollo demands, argued in conspiracies and the great rebellion of 1810, had a basis in natural law: the land by the grace of God, not men, provided the right to autonomy.

Spaces like hieroglyphs: the above and below

From the second half of the 17th century to beyond the middle of the 18th century, New Spain showed the fortunate effects of exploring and began to enjoy its own wealth from 1650 on. Mining booms and the slow but steady flow of goods produced by ranches and *haciendas* were noticeable in the unmistakable pride provided by the certainty of things of one's own. The vassals of the King, the Peninsular Spaniards, Criollos, Mestizos and castes had access to luxuries—lengthy for some, for others scarce—that trade and peaceful life made possible. Only the Indians kept themselves isolated in their political and everyday universe. Prosperity poked its face in the way of economic growth and an urbanization that combined the arrogance of the powerful lineages with the beauty of the palaces, which were then already raising their walls.[13] Quietly, almost as an unconscious suggestion, a sea of differences revealed itself between those born on either side of the Atlantic. Also, unlike the first Criollo generation, they never thought that the distance drawn between their identities could lead to civil struggle. In the shape of the Baroque city and its palaces and temples it was noticeable that the defense against possible attacks was the last of the considerations; the abundant arguments about Lutheran or heretic pirates raids proved that it was impossible for them to attack inland, but the threat of Criollo rebellions disappeared. Most feared, due to their relative frequency during the years of agricultural crisis and their effect on speculation and soaring prices, were riots, most of them ephemeral and localized. The specter of the Criollo conspiracy that haunted the authorities during Philip II's reign had dissolved.

In the Baroque cities settled powerful miners, *hacendados* and traders, who without the Christian shame and austerity of the early Counter-Reformation years, showed their social position through architectural profiles. The city and its people—whether Mexico City, Puebla, Antequera, Valladolid, Guanajuato, Zacatecas...—were living signs of prosperity; their intellectual and religious development would also be a sign. Spirit and matter, body and soul—in other words, mentalities—came together to trace the first profile of the Criollo homeland. Not without conflict, certainly: a social division in rigidly separated strata (a feature of a plural but not integrated society), the withdrawal of indigenous culture into the confined space of their sleepy towns, the most negative and fanatical traces of Trent, among other issues, collided with the dynamics of its daring explorers and hardworking missionaries in the immense north, of their proud identity with their native soil, with an expanding trade, with imagination in the service of curiosity and the confidence on the future of North America. Trust, in a word, seat of the successful civilization called the Western Paradise.

Two ways of thinking among extraordinary people can be an example that allows us to imagine the first part of the Baroque century: those of father Eusebio Kino and the Criollo scholar Carlos de Sigüenza y Góngora, locked in a dispute over the appearance of a comet within the timorous environment of the common people, who saw bizarre omens in the sky. The first one, a brave wayfarer of the hostile extensions of northern New Spain, was still rooted in purely dogmatic explanations; the second, towards the ripe fruits of the new way of seeing the universe, to the free opinion born of careful observation and reasoning. Both, however, lived in the deeply Catholic kingdom of this world. And for all, as Octavio Paz well wrote, was essential the enjoyment of the privileges of the view. At the heart of New Spain, Criollos environment was actually very far from the scene of the decisive events. Paz would rightfully say that for "Sigüenza, pacifism is the result of a state of civilization."

The American geographical horizon occupied the minds of people curious about the world's measures as much as of the royal administrators. They had the urge to know the size and wealth of the territory under the dominion of the King. But the rest of the inhabitants were probably more concerned about the "other geography," the one of an everyday life of piety, of the above and below, of the tripartite topography made of heaven, purgatory and hell. These vertical planes of the cosmos were not to be found

Map of the city of Zacatecas. One of the efforts of the Criollos and Spaniards was to find the routes that would lead them to mineral beds, which would support the importance of the venture of conquering the West Indies. Large deposits of gold, silver and other metals were found both in the Bajío (Guanajuato), as in the current states of San Luis Potosí, Guerrero (Taxco) and Zacatecas. The activity of mining and extracting metals determined the emergence of urban settlements of huge importance and constructive richness around the mining towns. [CAT. 75]

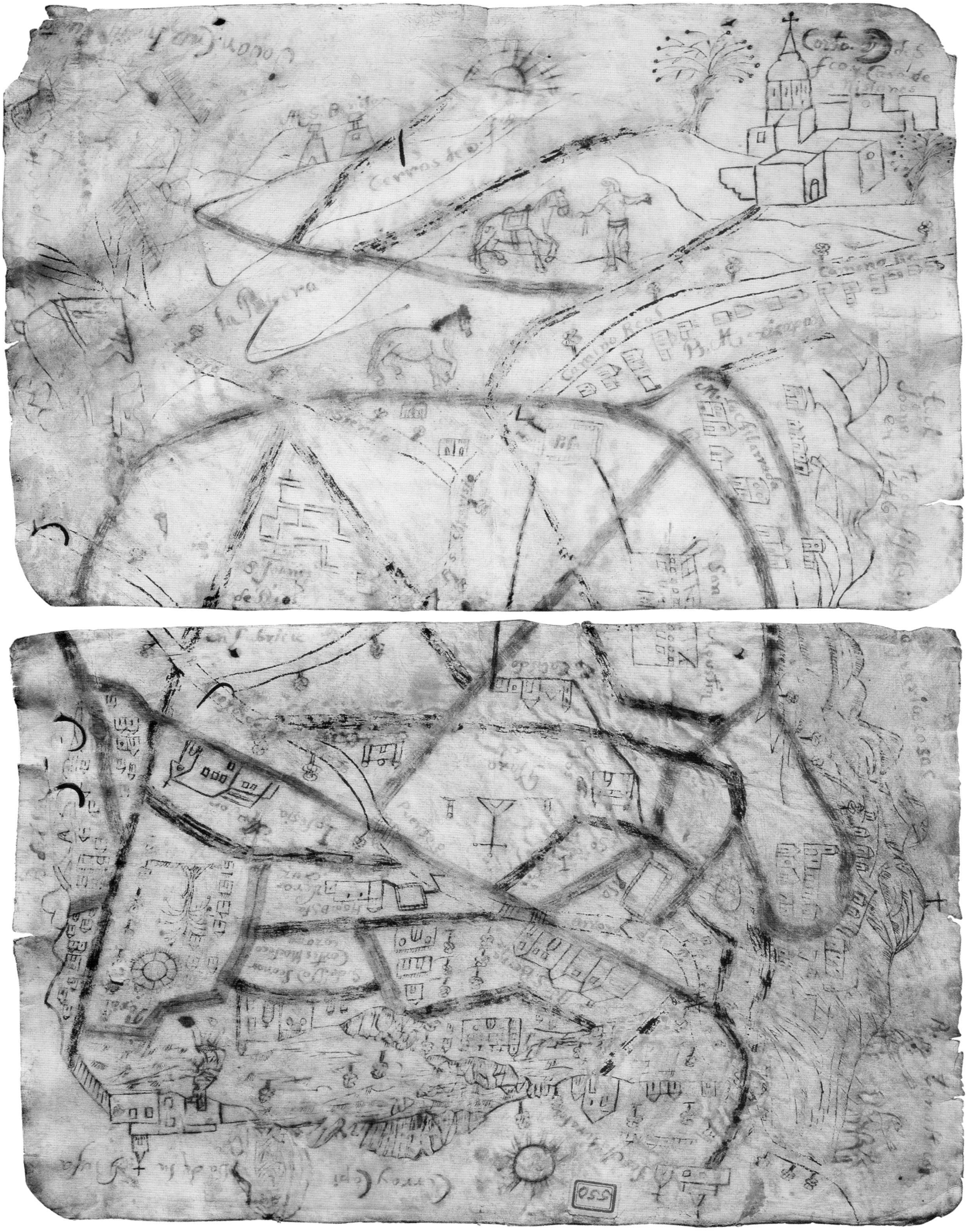
Conto. de S
Fco. y Casa de
Misiones
Camino Real
S. Juan de Dios
550

in the libraries of those scholars who were fond of mathematics and who deciphered the stars to predict the future; nor in the least consulted of the major monasteries and colleges; they populated family chapels, niches in the streets, churches... and imaginaries. Countless sculptural groups and paintings of all qualities and formats showed the imperfect living spirits the rigors of the temporal punishment inflicted on the gone souls. Perhaps the place more realistically sensed of this sacred cosmography was the purgatory, an ambiguous site in the inevitable transit to the Last Judgment, and therefore, profusely painted. To its dwellers they devoted prayers, vows, expiatory paintings and patronages, with the aim of obtaining indulgences for the ultimate destination. But it was also worthy to have contact with the celestial inhabitants. Thus, in the Baroque period, the New Spain society consumed with enthusiasm paintings and imageries: constantly asked for canvases and sculptures with themes such as the Immaculate Conception, or emblematic allegories for the catafalques, triumphal arches or sceneries; portraits that rendered proof of lineage as the basis of an economy of prestige, and its ostentatious qualities before the eyes of others—as the historians Yolanda Quezada and Tomás Pérez Vejo have suggested[14]—, or the heraldic of the religious orders were not rare.

Nothing different could be seen in this transposition of old Spain to the American one, except perhaps for the sounds and colors of the indigenous contribution to altars and statues of saints surrounded by fruits, sweet things and chilies; however, the difference existed: it established the relationship between that reality nominally separated between the Indians and the descendants of the Spaniards. The Criollo part had a special feature that would unfold into a habit of self-assertion: it appealed to the history of New Spain. An important example of this penchant for reflection from the mirror is provided by the scenes of the Conquest, in which, by reading the historians Antonio de Solís or Bernal Díaz, artists and their customers choose the sequence of transcendent moments of human acts, the so called "precise moments" of this "founding epic of the New Christian Spain," to uphold the rights of belonging to the land. In these accounts, the gestures of the main characters—Hernán Cortés and Moctezuma—had great importance, but also the determinant acts of other actors in the plot: the baptism of the women that the cacique granted to the Captain by the Mercedarian friar Bartolomé de Olmedo or the meaningful christening and vassalage of the Texcocan Ixtlilxóchitl.[15] These scenes were repeated from late 17th century until the end of 18th century, sometimes as simple and plain historiography, as in the folding screens, and sometimes as a sign of divine disposition, as in the paintings of baptisms of the lords of Tlaxcala and their glory breaks. One must imagine that world of beliefs, news from foreign lands, old premonitory fantasies, portents, loyalties, fervors, hierarchies and obediences, of castes and social divisions by skin color or ethnic origin, surrounded by colors and that lived demanding paintings, sculptures, rituals and religious orthodoxies. Everywhere were—and communi-cated—saints, angels and other beings emerged from the sacred history, readable due to the repetition of their

Initium S. Evangelij secundum Joannem.
IN principio erat Verbum, & Verbum erat apud
Deum, & Deus erat Verbum. Hoc erat in prin
cipio apud Deum. Omnia per ipsum facta sunt, &
sine ipso factum est nihil, quod factum est. In ipso
vita erat, & vita erat lux hominum: & lux in te-
nebris lucet, & tenebræ eam non comprehende-
runt. Fuit homo missus à Deo, cui nomen erat
Joannes. Hic venit in testimonium, ut testimonium perhiberet de lumine, ut omnes crederent
per illum. Non erat ille lux, sed ut testimonium perhiberet de lumine. Erat lux vera, quæ
illuminat omnem hominem venientem in
hunc mundum. In mundo erat, & mundus per
ipsum factus est, & mundus eum non cogno-
vit. In propria venit, & sui eum non receperunt. Quotquot autem receperunt eum, dedit
eis potestatem filios Dei fieri, his, qui credunt
in nomine ejus: qui non ex sanguinibus, neque ex voluntate carnis, neque ex voluntate viri, sed ex Deo nati sunt. (Hic genuflec
titur.) ET VERBUM CARO FAC
TUM EST, & habitavit in nobis: & vidi-
mus gloriam ejus, gloriam quasi
unigeniti à Patre plenum
gratiæ & veritatis.

These parts are essential in the celebration of Catholic liturgy. In New Spain, they were manufactured in molten silver, embossed and engraved; sometimes, lecterns could include filigree work. [CAT. 26]

The shields that the nuns commissioned to painters for their ceremony of profession show images of the saints the worshiped, usually related to the preferences of the order to which they entered. The central image corresponded to one of the advocations of the Virgin Mary. In this work, appear, surrounding the Immaculate Conception, Saint Joachim and Saint Anne (parents of the Virgin), Saint Joseph, the Holy Trinity and two small figures, one of which corresponds to St. Gertrude the Great, a devotion highly cherished by the Order of St. Augustine. [CAT. 140]

signs of identity, miracle workers, martyrs and virtuous men and women who died in the odor of sanctity. The Baroque was a world of feasts and festivities full of verses, written and painted stories, of amusements that even in excess were always directed to devotion and, as far as possible, continence.

Baroque Heaven had also reasonable and accurate Criollo contours. The wise Carlos de Sigüenza y Góngora was able to understand its natural phenomena without falling into the trap of forecasting disasters and apocalyptic predictions. Also the Hieronymite nun Juana Inés de la Cruz, influenced by Athanasius Kircher and inspired by her own exceptional talent, built with words her harmonic universe at the famed poem "First I Dream." Both views, of the scholar and the poet, discerned the behavior of the cosmos, of the sky seen from Mexico. Sor Juana, in a transcript summarized by the historian Elías Trabulse, wrote: "It being night, I fell asleep. I dreamed that I wanted to understand at once all things that make up the universe, but I could not even spot by its categories; not even one single individual; disillusioned, it dawned and I awoke."[16] However, she discovered much, despite human limitations. The talented Criollo nun dreamed the cosmos that is given to dreaming and reverie; she recounted the daydream, equilibrium of the universe. She dreamed that man woke up and the cosmos woke; God the architect, supreme intelligence, did not act capriciously, but with the logic of his great invention, geometry.

Another native, brother Diego Rodríguez, one of the most prominent figures of the educated circle of the 17th century New Spain, wrote a disturbing definition: "The volume of the world, namely the universe with its orbs and music spheres, can only be conceived and known as our image." The human ratio was measured according to the Divine Proportion, in words not unlike those used in his influential annual forecasts by Johannes Kepler for those same years.

For Criollo mentality, the design of New Spain was an abbreviation of the world. Under its skies were, summarized, all qualities of nature by work of its Creator. In the scheme of identity were drawn the guidelines of Christianity that barely separated the profane from the sacred, decorating it with environment provided examples: saints and angels, Marian devotions and exemplary stories were presented as readable and credible by its bid of Mexican flowers, fruits "of the land," by an abundance of unlikely colorful birds and American reptiles, of Indian crests and arrows. But it was also believed that, as everything on earth, America was a dangerous place: a place of temptations, hardships, testing for the soul. New Spain had also proved to be a theophanies site. A few years after the Conquest, according to a 17th century story, on the outskirts of Mexico City took place the greatest event of all in the continent: in times of Archbishop Zumárraga appeared the mother of Jesus, Mary in her advocation of Guadalupe. Divine gift and mystery, accepted as the patroness of the capital of the Kingdom from the mid-18th century, was accompanied by the Old Testament assertion: "Non fecit talliter omni natione." Before the turn of the century, she would become the symbol of Criollo identity, occasion for pilgrimages and offerings, model for a lavish visual production. In the last phase of the viceregal period, by imagining a curious Americanist theology was the beginning of the adventures of a protagonist of Independence, the Criollo Dominican friar Servando Teresa de Mier.[17] On December 12, 1794, during the religious celebration of the feast of Guadalupe, and before the authorities of the Church in New Spain, Mier said that "there the Ark of the Covenant of God with Israel, here the image of Guadalupe and the better Ark of the Covenant of the Lord and His Mother with the generation truly chosen and favored, their special people, with the Americans."[18]

Baroque art was extended as much as the very geography of New Spain. The need to furnish the world and fill it with visual messages was totalizing: it crossed social boundaries and spanned to all strata, it covered both the busiest roads of the kingdom and its ramifications as the most inaccessible corners—towns, ranches and haciendas, missions and forts. A sort of mania for colors and painted scenes invented a society that was identified by its artistic taste, a mania common to almost all and without eccentricities, separating the refined inclinations of the wealthiest and best educated within the trade centers or the more closed guilds from the considered "rustic" inhabitants of the mining towns and haciendas. That Baroque need to prevent a vacuum nourished with paintings and sculptures not only cloisters, cathedrals, churches and city palaces. Even the streets—site of the ephemeral collective, sign of civilization—and private houses were decorated with the red of *tezontle* (a red volcanic rock) or the white, gray, green and pink from regional quarries. Spaniards and Creoles alike became fond of the visual biographies of the saints or of family portraits that pointed out the ancestry of the name but also its European or American origin, each with its particular pride. Political rituals, honors to high-ranking officers as they arrived or left the cities, processions, family celebrations, festivities and mourning provided work for artists in a century of civilized explosion and hitherto unknown prosperity, unbalanced but spilling into all corners—and that perhaps would not be repeated until the 20th century. Criollo geography, in short, was similar to the European Catholic world, at least in its general features. Not so in its particular ones, where Mexican flora and fauna inhabited the celebrations and ritual customs. Heaven and hell were the intended final destination of the souls. The souls in purgatory, the *angelitos* (deceased infants and little children), and the prayers to armies of saints and blessed gave body to a religious ethos of its own, the one that is now called Mexican popular, the roots of which were Criollo before being Mestizo.

View of the Plaza and the Cathedral of Mexico as of the Year 1796/Copied from a print by Ignacio López Aguado, Mexico City, October 7, 1810. This piece of *papel picado* (perforated paper) is an interpretation of the print produced by the Valencian engraver José Joaquín Fabregat. In this view of the Plaza Mayor, the proportions are exaggerated in order to achieve further greatness; enhances the balustrade that demarcates an oval, in the center of which lies the equestrian statue of Charles IV, by another Valencian, Manuel Tolsá. Work in *papel picado* was developed in the late 18th century as a curious craft that produced watermark images of incredible finesse. It is possible that these pieces of *papel picado* adorned domestic settings. [CAT. 107]

The Baroque was a century in which even the war dressed in lace. Spain had been transplanted to America, almost like an echo, a whisper. The political struggles of the powers resented in empty territories, on the edge of civilization: the seas, path of goods from around the world and space for predating pirates, or the barely imagined inland that made borders without culture in Florida, Texas, Louisiana and its already famed New Orleans, or to the west, where the British and Russians fought over rugged but desirable territory due to the abundance of otter and beaver skins—highly valued among the peoples of harsh winters.

The watchful eye

The 18th century, a century of extreme contrasts, ended. The American land was then the echo of the new enlightened cult, the worship of nature. To the Spanish territories it arrived conveniently Christianized, without contradictions with the Catholic dogma, but with enough force to break the obsessive concerns of the minds fearful of change and aware of the hagiographic allegories. The change, which appeared in the visitor José de Gálvez's baggage in 1765—who had been sent by King Charles III—, and which asserted its preeminence in the last quarter of the century, under Charles IV, outlined Criollo identity and prefigured the Mexican sunrise. Nature, with its undeniable visual impact, with its absolute and ascertainable regularity, with science as its possibility for a secure and accurate reading, divided thought between the religious fervor and the recent devotion to rationalism. Enlightened New Spain minds, perhaps as a mechanism to shorten the distance with the faraway Europe of notable scientists and philosophers, welcomed the official requirements of scientific knowledge. The Royal Academy of San Carlos was one of its instruments. The success of formal education corresponded to the aggressiveness of Enlightenment thought. Confident, the men of the end of the century described the tastes and customs of their ancestors as useless waste, impossible for the requirements of life. In so doing, they also rejected, as aberrant, the old mating of reading art forms and the visual strength of the letter. The respect for precision became important, as well as for the preparation of the eye to see the wonderful spectacle of the world, not to access its divine machinery. The orderly nature could and should be analyzed and classified under its own laws—knowable—and features, with the solemnity of scientific logic.

The American environment was transformed. Among other things, changing the urban project. Although the spectral deposits of signs that the old palaces and temples were did not disappear, neoclassical buildings were built that gave the last shade to Criollo cities—a style that was the passage from New Spain to be Mexican. They also changed the ways of approaching the knowledge of space: as in the sixteenth century, the King demanded to know the secrets of his empire in order to dominate it. Spanish masters like Gerónimo Antonio Gil, Manuel Tolsá and Joaquín Fabregat conducted the new education of future engravers, painters, draftsmen, sculptors and architects. As in the European academies, with ecumenical ideals, the New Spain academy formed a gallery that turned art into a method of knowing the world inventory. Flowers, fruits, birds or insects, minerals and animals were classified accurately—a taxonomic obsession that recorded all visible things with a watchful eye, from the parts of a leaf to the signs that the new archaeology offered to the sight. Criollo pride combined the American natural wonder—that back then was thought as being diminished by Europeans—with the attractive and enigmatic geometry of the sculptures of gone civilizations—pagan, remote, but antecedents of the Criollo present. Again mainland eyes were used, but now the Criollos demanded participation. By excluding them from political life and marginalizing them from the spaces of decision-making on their own habitat, the sentiment of inequality and the dream of political autonomy were fermented again.

Fiercely, the struggle for independence began in September 1810 moving for a decade the difficult viceregal peace and separated New Spain—now an independent nation called Mexico—from the Spanish Crown. The ancient Criollo longings and social inequality fueled the desire for autonomy, first, and for independence later. Nearly half a century of war and violence was the cost of the first attempts of the old Criollos—now Mexicans— for directing their destinies in the territory that was their own. Cities, creatures of civilization, felt again, as in the days of the first Criollos, the frustration of the lack of defenses.

There were several attempts of take the cities. Within some they conspired, so the intimate enemy would use them as rebel platforms. Querétaro, San Miguel el Grande, Valladolid... History would indicate a different course: the town of Dolores, Guanajuato, was the tip of the fuse, with the call for Criollo insurrection led by the priest Miguel Hidalgo and the dragoon officer Ignacio Allende, the early morning of September 16, 1810. A few days later, without foreseeing it, the insurgents—Criollos, Indians and castes—captured with great violence the mining city of Guanajuato, capital of the wealthy administrative division. It ended an era. The next step would be the siege of Mexico City. The capital of the kingdom would be threatened by the many, inexperienced and undisciplined troops leaded by Hidalgo; the ghost of fear, as at the time of the plot of Martín Cortés, would wake up; its insomnia would last for more than a century. The effects of Creole patriotism, unfolded in the multicultural Mexican being, would live surrounded by the whirlwind of political conflict.

Criollos on the warpath

In February 1812, the priest José María Morelos y Pavón began to feel the grip of a siege. He was trapped in Cuautla. From there he unveiled, in a letter, the originating nature of his long—and ultimately decisive—struggle: the Criollo right against the *Gachupines*

PP. 70-71: The cartographer Abraham Ortelius was born in Antwerp and was cosmographer of the court of King Philip II. He was the author of the *Theatrum orbis terrarum*, a collection of 70 maps of the known world, which cited the sources from which they came and had several edition. [CAT. 1]

Lectori,
Partium longitudinis huius tabulæ initium non sumitur Ptolemaico more ab insulis Canarijs, versus Orientẽ; sed à Toletano Hispaniensis meridiano, Occidentem versus.
OCCIDENS.
Sinus
Magnus.
MERI
SE
CHAPALICVM MARE
Guachuchules gentes, nudę incedunt, sub dio habitant, venationibus tantum intenti
Terra incognita, et montibus asperrima.
Antropophagi sunt, qui his montibus habitant.
Tepecuanes gens fera, et sine legibus.
Coringa, prouincia.
Xurute prouincia
Cuanos gens fera.
Chiapoli prouincia
Tarosci hic habitant.
Antropophagi hic sunt
Tecoalium prouincia, gentes indomitę
Guaxacatecus prouincia montasa
Argenti fodine
Mechoacan paludes
Las monjas Insula deserta
Insulę desertę
Jn palude Mechoacan,
1. Capotitlan.
2. Amazcula.
3. Mezcacula.
4. Tepucuacan.
Xaliscus portus
Compostella
Guadalajara
Teconiorum prouincia
Tecaxquines populi.
Argenti et aeris fodinae.
Margaritarũ piscatio
Portus S. Antonij
Portus Natiuitatis.
Portus S. Jacobi.
Lacus salsus
Lacus aquę cali dę
Alpes
1. Tecomatlan.
2. Tampuchi.
3. Xenacatlan.
4. Asuacapan.
5. Siuacantepec.
6. Tecymachan.
7. Comiala.
8. Tecostitlan.
9. Coquimatlan.
a. Coxamatlan.
b. Epatlan.
c. Alimacingo.
d. Marocon.
e. Gualaxo.
f. Cuytlan.
110
109
108
107
106
23
22
21
20
19
18

HISPANIAE NOVAE SIVAE MAGNAE, RECENS ET VERA DESCRIPTIO. 1579.
Cum Imp. et Reg. Mtis priuilegio decennali
ORIENS
Deserta regio, et gens siluestris, animalium carnes putrefactas et sole semicoctas in delicijs habens. Bella inter se, ob messem et fructuum collectiones, sepius gerunt.
Chichimicas gens, passim vagans sub dio vitam degens.
Monsterium frat minoru.
S. Michael.
Queretaro
Magalia Hispanorum
Atacorin
Emenguaro
Amocotin
Aguandero
Mexico
Tescuco
Toluca
Angelorum ciuitas
Taxcala
Cuernabaca
Tlaxcala M.
Caçeres
Mexuacan, siue Tarascorum provincia.
MECHOA
SACATULA.
Coatalpanecas
Fodinæ argenti
Ayotecos M.
Fons
Catalutla
Notularum circa Mexico explanatio.
a. Escalpucolco.
b. Tucuba.
c. Istapalapa.
d. Ximaloaca.
e. Teutitlan.
f. Guytitlan.
g. Mexicalcingo.
h. Culiacan.
i. Catla vaca.
k. Nesquique.
l. Cinarantepec.
m. Xiquicpico.
n. Ocellotepec.
o. Vcicilapa.
p. Mimiapa.
q. Tecayuca.
r. Chalcontengo.
s. Tapalcapan.
t. Tisquiquiac.
u. Xilocingo.
x. Chiconantla.
y. Techistlan.
z. Calteca.

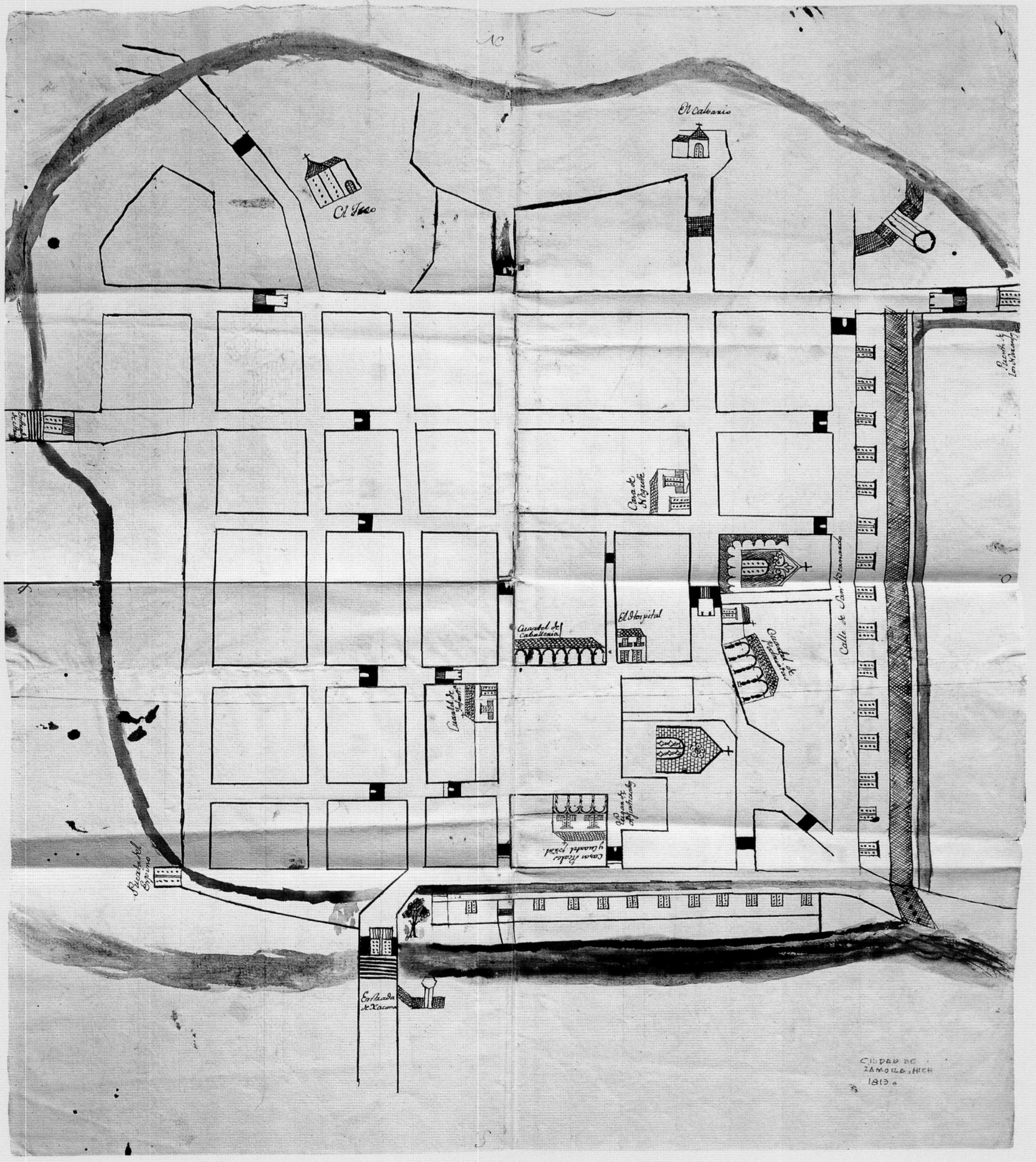

City of Zamora, Michoacán, José Sixto Verduzco was born in the city of Zamora, Michoacán, in 1770. Educated at the Colegio de San Nicolás in Valladolid, he devoted himself to the cure of souls. But Mexico's history remembers him for joining the ranks of the insurgency: he tried to seize Valladolid against the royalists, but was unsuccessful. This happened in the year 1813, for what he carefully devised a plan of attack through several maps that show his knowledge of the city and its region. In 1817 he was apprehended by troops of the viceroy Apodaca and, contrary to the fate of many insurgents, Verduzco was not executed or died in prison, but benefited from pardon and was later a senator for Michoacán. [CAT. 120]

(Spaniards), enemies of Hispanic America. Morelos wrote: "Beloved brothers: Our sentence is nothing but the Criollos rule the kingdom and that the *Gachupines* will go to their land or with their friend the French who intends to corrupt our religion. [...] We have sworn to sacrifice our lives and fortunes in defense of our holy religion and our country, until restoring our rights that for three hundred years have been usurped by the Spaniards. [...] Open your eyes, Americans, victory is ours!"[19]

The Creole rebellion spread and became a civil war. The once rich provinces of the Bajío felt uneasy. The change was abrupt. For example: At the beginning of the 19th century Criollo poets born in Zamora, Michoacán jurisdiction, were well-known in culteranist circles. The *Diario de México* published from 1806 on poems by the Franciscan friar José Manuel Martínez de Navarrete, "recognized innovator of the Spanish-language poetry, foreman of the Mexican Arcadia, poet of 'La mañana,' 'La inmortalidad' and 'La florecilla,' author of 'candid miniatures' so exquisitely mannered, in which mellifluous panpipes punctuate the sweet play of the shepherds and the lasses..."[20] They could not have imagined that only seven years later "the tiny, flowery valley" that inspired the poet's bucolic picture would be the landscape of civil war. Before a month after the Grito de Dolores the uprising ignited in the Bajío around Zamora leaded by some priests, ranchers and soldiers. The parish priests of La Piedad (Antonio Macías), La Palma (Marcos Castellanos) and Cotija (Luciano Farías) stirred up their congregations. Something similar did others with their peons or troops, as the case. Don Toribio Huidobro seized Zamora in the same month of October, "by the time that the residents of the village learned, by an official letter from Valladolid, that the officers' junta of the Ejército Grande de América had organized the arms contingents for the greater success of the insurgents and the orderly conduct of the troops, and had therefore appointed the priest Don Miguel Hidalgo y Costilla as *generalísimo de las Américas*."[21] Hidalgo passed through Zamora on his way to Guadalajara on November 21, 1810. There, according to prominent Criollos, he designated the hitherto village of Zamora with the title of "city." But just a few days later, the royalists recaptured the place. It was only the beginning of a long history of violence, arrivals and departures of insurgents and royalists, under the dubious rules of civil war.[22]

The insurgent José Sixto Verduzco, a clergyman from Zamora who graduated of the College of San Nicolás de Valladolid, led the rebel forces to the siege of Zamora in 1813. He used the knowledge of his environment: the intersections and their square lines, the center open to the main square, the heights from which they could be spotted, the possible defenses... The city without walls had to withstand. Verduzco was not a successful military man; the Criollos of Zamora decided to support royalists from 1815 until the end in 1821.[23] But the effects of war were certainly felt: famine, as in 1818, and banditry "acting in the shadow of insurgency" blurred the once bucolic Criollo landscape. Verduzco, incidentally, was pardoned before the consummation of Independence and returned to his hometown.

The view of the Criollo rebel on his hometown and on the capital of Michoacán can be compared with that of Cortés three hundred years before. Both admired the city, scrutinized its nooks and crannies, recorded the image on the geographical code that made them intelligible—in maps seen from above, bird's eye views—and ambitioned to capture them. Straight streets and main buildings outlined as what they were: a triumph of civilization, trenches, and heights as potential watchtowers, among other graphic elements that allowed reading the city as a target in a war of conquest. Verduzco's drawings, like those of Cortés, were not maps on neglected papers. A touch of beauty discovers the wonder of what was going to be destroyed and rebuilt afterwards—the objective of war is the postwar period, not total annihilation, as Le Roy Ladurie reminds us.[24]

The cycle seemed to close, as if history was a fatality. The Criollo rebels threatened the city of the King's vassals. This time, however, the targeted cities were torn between being Spanish American or—a serious novelty—being Mexican. The priest Verduzco, unlike Cortés, could never take the besieged cities of Michoacán. He lost the battles. His party, the Criollos, won the war.

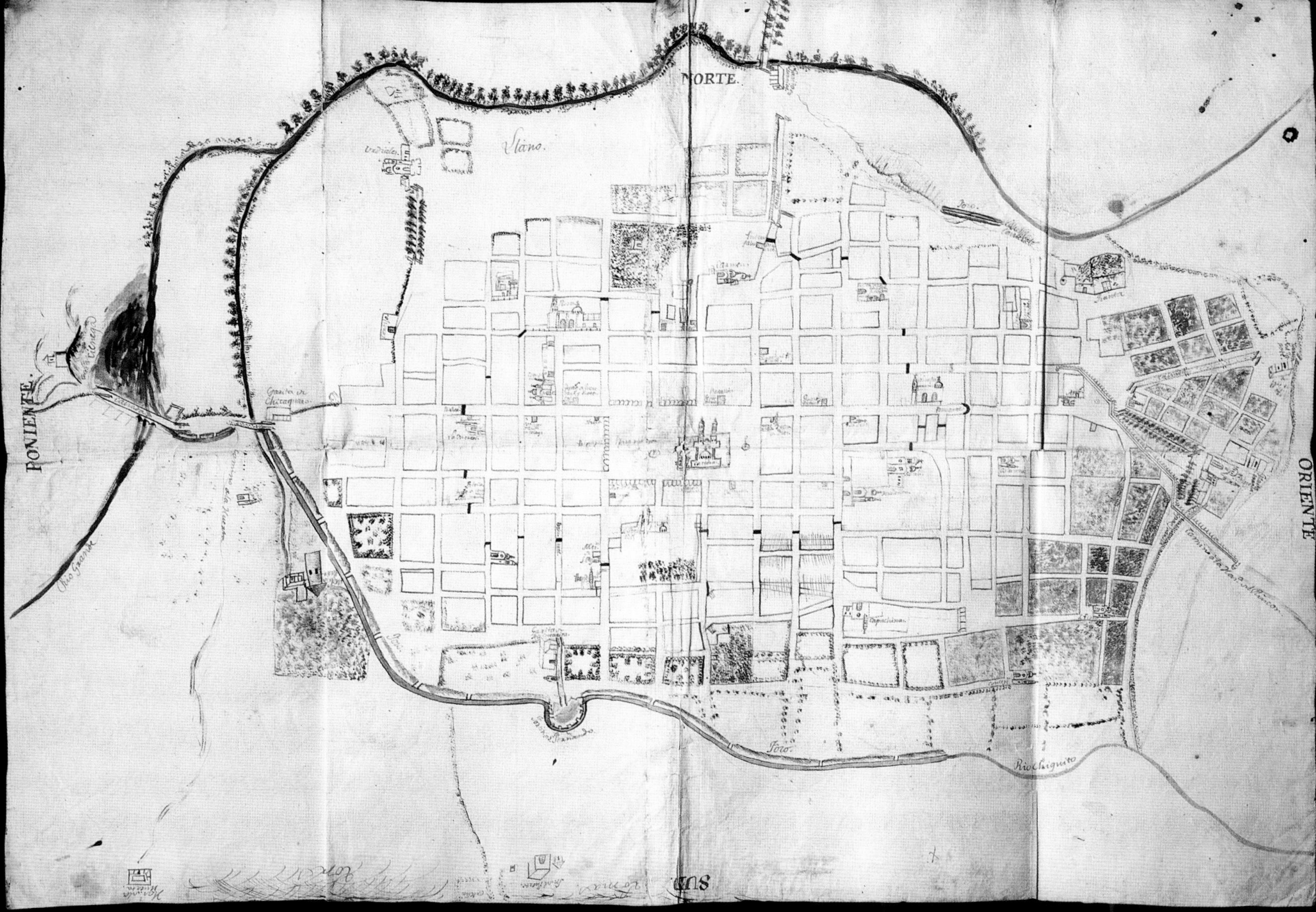

City of Morelia. Formerly known as Valladolid de Michoacán, this city was an important urban center in the West of the Viceroyalty of New Spain. It was founded in 1541 near Pátzcuaro, an important Indian settlement. Towards the end of the 16th century, Valladolid had grown in population and development due to the transfer of powers and institutions that had been consolidated in Pátzcuaro. The construction of the cathedral took place between 1660 and 1744. This map is dated 1813, when José Sixto Verduzco, a priest linked to the insurgency, planned to attack the city. [CAT. 119]

NOTES

1. See José Luis Martínez, *Hernán Cortés*, 5 vols., Mexico City: Fondo de Cultura Económica, 1993, pp. 306–308.
2. *Ibid., Documentos cortesianos*, I, doc. 15, p. 156.
3. *Ibid.*, t. I, p. 548.
4. See the splendid book by José Luis Martínez, *Pasajeros de Indias. Viajes trasatlánticos en el siglo XVI*, Mexico City: Fondo de Cultura Económica, 1999.
5. Italo Calvino, *Invisible Cities*. There are several editions of this wonderful tale of fantasy.
6. Octavio Paz, "El tres y el cuatro", *La utopía mexicana del siglo XVI. Lo bello, lo verdadero y lo bueno*, Mexico City: Azabache, 1990, p. 13.
7. Guillermo Tovar y de Teresa, "La utopía del virrey de Mendoza...," in *ibid.*
8. *Ibid.*, p. 20.
9. *Ibid.*, pp. 28–36. See also in this book the essays by Miguel León Portilla, "Fray Juan de Zumárraga y las lenguas indígenas en México," and Silvio Zavala, "La Utopía de Tomás Moro en la Nueva España."
10. *Ibid.*, p. 38. See also Luis González Obregón, *Semblanza de Martín Cortés*, Mexico City: Fondo de Cultura Económica, 2005, and Juan Suárez de Peralta, *La conjuración de Martín Cortés*, Mexico City: UNAM, 1994.
11. See David Brading, *Orbe indiano. De la monarquía católica a la república criolla, 1492-1867*, Mexico City: Fondo de Cultura Económica, 1991 (The First America: the Spanish Monarchy, Creole Patriots and the Liberal State, 1492–1867, Cambridge: Cambridge University Press, 1991). By the same author, *La Virgen de Guadalupe. Imagen y tradición*, Mexico City: Taurus, 2002 (*Mexican Phoenix. Our Lady of Guadalupe: Image and Tradition Across Five Centuries*, Cambridge: Cambridge University Press, 2001).
12. Enrique Florescano, *El Escudo Nacional...*
13. Francisco de la Maza, *La ciudad de México en el siglo XVII*, Mexico City: Fondo de Cultura Económica, 1985
14. Tomás Pérez-Vejo and Yolanda Quezada, *De novohispanos a mexicanos, retratos e identidad colectiva en una sociedad en transición*, Mexico City: Museo Nacional de Historia, INAH-Conaculta, 2009.
15. In this regard, see the suggestive study by Jaime Cuadriello, "Destino de Moctezuma II," in *El Éxodo mexicano. Los héroes en la mira del arte*, Mexico City: Museo Nacional de Arte-UNAM, 2010. Also, on these historiographical paintings, my essay "El olvido en la historiografía. El caso mercedario novohispano," in Revista Historias, Mexico City: INAH, 2000. See also *Pinceles de la historia. De la patria criolla a la nación mexicana*, Mexico City: Museo Nacional de Arte, 2000.
16. Elías Trabulse, *El círculo roto. Estudios históricos sobre la ciencia en México*, Mexico City: Fondo de Cultura Económica, 1996, pp. 75–91.
17. Brading, *Orbe indiano, op. cit.*, pp. 627–635. See also Christopher Domínguez Michael, *Vida de fray Servando*, Mexico City: Ediciones Era-Conaculta-INAH, 2004.
18. *Orbe indiano, op. cit.*
19. In Carlos Herrejón, *Morelos. Antología documental*, Mexico City: Secretaría de Educación Pública, 1985 (Cien de México), p. 76.
20. Luis González y González, *Zamora, Zamora: Gobierno del Estado de Michoacán*, 1978 (Monografías Municipales), p. 74.
21. *Ibid.*, p. 84. See Guadalupe Jiménez Codinach, *México, su tiempo de nacer. 1750-1821*, Mexico City: Fomento Cultural Banamex-Corporación San Luis, 1997.
22. González, *op. cit.*, p. 85.
23. *Ibid.*, p. 86.
24. "La guerra es un camaleón", *Entre los historiadores,* Mexico City: Fondo de Cultura Económica.

Documents like this one settled government measures for the ministry of water in urban and rural areas. The opening through which the water came to a property could have different sizes, which were rated in terms of its capacity. The size of the frame or *data* (which is the name of the opening) was assigned according to the area to be irrigated. [CAT. 118]

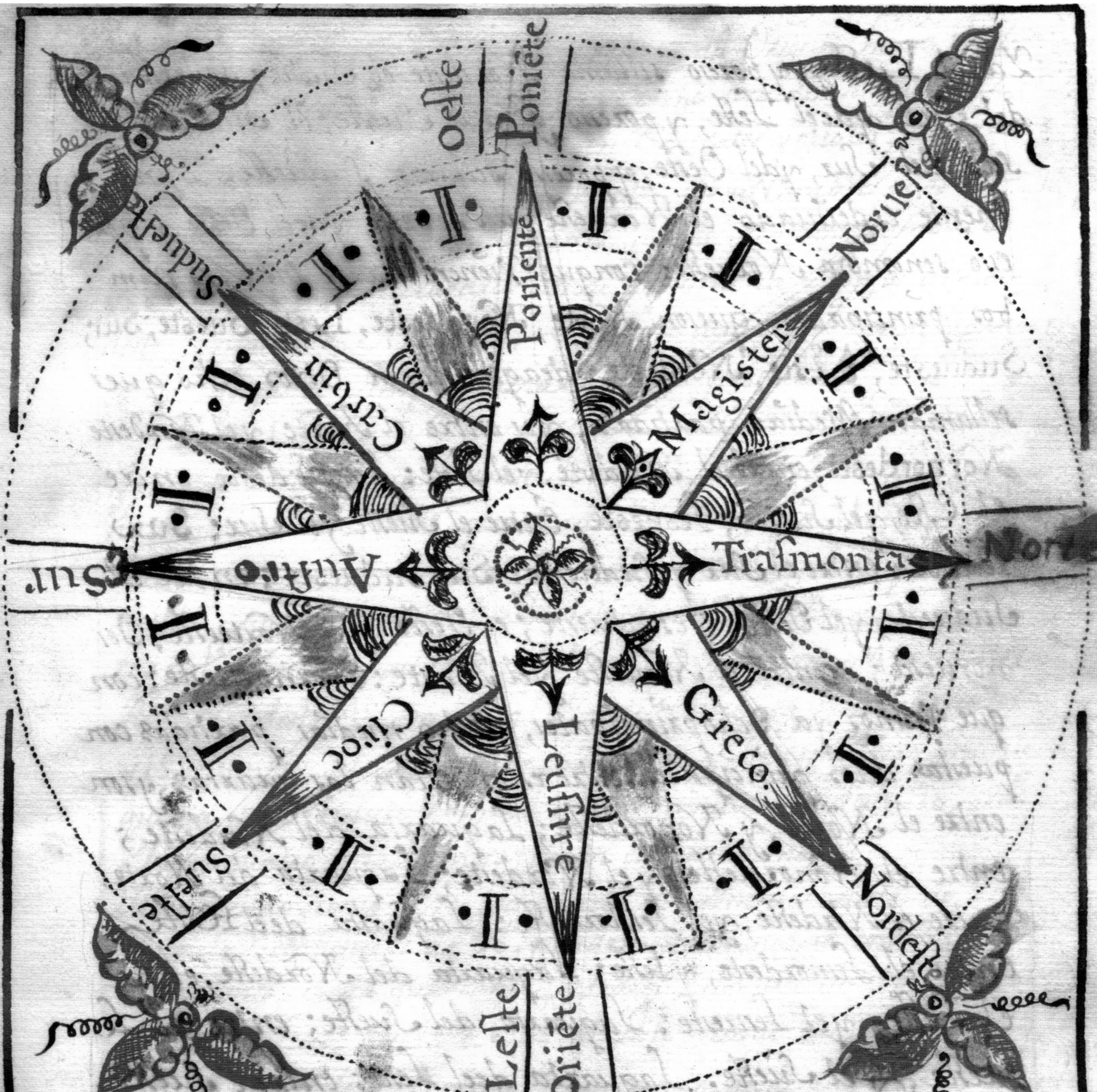

Explicaciō delos Rumbos dela Abuja

Combiene aduertir la diferencia que ay entre Rumbo, y Viento, antes de tratar delos Rumbos dela Abuja, para excusar el Equivoco. Lo que se deue entender por Rumbos: son los quatro principales: Norte, Sur, Leste, Oeste; Pero son Rezeuidos quatro mas, que son Nordeste, Sudueste, Norueste, Sueste; que aunque son compuestos delos quatro principales tambien seles dâ el atributo de principales el Nordeste es compuesto de el Norte, y de el

IV

Si indigna copa
a metros raudales]
la atención se recata,
temerosa]
de investigar con
números mortales]
la inmortal primavera
de una rosa.]

Al acorde murmullo
de cristales,]
que Hipocrene
dispende vagarosa,]
afecte dulce el
de Libetra coro]
la voz de plata,
las cadencias de oro.

The Criollo sentiment

Métissage and caste in the society of New Spain

Manuel Ramos Medina

The Criollo phenomenon in New Spain forces us into a very complex subject, for a good number of reasons. Chiefly amongst them is the social composition that grew after the Conquest. Before the opening of the American continent to the West, only Native Americans dwelled here, and they had had no contact whatsoever with the rest of the world. But since Columbus travels, settlers from Europe, Africa and even Asia arrived to the new continent. The mixing of different human groups resulted in a new type of society.

In Mexico, understood then as New Spain (1521-1821), such circumstances originated the different strata that grew ever more complex in their configuration as the years of the Viceroyalty passed. In those years a minority formed by mainland Spaniards ("Peninsulares") was the most powerful group. Their descendants were called "Criollos," while Indians, Africans and people from Asia shaped the rest of the population. In the following pages I will refer solely to the Criollos.

The term Criollo, in the Viceroyalty of the New Spain, defined those born in these parts from Spanish descent, who eventually would identify themselves completely with the new lands, while inheriting Western culture, to which they would provide their own shade. Such a definition transformed itself throughout the 300 years that the Viceroyalty of the New Spain lasted. Since the Independence and during the 19th century, the name Criollo gained a nationalistic connotation, which formed the patriotic awareness that even spread into the 20th century. It was not in vain that Vasconcelos spoke about the existence of a cosmic race.

Edmundo O'Gorman, in his *Meditaciones sobre el criollismo*,[1] defined *criollismo* as the embodiment of the New Spain being. He defined it not as a mere racial or roots category but as a "sentiment" of identity, of appropriation of the conquered, peopled and racial mixed places, a pride of having a country that could be favorably compared with the very best in the world. It is not surprising therefore that, until recently, Criollos were only the children of Spaniards who were born in Mexico. Great writers of the 19th century, such as Lucas Alamán, Carlos María de Bustamante and Vicente Riva Palacio, among others, echoed this vision. When referring to the history of the viceregal period, they said that with:

> [a] higher placed in the social rank and proud of the European blood in their veins, many of the direct descendants of Spaniards with no Indian blood, inheritors of the vast and prosperous properties directly derived from the Conquest, considered themselves naturally committed to the continuity of a political order that, apart from being looked as good, just and legitimate, assured them their preeminence and their dignities, the more coveted as they were rarely bestowed.[2]

On the other hand, 19th century liberals strongly disdained the viceregal era, defining it as a time of decline when métissage took place and had, as a result, a clear separation of

The social composition of New Spain became in a few years after the Conquest highly complex and crystallized in caste classification. With command and control purposes, rules were issued to regulate the behavior and dress of some of them; thus, for example, Indians and mestizos could not wear a hat or carry weapons or ride horses. However, there were Indians and mestizos, descendants of prominent families that claimed the validity of their titles, and which commissioned portraits in the Spanish style, as in this painting, which shows a woman with attires associated with the Indian tradition, richly ornamented and with the sign that identifies her, based on her lineage. [CAT. 69]

Retrato. de Sebastiana
Ynes. Josepha. de Sn. Aug- tin
Hija legitima. de Dn. Mathi as
Alexo. Martinez y de. Dña.
Thomasa. de Dios. Y=
Mendiola. de Edad. de
16 años. del. Año
de 1757 años....

Folding screen of the Conquest. Folding screens are furniture arising from the exchange between the West Indies and Asia. Its Spanish name comes from Japanese and means "protection from the wind." In New Spain, these screens did not have this purpose but to divide domestic spaces and be carriers of complex ornaments and emblems for the moral edification of the inhabitants of the house. Also, several screens were worked out with the technique of mother-of-pearl inlay and depicted in their panels historical scenes, preferably of the conquest of Mexico. [CAT. 24]

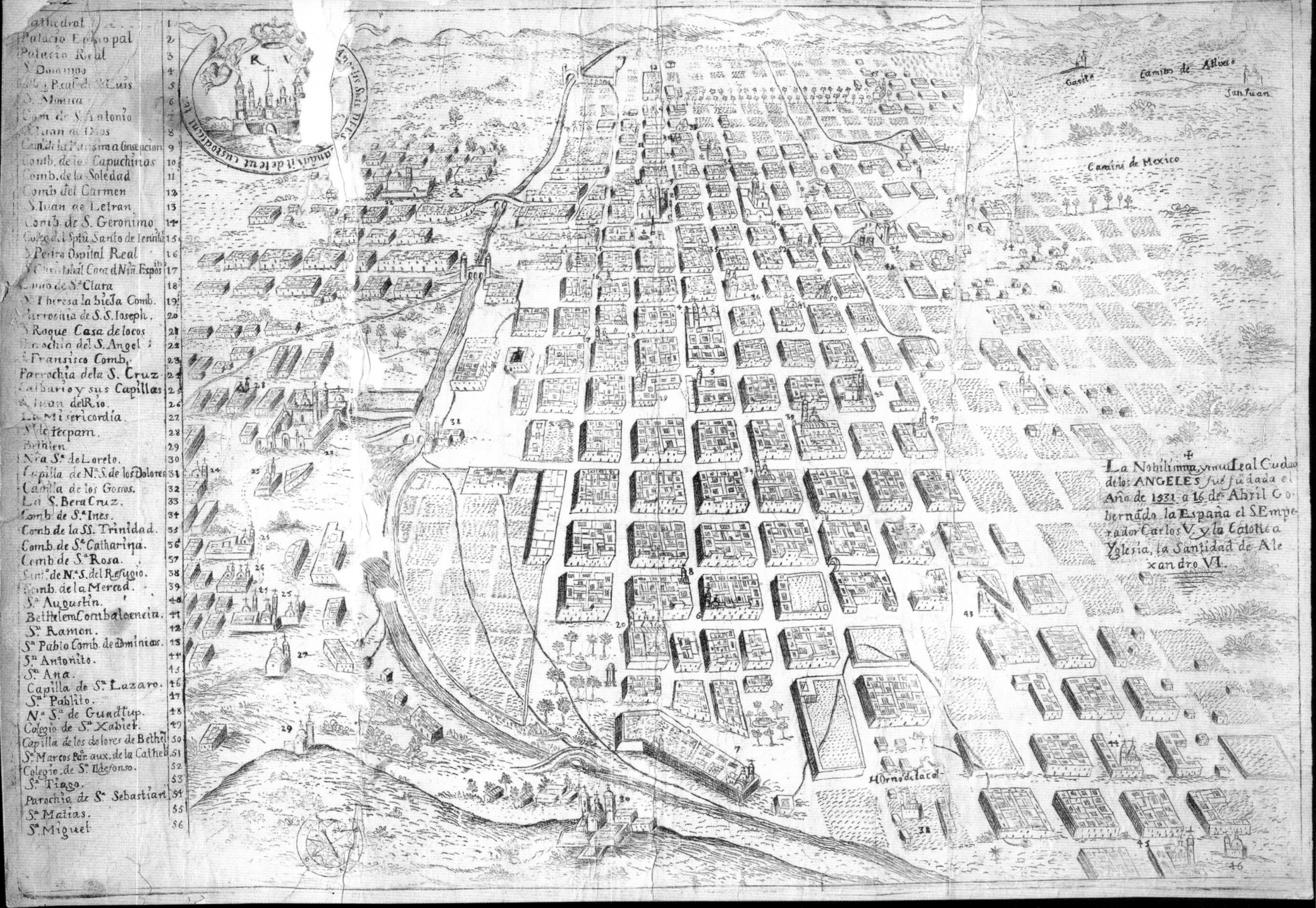

The most noble and loyal city of Los Ángeles. Puebla de los Ángeles was founded in 1531. Because of its location, it was a site of great political and commercial importance, as it stands somewhere between the port of Veracruz and Mexico City. Since shortly after its founding, Puebla disputed the supremacy to Mexico City. Its supporters claimed that it was placed in a privileged position since it was not subject to the constant risk of flooding that the former Tenochtitlán had to face. In fact, during the floods of 1624, the capital of the Viceroyalty was affected in its many buildings and streets and everyday life, which was essentially outdoors. Some residents of Mexico decided to migrate to Puebla and settle there. [CAT. 42]

those who arrived from Europe: the conquerors, who were bestowed with great economic and political privileges.

Castes were the result of racial mixing between Indians, Africans, Europeans and Asians, strongly marked during the 17th century. The names that defined and classified those castes during the 18th century were very curious: *Mestizo*, *Castizo*, *Mulato*, *Morisco*, *Albino*, *Lobo*, *Barcino*, *Coyote*, *Chamizo*, *Torna atrás*, *Chino cambujo*, *Sambiguo, Tente en el aire*, *Ahí te estás*, *No te entiendo*, *Salta atrás*, among others. But among these mixes, the white element stood out.

Indian nobles who accepted the Conquest preserved, in most cases, their rights, and the Spanish Crown recognized their titles. The Indian nobility maintained certain ancient traditions, such as their dresses, foods and languages, but some of its members adopted some European cultural ways, in other words they gradually transformed themselves.

Originally, most Criollos belonged to the elite. Born in these parts they formed an important group mainly characterized by the color of their skin and their identification with European customs. Notwithstanding their status, since the 16th century they gradually mixed with Indians, although their children felt closer to the world of their fathers, that is, the West. We can state then that even when these grandchildren of Spaniards were not exclusively Iberian descendants, the assimilation to European culture made them Criollos: they belonged to and identified with the land where they were born.

During the viceregal era, Spaniards were at the top of the social pyramid, and Criollos were displaced from the key positions in the political sphere. In mid-16th century, the Crown issued a series of restrictive measures aimed at separating the sons of the conquistadores from the posts they had had until then; it was a provision made to overcome the inconveniences of living so far from the metropolis, and to prevent possible behaviors contrary to the interests of Spain.

During the Viceroyalty, especially during the 17th century, Criollos became aware of their singularity regarding the Spaniards that arrived to the New Spain in the service of the King: this is the reason why they constantly struggled to repair the affronts that the Spanish government imposed on them because of their New World condition. The Crown integrated Criollos—prevented from holding the most important posts—into its growing bureaucracy, always subordinated to mainland Spaniards. Many became civil servants and occupied positions at the Audiencia de México, but the King never allowed Criollo judges to become a majority. In the same way they were incorporated into the city councils, composed by various majors, aldermen and syndics that looked for the interests of the corporation. They could have judicial functions in courts of first instance and even appeals, in which they hold the main posts and devoted themselves to the government of the cities.

Preferably, Criollos inhabited urban areas, founded by their ancestors, the conquistadores during the 16th century. The most important Criollo cities were Puebla, Querétaro, Celaya, Salvatierra, Guadalajara, Guanajuato, Mérida, San Luis Potosí, Valladolid,

PP. 88-89. The concept of *hidalguía* has its roots in the medieval Iberian Peninsula. At first, a *hidalgo* was the son of a wealthy man, but over time it began to name all those descendants of prominent families who had not inherited the estate. It is said that to New Spain came many *hidalgos* to seek their fortune, but, echoing the medieval tradition, they strived to prove the purity of their bloodline by this kind of patents. [CAT. 89]

ON FE LI PE

Por la gracia de
Dios rrei de cas
tilla de leon de
aragon de las
dos secilias de je
rusalen de naua
rra de granada
de toledo de va
lencia de galizia
de mallorcas de seuilla de cerdeña de cordoua
de corcega de murcia de jaen del algarue de alge
zira de gibraltar de las yslas de canaria de las
yndias yslas e tierra firme del mar oceano con
de de barcelona señor de bizcaia e de molina
duque de athenas e de neopatria conde de rru
sellon e de cerdania marques de oristan e de go
ciano archiduque de austria duque de borgoña
e de brauante e milan conde de flandes e de tirol e c.

ALMY Justicia maior //
E a los del mi co
sejo presidentes
E oidores de las
mis audiencias alcaldes alguaziles
de la mi casa y corte E chancellerias
// E a todos los concejos corregidores asistentes
governadores alcaldes alguaziles merinos E
otros juezes E justicias quales quier ansi de la
villa de canatalaçor como de todas las otras
ciudades villas E lugares destos mis reinos E
señorios que agora son o seran de aqui adelan
te E a qual quier o quales quier que cojen rre
caudan y empadronan E an cobieren de coger
E de rre caudar y empadronar en renta o en //
fialdad o en otra qual quier manera agora E de
aqui adelante las mis monedas pedidos E ser
vicios E los otros pechos E derechos E tributos
quales quier mios E concejales que los buenos
hombres pecheros de la dicha villa de Cañata
laçor E de todas las otras ciudades villas E lu
gares de los mis reinos E señorios entre si he
charen E rrepartieren E derramaren en qual
quier manera ansi para mi servicio como pa
ra sus menesteres E a todos E a cada uno de vos
en vuestros lugares E juridiciones a quien esta
mi carta E executoria fuere mostrada o su tresla
do signado de escribano publico sacado en
publica forma con autoridad de juez en ma
nera que haga fee SALUD
E gracia sepades q
pleito paso y esta
to en la mi corte E chan
celleria que esta E rreside en la villa de vallado
lid ante los mis alcaldes de los hijos dalgo E no //
tario del rreino de castilla que del primera men
te conoscieron y en grado de apelacion E supli
cacion ante el presidente E oidores de la dicha

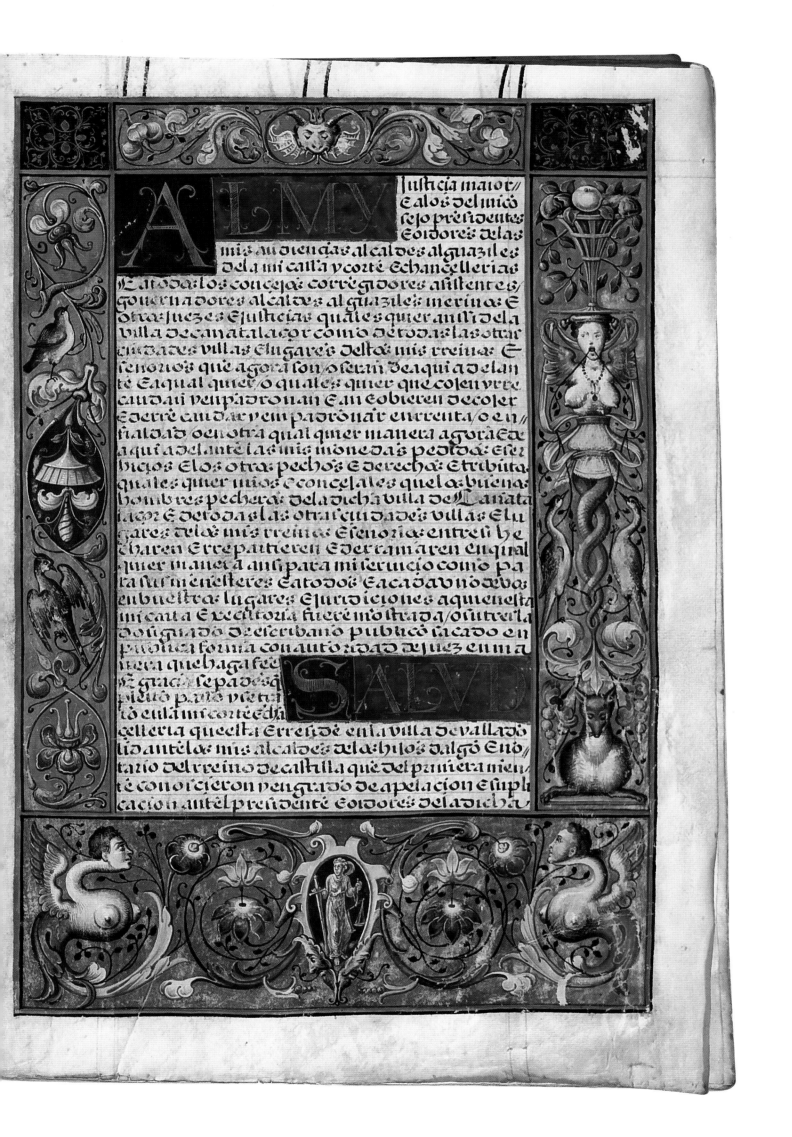

Zacatecas and the capital of the Viceroyalty. Criollo patrimonies started with inherited *encomiendas* of great prestige and strong earnings due to the work of Indians and slaves, but, as time went by, Criollo occupations diversified. A wide range of occupations opened for them, although many became impoverished. Criollos worked as blacksmiths, silversmiths, carpenters, retail merchants and other activities. Not all of them got rich, but lived from their modest incomes that allowed a decent living. Thus, far from maintaining zeal for their origins, they continued the process of métissage and the number of *acriollado* inhabitants grew significantly.

However, being displaced by Spaniards, Criollos began, since the 16th century, to search for their own values, identifying themselves with the country where they were born. At first, this manifested itself within the religious orders, where equality among individuals was preached. Even in a pro-Spaniard order as the Discalced Carmelites, Criollo pride broke out, but was severelyrepressed: that seed was even implanted in young Spaniards, recently arrived to the Viceroyalty, waiting to be admitted in the Carmel.

Another open space for Criollos was the ecclesiastical councils. The diverse realms that constituted the New Spain had as the foremost ecclesiastical authority the Episcopal sees, most of them founded during the 16th century. Representation lay in the person of the bishop, the supreme ecclesiastical dignity and its architectural symbol, the cathedral. Every church endowed with such a dignity included for its government a bishop and a collegiate body of clergymen, the cathedral council. This was a permanent body, and, unlike the bishops, most of them Peninsulares, who could be removed from their sees, their members were not frequently removed. Cathedrals councils were depositaries of government and administrative traditions and when the see was vacant or the bishop absent, their significance grew. A strong corporative spirit and a sense of identity with their country characterized Criollo clergymen.[3]

Educated Criollos and middle classes sought symbols of identity that could distinguish and even privilege them. Subsequently they spread those symbols in many cities,

PP. 92-93: **Folding screen of the nations**. The allegorical series drawn by Paul Decker and engraved by Pintz and Engelbrecht, published under the title of *Strengths and weaknesses of the European peoples*, inspired the images of this screen. The publication dates from 1739. In the images selected for the decoration of the screen, it is noticeable the desire to establish a moral classification, where the strengths and weaknesses stem from the mixture of bloodlines of individuals from different "nations," that is, communities who share territory and culture. [CAT. 25]

reaching the most needy layers of society: castes, Indians and Africans. The most important Criollo symbol, although not the only one, was the Virgin of Guadalupe cult. Regardless of the authenticity of the miracle of the apparitions of Jesus' mother, in those times there was no doubt about the reality and veracity of them. In the 17th century, for the first time, the tradition of Guadalupan apparitions was compiled and published. The first of these works was printed in 1648 as: *Imagen de la Virgen María Madre de Dios de Guadalupe, milagrosamente aparecida en la Ciudad de México. Celebrada en su Historia, con la Profecía del capítulo doze del Apocalipsis*, and was written by Miguel Sánchez. One is powerfully attracted by to the cover of this work: the distinctive symbol of the Virgin on a nopal cactus while two flanking Indians hold her mantle. The Habsburg double-headed eagle was sometimes confused with wild ducks in the central region of the Viceroyalty.

After Sánchez's work came the best known of the apparition books: the *Nican Mopohua,* by Luis Lasso de la Vega, chaplain of Guadalupe's sanctuary, who, in 1649, wrote about the Guadalupan history in Nahuatl, in order that the Indians could read in their own language about the miracles. Starting from these works, the writing of books and sermons (many of them unpublished) multiplied: the aim was to spread the privilege that the Virgin had offered to Novo-Hispanic people, a privilege that distinguished the New Spain from the rest of the world.

Between 1660 and 1770 there was an enormous growth in the number of panegyrical sermons preached in honor of the image of the Virgin of Guadalupe: most of them were written by elite members of the University and the Cathedral's council to promote the cult. The patriotic zeal of the Criollos made some assertions close to heterodoxy. It was taken as a fact that Mexico had been chosen among all nations in the world to receive the patronage and the special protection of the Mother of God. And even more: that the Virgin of Guadalupe was the most faithful portrait of the Virgin, and therefore the eternal image in Juan Diego's *ayate* was a miracle closely resembling that of the transubstantiation of the Eucharist. They even maintained that the miraculous image constituted the third step in the process of divine revelation.[4] The Society of Jesus also sustained such efforts: some of their most important preachers were responsible for the rise of true Guadalupan devotion.[5] This was the appropriation of

an image that could not be compared with events in the rest of the world: it was a Criollo creation par excellence that had an influence over the entire population of the New Spain and became a tradition that even today rallies the Mexican population around it, giving them an icon for their history.

However, the Virgin of Guadalupe was not the only Criollo religious symbol. Other sanctuaries of relevance opened during the 16th century. In Mexico City three places of devotion acquired great importance among the urban population: Los Remedios, La Piedad and La Bala. The image of Nuestra Señora de los Remedios was worshipped in a sanctuary located west of the city, at the top of a hill called Otomeapulco. The sanctuary of Nuestra Señora de la Piedad was within the church of a Dominican Recollects monastery, founded in 1595, south of the city, and the sanctuary of Nuestra Señora de la Bala was located east of the city limits, in Iztapalapa, where she is still the patroness. Nuestra Señora de la Bala (Our Lady of the Bullet) was called like this because a bullet fired by a jealous husband pierced his woman's head and ended up in the plinth of the Virgin where "it stuck and stayed where it can still be seen today [...] and even when it moves and turns round, it has never been taken out of joint."[6] Thus, all four cardinal points had its own devotion.

The founding of sanctuaries continued a Spanish tradition, especially in the Kingdoms of Castille and Catalonia, where we find a great number of accounts from the 14th and 15th centuries supported by the clergy. They where, and some still are, visited by numerous pilgrims. The Counter-Reformation brought a major impulse to public worshipping and Marian images multiplied abundantly. Spanish literary models crossed over to the New Spain, where they were renovated and enriched with the culture developed in these parts.

The above-mentioned tradition, apparently supernatural, continued in the Viceroyalty with the founding of many sanctuaries in the most important cities of the Kingdom, usually inside the urban traces related to a pilgrims path, for instance, Izamal, San Juan de los Lagos and Zapopan. The sanctuary of the Virgin of Ocotlán, in the outskirts of the city of Tlaxcala, deserves special attention. In 1537, the Tlaxcaltecans were granted privileges by the Spanish Crown: Charles V issued a Royal Decree of Graces conferring Tlaxcala with a coat of arms and its recognition as noble and loyal city, in appreciation of their support in the Conquest of Mexico and the lands to the north. The Tlaxcaltecans were conquistadores and accepted to be vassals of the Spanish Crown. Tlaxcala is a special case because it could combine Western culture with their own pre-Hispanic traditions.

Since the beginning of the 16th century we find a mariophany that is still one of the most visited sanctuaries in Mexico: Ocotlán. The Spanish tradition found its way among the Tlaxcaltecans in a very similar way to the apparition of the Vrigin of Guadalupe in Tepeyac. Even the Indian to whom the Virgin of Ocotlán appeared was called Juan Diego, and, unlike the one from Cuautitlán, his remains were buried in the sacristy of the church of Santa Isabel Xiloxochtlán.

A New Spaniard man of letters, Cabrera y Quintero devoted his knowledge of ancient languages like Latin, Greek and Hebrew to the creation of eulogies and hymns, among which stands out "Hymni omnis, generis et mensurae ad inn-tationem Prudentii, Christiane Poetae." He is also the author of several moral sermons and of the famous work *Escudo de armas de la Ciudad de México*, which evidences the protection provided to the city by the Virgin of Guadalupe during the *matlaltzáhuatl* epidemic in the 1730. [CAT. 82]

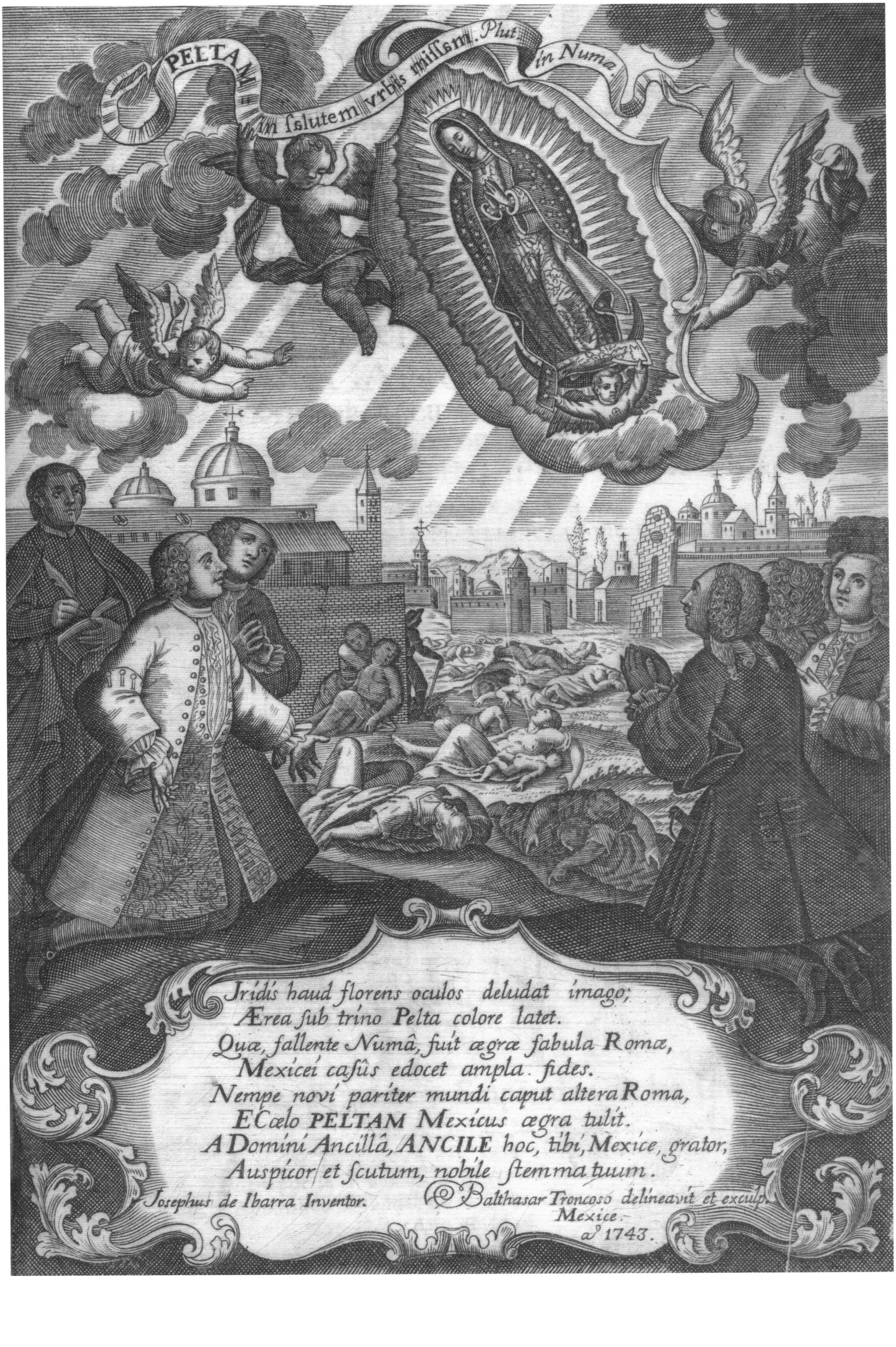
PELTAM in ſalutem vrbis miſſam. Plut. in Numa.
Iridis haud florens oculos deludat imago;
Ærea ſub trino Pelta colore latet.
Quæ, fallente Numâ, fuit ægræ fabula Romæ,
Mexicei caſûs edocet ampla fides.
Nempe novi pariter mundi caput altera Roma,
E Cœlo PELTAM Mexicus ægra tulit.
A Domini Ancillâ, ANCILE hoc, tibi, Mexice, grator,
Auspicor et ſcutum, nobile ſtemma tuum.
Josephus de Ibarra Inventor.
Balthasar Troncoso delineavit et exculp.
Mexice.
aº 1743.

America
CON
DI
TA
MANV
ORE
HISTORIA VERDADERA
DE LA CONQVISTA DE LA
NVEVA ESPAÑA.
Escrita
Por el Capitan Bernal Diaz del
Castillo, Vno de sus Conquistadores.
Sacada a luz,
Por el P. M. Fr. Alonso Remon, Pre-
dicador y Coronista General del Orden de
N.S. de la Merced, Redencion de Cautiuos.
A la Catholica Magestad del
Mayor Monarca D. Filipe
IV. Rey de las Españas y
Nuevo Mundo N. S.
Con Priuilegio, En Madrid, en la Emprenta del Reyno.
D. Fernando Cortes.
P. Fr. Bartolome de Olmedo.
MEXICO.

Criollismo and its repercussions in the Enlightenment

For the free vassals of the King, mostly descendants of Spaniards, Charles V created the Royal and Pontifical University on September 21, 1551, in Mexico City—the first American university—, although it was inaugurated in 1553, in order to teach all sciences so that "the naturals and the sons of Spaniards were taught the things contained in our saintly catholic faith and in the other faculties."[7] This foundation had as its main purpose to create a center for the learning of young people born in the Viceroyalty, without excluding others. Facing the dying Colegio de Santiago Tlatelolco, the University was an option for the sons of the Indian nobility who lived together with the other students, another proof of the perception we introduced at the beginning: Indian students became Criollo-like. Therefore, racial origin was not a determining factor, while cultural identification with the West was.

The University granted the titles of *bachiller*, *licenciado*, *maestro* and *doctor*. From its classrooms distinguished pupils graduated as doctors, lawyers, teachers, theologians, philosophers, and in other fields of knowledge. It was constituted in four major faculties: Medicine, Canon law, Law and Theology. There was also a minor faculty: the Arts, a sort of high school today. The members of the cathedral council as well as the judges of the Real Audiencia of Mexico, were, mostly, Criollo teachers in the university. The mid-18th century Bourbon reforms did not alter this institution at all.

The Society of Jesus had founded, since its arrival to the New Spain in 1572, the Colegios Mayores. Every viceregal city had as one of its major concerns the education of young criollos. The great pedagogic tradition of the Jesuits allowed them to educate the colonial elite with the most advanced methods of their time, preparing them for the university. The Society soon increased the number of its members with people born in Mexico. Unlike other religious orders, the Jesuits never applied for the alternative rule, as most of its members were Criollos. In the 18th century, the twenty-five Colegios Mayores became true seedbeds of Criollo consciousness and brought modern thought to the Viceroyalty. Even after their expulsion in 1767 their imprint lasted, their precepts, at the beginning of the 19th century stirring many of the priests that would later start the Independence process. The most significant case was that of father Miguel Hidalgo y Costilla.

The culmination of the educative role of the Jesuits resulted in the enlightenment of Criollo society. The Jesuits, identified with modernity, were the foremost teachers of a generation that asked the King for new scientific and artistic institutions. By the middle of the 18th century the number of Jesuits in the New Spain amounted 625; the Society owned the Casa Profesa, eight seminars and 25 colleges. Undoubtedly, the Mexican province was the largest outside Europe, and it was almost entirely made of Criollos.[8]

The education of the Novo-Hispanic elite received the influence of the Society of Jesus. Their students acquired, during their education, a Criollo consciousness, a sense of

The True History of the Conquest of New Spain, Madrid, Imprenta del Reyno, 1632.
Bernal Díaz del Castillo participated in the campaigns of conquest on the way to the city of Tenochtitlán. With great narrative skills despite lacking the education of the noble Spaniards like Cortés, Díaz del Castillo gives an account of the exploits of the Spaniards in a rugged terrain that placed them at any time, at the mercy of the violence of the natives. Recounts the battles in its harshness, but also contributed to the myth of the feats of the Europeans and of the amazement the Indians showed at their weapons, armors and horses, "because they had never seen horses or men like us." [CAT. 72]

pride and admiration for their own past, even the pre-Hispanic one, which allowed them to compare favorably with Europeans. If the latter had the glory of Greece and Rome, New Spaniards had their own ancient cultures, and they saw them as similar to those in Europe.

The expulsion of the Jesuits in 1767 did not put an end to Criollo education, since Jesuit colleges were not the only existing instances of culture and learning. The New Spain had grown mature and evolved, and had other institutions that gave continuity to the education. Some of the closed colleges opened their doors again a few years later, now administered by the clergy. The blossoming Tridentine seminars and, in the capital, the University must be taken into account.[9] Criollos maintained their superior education until the end of viceregal times. We can assure today that Criollos, originally defined as the descendants of Spaniards, mixed themselves throughout those three centuries; and that this phenomenon gave as a result the actual Mexican population.

NOTES

1. Edmundo O'Gorman *Meditaciones sobre el criollismo* (inaugural address as member of the Academia Mexicana de la Historia, corresponding branch of Spain's Real Academia de la Historia), Mexico City: Centro de Estudios de Historia de México Condumex (today Carso), 1970.
2. Vicente Riva Palacio, *México a través de los siglos...*, vol. III, p. V.
3. For more on the subject, see Óscar Mazín, "La catedral de Valladolid y su cabildo eclesiástico", in Nelly Sigaut (ed.), *La catedral de Morelia,* México: El Colegio de Michoacán & Gobierno del Estado de Michoacán, 1991, pp. 17-63.
4. David A. Brading, *Nueve sermones guadalupanos*, Mexico City: Centro de Estudios de Historia de México Condumex (today Carso), 2005, p. 13
5. Ibídem, p. 25.
6. Mariano Fernandez de Echeverría y Veitia, *Baluartes de México. Descripción histórica de las cuatro milagrosas imágenes de Nuestra Señora que se veneran en la muy noble, leal e imperial ciudad de México,* Mexico City: Imprenta de Alejandro Valdés, 1820, pp. 13-14.
7. Francisco de la Maza, "Las tesis impresas", *apud La Universidad Nacional Autónoma de México, la Primera Universidad de América. Orígenes de la Antigua Real y Pontificia Universidad de México. XXX Aniversario de su restablecimiento como Universidad Nacional de México,* Mexico City: Imprenta Universitaria, 1940.
8. María Cristina Torales Pacheco, "Los jesuitas, la RSBAP y la identidad patria americana," in *Ilustración en el mundo hispánico. Preámbulo de las independencias,* Mexico City: Gobierno del Estado de Tlaxcala, 2009, pp. 337-357.
9. Enrique González y González, "La expulsión de los jesuitas y la educación novohispana. ¿Debacle cultural o proceso secularizador?," in *Ilustración en el mundo hispánico..., op. cit.*, pp. 255-275.

The *herma* or *términos* are ornamental elements that emerged from the landmarks that, in antiquity, were usually placed on roads and open fields to invoke the protection of the god Hermes. The *términos* consisted of a simple column, the top of which was eventually occupied by the carved image of the god of roads. As a decorative motif in Renaissance, plateresque and Baroque repertoires, the *herma* or *términos* refer to a type of carved column that shows a male torso without limbs, and whose lower body does not continue but as a frankly ornamental configuration of architectural elements, as in the example offered here. These images were also used in borders of illuminated books and engraving plates. [CAT. 89]

V

Matiz mendigue
de la primavera,]
que afectuoso venero,
humilde canto]
de Amaltea la copia
lisonjera]
el de Fabonio colorido
manto.]

Mientras clarín
de superior esfera,]
en fijos polos,
el florido espanto,]
publica del invierno,
que volantes]
copos, anima
en flores rozagantes.

D. Carlos de Siguença y Gongora

1676

3 p. 4.

Carlos de Sigüenza y Góngora

In benefit of the Criollo homeland

Mitchell A. Codding

The well-known polymath Carlos de Sigüenza y Góngora (1645-1700) was one of the most renowned and published Criollo authors during the viceregal era. Throughout his life he brought to print thirteen poetic, historic and scientific works, as well as thirty predictions, lunar calendars and almanacs with his own name or under the pen names "El Mexicano" or Juan de Torquemada. Above all, thanks to the figure of Sigüenza y Góngora, the glorification of the Mexican homeland became for the first time not a mere occasional subject for a Criollo writer, but a unifying theme. Sigüenza also stands out along the 17th century due to his obvious efforts to assimilate the indigenous cultural history to Criollo mythology. Throughout the 17th century, in the works of his precursors and contemporaries, it is possible to find expressions of patriotic pride while exalting the natural splendors of Mexico and the achievements of its people, like Bernardo de Balbuena in *Grandeza mexicana* (Mexico, 1604), Arias de Villalobos in *Obediencia* (Mexico, 1623), Miguel Sánchez in *Imagen de la Virgen María* (Mexico, 1648), Francisco de Florencia in *La estrella del norte de México* (Mexico, 1688) and Agustín de Vetancurt in *Teatro mexicano* (Mexico, 1698). What distinguishes Sigüenza's work is that he dared to state at all times the Mexican cultural, religious and intellectual superiority, while for his contemporaries it was enough to make some prudent and routine suggestions about equality in the growing rivalry between Americans and Europeans. As Jacques Lafaye notices: "Mexican 'preeminence' is a notion formally born from Sigüenza y Góngora's pen; it will become one of the guiding ideas of 18th century religious-patriotic faith."[1]

According to his own statement, Carlos de Sigüenza y Góngora was born in Mexico City on August 14, 1645, a fact that he recorded himself for posterity in a note in folio 111 verso of Mexico City's *Primer libro de actas de Cabildo*, the most old and important book he saved from the flames when the viceregal palace was set on fire during the riots of 1692.[2] His father, Carlos de Sigüenza, native of Madrid, had been the first writing tutor of prince Baltasar Carlos before leaving for the New Spain with the entourage of the new viceroy, Marquis of Villena. In Mexico, he spent most of his life as second officer of the Ministry of Government and War. The young Sigüenza began his formal education in 1660, when he entered the novitiate of the Society of Jesus in Tepotzotlán, where he studied rhetoric in its college. In 1662, at the age of 17, he took the simple vows of the Jesuits and continued his academic education by studying philosophy at the Colegio de San Pedro y San Pablo in Mexico City. The highly promising career of the young Jesuit ended abruptly in 1667, when he was expelled from the Society of Jesus after sneaking out a few times at night while teaching at the Colegio del Espíritu Santo in Puebla.

This reversal of fortune did not thwart the ambitions of the Criollo prodigy, but forced him to seek fame outside the powerful Society of Jesus. Promptly, he resumed his studies on canon law that he had started the same year at the Royal and Pontifical University of Mexico, and privately devoted to the studio of mathematics, astronomy and astrology. In 1672 he obtained the chair of astrology and mathematics at the University of

Detail of the **Folding screen of the Conquest** (reverse). In this relation it is enhance the Cathedral, with the number 1, and at the bottom, a landscape of the street of the Archbishopric, a street that Carlos de Sigüenza y Góngora surely walked through in many occasions. [CAT. 24]

26
27
28
29
67
1

This work, published in 1698, bears witness to the grandeur of Mexico City and the achievements of its residents in regard to the embellishment of it, after its founding by the Spaniards in 1521. It collects the highlights of the city of Puebla and noteworthy events in America. Its author was the Franciscan Agustín de Vetancurt, who also wrote and account of the Province of the Santo Evangelio. [CAT. 5]

Mexico, even being self-taught in these subjects. At the time, Sigüenza also became interested for pre-Hispanic civilizations in the Valley of Mexico, and began his collection of indigenous codices and manuscripts that soon would became the largest in its subject. As his fame grew, he accumulated new positions and titles, most of them more prestigious than remunerated: royal cosmographer (1680), general artillerymen examiner (1680), chaplain at the Hospital del Amor de Dios (1682), accountant of the University (1690) and general book examiner for the Holy Office of the Inquisition (1699).

Barely a year after leaving the Society of Jesus, Sigüenza started his literary career at the age of 22 by publishing an epic poem dedicated to Our Lady of Guadalupe, *Primavera indiana* (1668), composed in 1662 when he hadn't taken the Jesuit vows yet. This publication wouldn't have been possible without the patronage of the eminent Criollo Pedro Velázquez de la Cadena, the very same patron who paid Sor Juana Inés de la Cruz's dowry when she entered the convent of San Jerónimo in 1663. His first printed work enabled him to begin to restore his public image, and to distinguish his poetry and himself by adopting the surname of an illustrious maternal relative, the renowned Spanish poet Luis de Góngora. He utilized the title page of *Primavera indiana* to use for the first time his double last name: Carlos de Sigüenza y Góngora. Although the precise relationship between Luis de Góngora and Sigüenza must still be confirmed, his friend Francisco de Florencia stated in his Guadalupan treatise *La estrella del norte* (1688) that the most distinguished Spanish poet was Sigüenza's uncle.[3] The sole document in which his mother is mentioned with the surname Góngora—"Doña Dionisia Suárez de Figueroa y Góngora"— is the biographic note he left in Mexico City's *Primer libro de actas de Cabildo*.[4] Sigüenza only once referred to his famous "uncle" when he mentioned incidentally, in his *Teatro de virtudes políticas* (1680) that Luis de Góngora was "my relative."[5]

The cult of Our Lady of Guadalupe, which arose around mid century, became the center of the most vigorous and dominant expressions of Criollo patriotism, from its beginning until Mexican independence. The spread of the cult was promoted mainly by the writings of four members of the Criollo clergy: Miguel Sánchez (*Imagen de la Virgen*, 1648), Luis Lasso de la Vega (*Hvei tlamahviçoltica*, 1649), Luis Becerra Tanco (*Felicidad de*

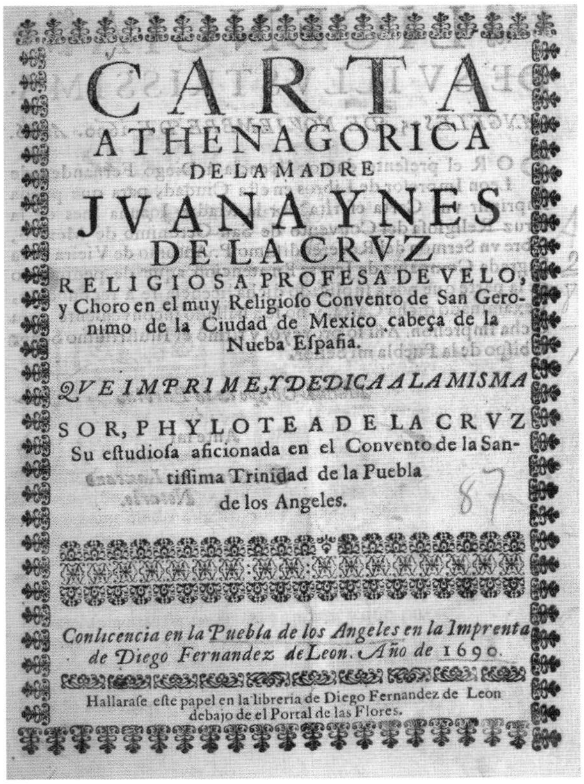
CARTA
ATHENAGORICA
DE LA MADRE
JVANA YNES
DE LA CRVZ
RELIGIOSA PROFESA DE VELO,
y Choro en el muy Religioſo Convento de San Geronimo de la Ciudad de Mexico cabeça de la Nueba Eſpaña.
QVE IMPRIME, Y DEDICA A LA MISMA
SOR, PHYLOTEA DE LA CRVZ
Su eſtudioſa aficionada en el Convento de la Santiſſima Trinidad de la Puebla de los Angeles.
Con licencia en la Puebla de los Angeles en la Imprenta de Diego Fernandez de Leon. Año de 1690.
Hallaraſe eſte papel en la libreria de Diego Fernandez de Leon debajo de el Portal de las Flores.

Sor Juana Inés de la Cruz, Carlos de Sigüenza y Góngora and Juan Ruiz de Alarcón, all three were very emphasized in the Novohispanic literature. Sor Juana Inés de la Cruz, poet and dramatist, was Known as the "Tenth Mexican Muse". She died in 1695 in Mexico City. [CAT. 132]

México, 1685) and Francisco de Florencia (*La estrella de el norte de México*, 1688). The image of Our Lady of Guadalupe, venerated in a small chapel in Tepeyac—or Tepeaquilla, as it was known at the time—had only been subject of local devotion from 1648 on, when Miguel Sánchez published his *Imagen de la Virgen*. In the first book devoted to Our Lady of Guadalupe, Sánchez formalized one century of oral tradition about the Virgin's apparitions to Juan Diego, and also dated them between December 9 and 12, 1531. In his treatise, Sánchez established that his purpose wasn't just to narrate any Marian story, but to interpret the transcendence and symbolism of this miraculous visitation to his Criollo homeland. He expounded the discovery and conquest of Mexico as part of a divine plan so that the Virgin of Guadalupe, God's most perfect image, appeared on His chosen land. The arrival of Guadalupe transformed Mexico into a new Holy Land, and made of his children, as with the former Israelites, the chosen people of God. The impact of Sánchez's work on the religious, cultural and political history of Mexico can not be exaggerated, because *Imagen de la Virgen* did not only invent the cult of Our Lady of Guadalupe, but laid the foundations of the Mexican homeland.

For the dates of its composition and publication, *Primavera indiana* is the first significant literary work devoted to the Mexican Virgin. By using the word "*indiana*" in the title, Sigüenza didn't refer to the Indian population but to the Criollos, or *Indianos*, according to popular terminology in Spain during the viceregal era. Sigüenza aimed his poem for the Criollo population, for whom the miracle of Guadalupe had a larger importance. It is probable that Sigüenza developed his devotion for Guadalupe during his first years as novice in Tepotzotlán, since the Jesuits were among the main promoters of her cult. Due to the prophetic interpretation of the Virgin's apparitions, it is clear that the young Sigüenza was inspired by Sánchez's *Imagen de la Virgen* for his *Primavera indiana*. Based on the apocalyptic images of Sánchez, the "*Indiana* spring" by Sigüenza marked Guadalupan tradition with a millenarianist symbolism. In his "sacred-historical poem," the Mexican winter of paganism yields to the eternal redemptive spring of Guadalupe, symbolized by the miraculous image of the Virgin's flowers, to cause the dawn

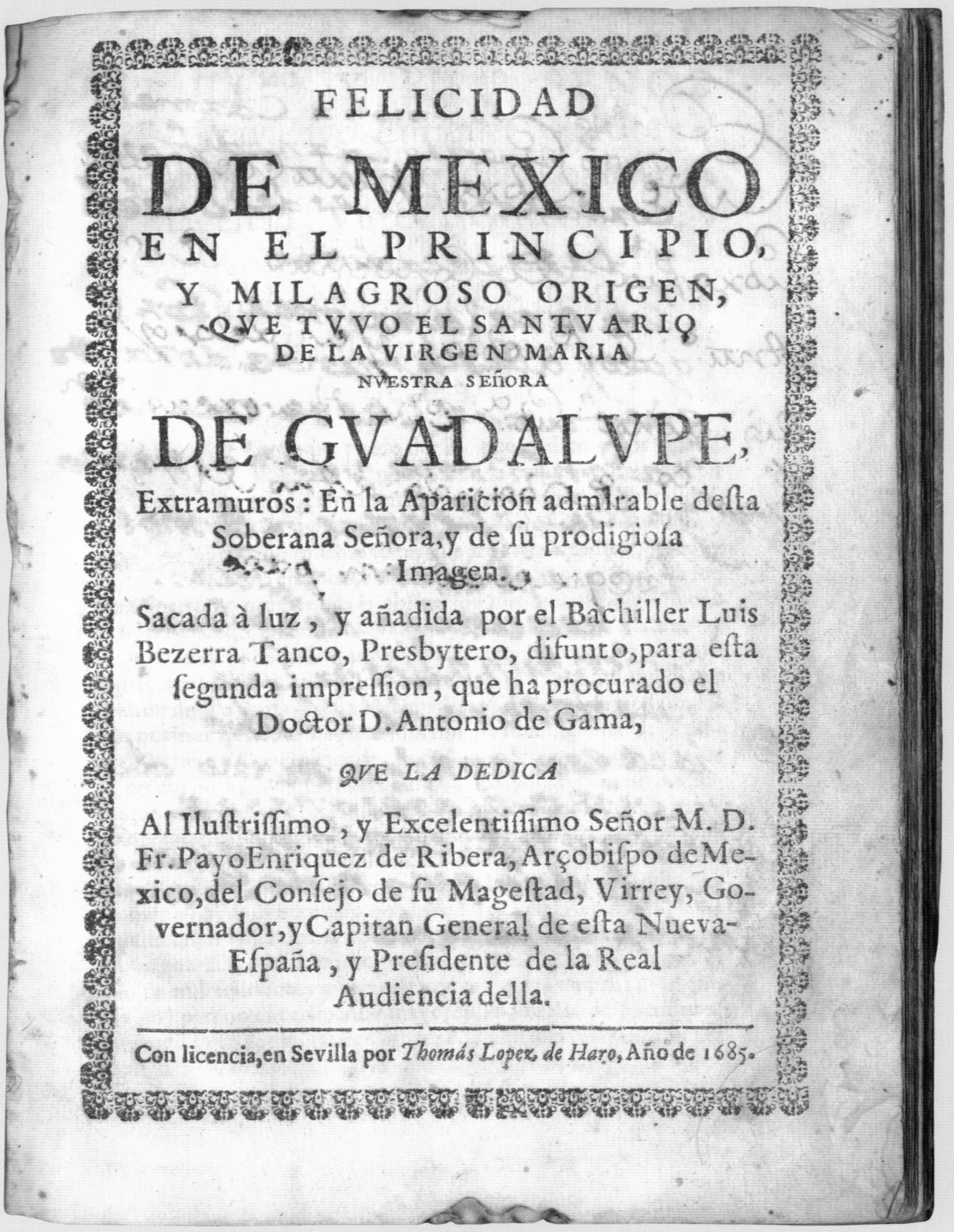

FELICIDAD

DE MEXICO

EN EL PRINCIPIO,

Y MILAGROSO ORIGEN,

QVE TVVO EL SANTVARIO

DE LA VIRGEN MARIA

NVESTRA SEñORA

DE GVADALVPE,

Extramuros: En la Aparicion admirable desta Soberana Señora, y de su prodigiosa Imagen.

Sacada à luz, y añadida por el Bachiller Luis Bezerra Tanco, Presbytero, difunto, para esta segunda impression, que ha procurado el Doctor D. Antonio de Gama,

QVE LA DEDICA

Al Ilustrissimo, y Excelentissimo Señor M. D. Fr. Payo Enriquez de Ribera, Arçobispo de Mexico, del Consejo de su Magestad, Virrey, Governador, y Capitan General de esta Nueva-España, y Presidente de la Real Audiencia della.

Con licencia, en Sevilla por *Thomás Lopez de Haro*, Año de 1685.

The author of this work is Luis Becerra Tanco. It was published in 1685. Becerra Tanco was a connoisseur of ancient languages like Hebrew, Latin and Greek as well as Nahuatl and Otomi, which allowed him an approach described by Francisco de la Maza as "scientific" to the miracle of the Guadalupan apparition. In his text, he admits that he seeks to narrate the "true" and adhere to sobriety in the speech. [CAT. 139]

of a Criollo paradise. The deepest impact of *Primavera indiana* among the Criollos came from the promulgation of the pre-eminence of the Mexican homeland.

The second main work by Sigüenza, *Glorias de Querétaro* (1680), in which he recounts the consecration of a new Guadalupan temple in Querétaro in 1680, approved by archbishop-viceroy Payo Enríquez de Ribera, highlights the growth of the cult outside the Valley of Mexico. *Glorias de Querétaro* made him possible to publish a Guadalupan "song" that he had composed as a homage to the archbishop, his sponsor; besides, it enabled him to release a new revised edition of *Primavera indiana*. Sigüenza's initial difficulties were thwarted and clearly benefited from the spread of the cult of Guadalupe and the archbishop's sponsorship. Sigüenza's contributions to the development of the Guadalupan cult did not end with these literary works, because he would later have a main role in the historical authentication of the apparitions.

In the mid-1680's, Sigüenza acquired the manuscripts collected by Fernando de Alva Ixtlilxóchitl, which included the earliest Guadalupan report: the *Nican Mopohua*. This acquisition placed him at the center of the controversy about the authorship of this anonymous manuscript. The lack of ecclesiastical documentation contemporary to the apparitions, and particularly the remarkable silence of bishop Juan de Zumárraga, had motivated the anti-apparitionist debate from the publication of *Imagen de la Virgen* on, by Sánchez. Therefore, the identification and authentication of the original Guadalupan account became the deepest concern for Criollo patriots like Sigüenza, because only that original account could justify the miracle that had defined their religious and cultural independence from Europe.

In what turned out to be a historic revelation, Sigüenza swore in his *Piedad heroyca*, completed around 1694, that the real author of the original account was not the Franciscan apostle Agustín de Mendieta—as Francisco de Florencia declared in *Estrella de el norte de México* (1688)—, but the 16th century erudite Indian Antonio Valeriano.[6] Born around 1531, Valeriano was educated at the Colegio de Santa Cruz de Tlatelolco, was one of the main collaborators of Bernardino de Sahagún in the *Historia general*, and as teacher he had Juan de Torquemada as one of his disciples.[7] The truthfulness of his report, dating from mid-17th century, was not called into question since his oral sources were contemporary witnesses and even original participants. The conclusive identification of Valeriano's manuscript by Sigüenza finally provided the historical validation that the Criollos had sought for decades. After the death of Sigüenza in 1700, when the holographic manuscript by Valeriano disappeared, his testimony about the authenticity of the *Nican Mopohua* has been the basis for documenting the Guadalupan miracle from the 18th century on.[8] Therefore, generations of Guadalupan devotees have immortalized Sigüenza as a key figure in the shaping of the most transcendental religious movement in Mexico's history.

The year of 1680 marked the height of Sigüenza's efforts to assert his Criollo patriotism, especially in his attempts to claim Mexico's Indian history for the Criollos, and it was

Many images of the Virgin of Guadalupe were to be "touched" by the original. This means that, whether a sketch on canvas, or a piece with shell inlay like this, some part of the work had the opportunity to touch for a few moments the *tilma* venerated in the Basilica of Guadalupe. As it was believed that the *tilma* communicated sacredness to the objects it touched and gave them a miraculous nature, the artists who produced "touched" images took care to state that aspect on the piece, which, of course, would not have the same value if it had not undergone such treatment. [CAT. 4]

during this same year that he composed his most daring works. The "song" in *Glorias de Querétaro* (1680), which he dedicated to the archbishop, gave him the opportunity to openly introduce the issue of Mexican supremacy, expressing in his statement:

Embaraço del ayre
De Querétaro nobles suspensiones,
Sin mendigar a Europa perfecciones,
Ni rezelar del tiempo algun desayre[9]

It was also in the title page of *Glorias de Querétaro* that he introduced for the first time his engraved emblem with the winged horse Pegasus and the Latin motto *Sic itur ad astra* ("So it goes to the stars"), which he used in all his subsequent publications. The use of a personal emblem in his works was another sign of his Criollo spirit, since traditionally the use of emblems was restricted to European nobility. By adopting the Pegasus emblem for his works, Sigüenza took over an acknowledged symbol of European superiority and turned it into an expression of the intellectual and cultural equality of the Criollos. It seems that this novelty introduced by a Criollo scholar caused quite some curiosity among the Novohispanic elite, because Sigüenza offered his readers an explanation on the patriotic symbolism of his emblem on two occasions in 1680: a brief one in his *Lunario* for 1681, and an enlarged version in the "Preludio II" of *Teatro de virtudes políticas* (1680). In short, Sigüenza explained that he had chosen the Pegasus' emblem as personal symbol because it represented the individual that always strains his soul towards the sublime in benefit of his homeland.

In the New Spain existed the long tradition of receiving in the new viceroys with triumphal arches sponsored by Mexico City's Council and Cathedral. Traditionally, triumphal arches were ephemeral monumental structures made of wood reaching 25 meters high, 14 meters width and three and a half between its facades. Inspired by ancient Roman models, triumphal arches had three bodies or levels, incorporating classic columns, and decorated and/or painted simulating veined marble and bronze. This entire splendor served as frame for allegorical paintings with poems or emblems, which represented the virtues of the new viceroy. In 1680, for the arrival of Viceroy Tomás Antonio de la Cerda y Aragón, Count of Paredes and Marquis of La Laguna, two prominent erudite Criollos were entrusted with the design of the arches of the City Council and the Cathedral: Sigüenza and Sor Juana Inés de la Cruz, respectively. According with the tradition, Sor

Carlos de Sigüenza y Góngora introduced in this work, for the first time, an engraved emblem representing a winged horse—the Pegasus of the classical tradition—, with the Latin motto *Sic itur ad astra*, which means "So it goes to the stard," referring to the improvement of the individual, always seeking higher aims. [CAT. 81]

GLORIAS DE QUERETARO

EN LA

NUEVA CONGREGACION

Eclesiastica de MARIA Santissima de Guadalupe, con que se ilustra:

Y

EN EL SUMPTUOSO TEMPLO, QUE dedicò à su obsequio

D. JUAN CAVALLERO, Y OCIO

Presbytero, Comissario de Corte del Tribunal del Santo Oficio de la Inquisicion.

ESCRIVELAS

D. Carlos de Siguenza, y Gongora

Natural de Mexico, Cathedratico proprietario de Mathematicas en la Real Universidad de esta Corte.

EN MEXICO:
Por la Viuda de Bernardo Calderon.

IXI DC LXXX

THEATRO
DE VIRTVDES POLITICAS,
QVE
Constituyen á vn Principe: advertidas en los Monarchas antiguos del Mexicano Imperio, con cuyas efigies se hermoseó el
ARCO TRIVMPHAL,
Que la muy Noble, muy Leal, Imperial Ciudad
DE MEXICO
Erigiò para el digno recivimiento en ella del Excelentissimo Señor Virrey
CONDE DE PAREDES,
MARQVES DE LA LAGVNA, &c.

Ideòlo entonces, y ahora lo descrive

D. Carlos de Siguenza, y Gongora
Cathedratico proprietario de Mathematicas en su Real Vniversidad.

EN MEXICO: Por la Viuda de Bernardo Calderon.
∞ DC LXXX.

Juana chose a god from classical mythology, Neptune, to symbolize the virtues of the new viceroy. The symbolism was appropriated, since the Marquis of La Laguna had arrived to rule a kingdom whose capital was founded by the Aztecs on an island in the Texcoco lake. Sor Juana described and explained her creation on a pamphlet entitled *Neptuno alegórico, océano de colores, simulacro político* (1680).

The triumphal arch commissioned by the City Council to Sigüenza, described in his *Teatro de virtudes políticas* (1680), one of the most daring treatises printed during the entire viceregal era, offered to the new viceroy and Mexico's entire population the Aztec monarchs idealized as symbols of princely virtues. With this unprecedented act, he declared that the indigenous cultural heritage of his homeland equaled in esteem and symbolic value the Greco-Roman heritage of the Old World. Before God, King and country, Sigüenza publicly claimed the history of ancient Mexico for himself and for all the Criollos. Even if, from a modern perspective, it is easy to notice political purposes to his acts, Sitgüenza's aim was not to start a rebellion but to provide the Criollos with a historical past as valuable as the glorified present. If the native population had been perceived as a threat at the time, the potentially inflammatory allegory by Sigüenza wouldn't have been carried out. Sigüenza's Indians were not those of contemporary Mexico but belonged to an indigenous past that was being mythified by erudite Criollos.[10]

In anticipation to the criticism of his work by the Novohispanic elite, Sigüenza used the "Preludio II" of *Teatro de virtudes políticas* to justify his use of historical figures, instead of mythological ones, as symbols of princely virtues. The title of his essay clearly stated his intentions: "Love owed to the country is the reason for, disdaining fables, looking for a more praiseworthy idea to embellish this triumphal facade." In his essay, Sigüenza rejected the practice of his predecessors of looking for inspiration in classical mythology when he wrote: "A style common to American talents has been to beautify with mythological ideas of lying fables most of the triumphal facades erected to welcome the princes."[11] After saying this, Sigüenza had to devote another essay, "Preludio III", to defend his fellow countrywoman Sor Juana for choosing Neptune as symbol of the viceroy, all summed up in its title: "Neptune is not a faked god of pagans, but son of Misraim, grandson of Cam, great-grandson of Noah, and parent of the West Indians."

As it's possible to imagine, Sigüenza had not to wait too long before his arch was criticized. The Criollo Juan Antonio Ramírez Santibáñez printed his own versified account about the arrival of the viceroy: *Relación piérica de la solemnidad con que recibió México a su virrey el Conde de Paredes* (1680), in which he expressed what was probably common opinion about Sigüenza's arch:

Un arco bien levantado
la ciudad sin interés
aquí le tuvo formado,
que alabándolo cortés
no dejó de estar aindiado.[12]

In this work, Sigüenza refers to the former Indian nobility, in an effort to dignify and place it at the same level as the great leaders of the Greco-Roman antiquity. The figures of the Mexica characters were inserted as part of the iconographic program of the triumphal arch erected to honor the arrival of the Viceroy Conde de Paredes, Marquis de la Laguna. [CAT. 80]

Even sixteen years later, another Criollo writer of certain fame, Alonso Ramírez de Vargas, offered a subtle censure of the "Indian-like" arch in relation with the arch made for the arrival of the Viceroy Count of Moctezuma, *Zodiaco ilvstre de blasones heroicos* (1696):

> That the swans of this Mexican Cayster have exhausted in arguments the ideas of the greatest heroes of pagan times in praiseworthy welcomes and triumphal arches, that have been erected by the courtier for Their Excellencies the Viceroys until now, doesn't seem, perhaps, but providence.[13]

By referring to the "swans," Ramírez de Vargas alluded to the well-known sonnet "Dulce canoro cisne mexicano" ("Sweet, canorous Mexican swan") that Sor Juana dedicated to Sigüenza in 1680. Although his manifestation of Criollo patriotism in *Teatro de virtudes políticas* was received with disdain by many of his contemporaries, over a century after his death Sigüenza was still a vital source of inspiration for Criollo patriots like Friar Servando Teresa de Mier and Carlos María de Bustamante, who gave political character to Sigüenza's benign glorification of ancient Mexican civilizations in order to defend Mexican nationalism during the insurgency of 1810.[14]

A celestial phenomenon in 1680 drove some of the most transcendental expressions of Sigüenza's Criollo spirit in his *Libra astronómica y filosófica* (1690). Between November 15, 1680, and January 1681, a comet appeared in the sky over Mexico and sparked an intense debate about the nature of comets among professional and amateur astronomers residing in the New Spain. The following controversy provoked a confrontation between traditional and modern scientific beliefs about cometology. Sigüenza headed the debate to ease the public hysteria, fed by the superstition that comets were omens of disasters and bad luck. The Vicereine Countess of Paredes was among the alarmed citizens for whom Sigüenza printed a pamphlet entitled *Manifiesto filosófico contra los cometas despojados del imperio que tenían sobre los tímidos* (1681). His brief treatise, based on the most modern scientific theories, explained that comets were mere stars ruled by nature's laws to be found in extremely eccentric solar orbits. This manifest incited the debate that confronted Sigüenza with three astronomers—one Criollo and two Europeans—, which resulted in a competition of Criollo pride and intellectual equality.

The first and most prestigious to reply to him was the German Jesuit Francisco Eusebio Kino, who had recently arrived and quickly prepared his own study, dedicated to the viceroy: *Exposición astronómica del cometa* (1681), partially based on the observations of the comet he had made in Cádiz. Kino's treatise stated the scientific beliefs still prevailing in Europe, in which comets represented malevolent forces. This conviction placed him in direct opposition with the more progressive beliefs of Sigüenza. The other participants in the debate issued pamphlets and manuscripts with the same scientific point of view as Kino. Sigüenza kept his real intellectual fury against Kino and expressed it in his erudite

As cosmographer and mathematician at the service of King Charles II, Sigüenza spent time in this work to expound on the relationship between comets and the Apocalypse. A circumstance that marked the publication of *Libra astronómica...* was precisely the passage of a comet in the year 1680, a phenomenon that alarmed many people, including the Viceroyalty of New Spain. [CAT. 78]

LIBRA ASTRONOMICA, Y PHILOSOPHICA

EN QUE

D. Carlos de Siguenza y Gongora

Cosmographo, y Mathematico Regio en la Academia Mexicana,

EXAMINA

no solo lo que à su MANIFIESTO PHILOSOPHICO contra los Cometas opuso el R. P. EUSEBIO FRANCISCO KINO de la Compañia de JESUS; sino lo que el mismo R. P. opinò, y pretendio haver demostrado en su EXPOSICION ASTRONOMICA del Cometa del año de 1681.

Sacala à luz D. SEBASTIAN DE GUZMAN Y CORDOVA, Fator, Veedor, Proveedor, Iuez Oficial de la Real Hazienda de su Magestad en la Caxa desta Corte.

En Mexico: por los Herederos de la Viuda de Bernardo Cal deron

IXI. DC. XC.

treatise *Libra astronómica y filosófica*, which for lack of sponsor was not printed until 1690. Based on his observations of the comet in 1680 and 1681, and supported on Aristotle's authority, Sigüenza destroyed methodically Kino's cometological theories. *Libra astronómica*, a milestone in Mexico's science history, gave Sigüenza the opportunity to state the Criollo intellectual superiority by sarcastically attacking the Old World stereotype, embodied by the beliefs of Kino:

> In some parts of Europe, specially in the Northern ones, even if remote, think that not only the Indians, the original inhabitants of these countries, but also those of us of Spanish parents that were born in them by chance, walk on two feet by divine dispensation or that even making use of English microscopes hardly can the rational be discovered in us.[15]

Sigüenza's definite victory upon publishing *Libra astronómica* was to scientifically demystify the skies for his Novohispanic fellowmen and to demonstrate that a Mexican Criollo was more erudite, more progressive and more advanced in theories than a Jesuit scholar from the University of Ingolstadt.

Sigüenza's scientific contributions to his homeland did not end with *Libra astronómica*. After centuries of exploration and colonization of the New Spain there was still a lack of accurate maps of most of the viceroyalty. Sigüenza, watching for his duties as royal cosmographer, made an effort to improve the geographical knowledge of the New Spain. Several of his maps served to document in more detail some of the farthest frontiers of the viceroyalty. He prepared maps of the 1689 and 1690 expeditions carried out by Alonso de León, governor of Coahuila, to the new province of the Tejas Indians, the current state of Texas in the United States.[16] By order of the viceroy, Sigüenza took part in an expedition to Florida in 1693 with the purpose of identifying the site for the founding of a new town in Pensacola bay. He prepared the official account and made a map of the bay based on his direct observations.[17] It is also documented that Sigüenza surveyed Me xico City twice, in 1688 and 1692, by order of the viceroy.[18] His two more important and influential maps only survive in 18th century copies: the "Mapa general de todo el reyno", the first one covering the entire New Spain traced by a Criollo, and the map of the Valley of Mexico.

Around 1668, while Sigüenza was working on his "Mapa general de todo el reyno", he had access to all the accounts of official expeditions and manuscript maps in government archives, not to mention other available sources in monastic, school and private libraries, but he didn't just rely upon others' documentation. He made his own astronomical observations whenever possible to obtain more accurate calculations of the latitude and longitude of any site. Although his original map is missing, Sigüenza influenced many 18th century New Spain cartographers through the manuscript and printed maps of the

PROVINCIA DE TESCUCO.

Aotonba.
Ostotipac.
Quatlipan.
Venta de Cordova.

Macueso
Veleri.
Tapetlastic.
S.Loranço
S.Marcos.

Teotiteguq
Chometla.
S.Diego.
Coatinchen
Coatepec.
Venta del Chal

S.Maria
Chiauta
S.Cruz
Guapatla.
Istapaluca.

cal co.
Papalotla
S.Simon
Chicoloapan
Atipac.
S.Augustin
Trapac
Ayotla

S.Pablo
Tololcingo
Tepapa
Magdale
Purificacion
S.Bernardino
Chimalguacan
Tlapinaguia
Venta nie

Chiconautla
Teapa
S.Miguel
S.Maria

S.Juan
quanal
NORTE SUR

LAGUNA
S.CHRISTOBAL
Peñol del Marqs
S.Maria

LAGUNA DE TESCUCO
S.Maria
Istaguacan
istapalapa

pomqu berri el nõ
de Guautitlan y
Avenidas de Pa-
chuca a Mexico.

S.Xpobal: S.clara
S.Pedro
Santiago
Peñol dlos lados
Mexicalsingo
Culhacan

S.Juan
Guadalupe
Albarrada agua de los Indios
Itzapalco
Aciendas

S.Cicilia
MEXICO
Piedad
S.Mateo Reyes

S.Barbara
Tudtulan
Chapultepec
Miscoaqu
Tacubaia
S.Jacinto

Cuautitlan
Molino
Teneuco
S.Monica
barranca de Jaltocan
S.Fe
S.Geronimo
S.Bernabe
S.MISCUAQUE

repartidor
Totolpan
S.Martin
S.Maria
Reme dios
Vatan

S.Cruz
Jesus del Monte

Coacan
Chimalpa

Tepatlq

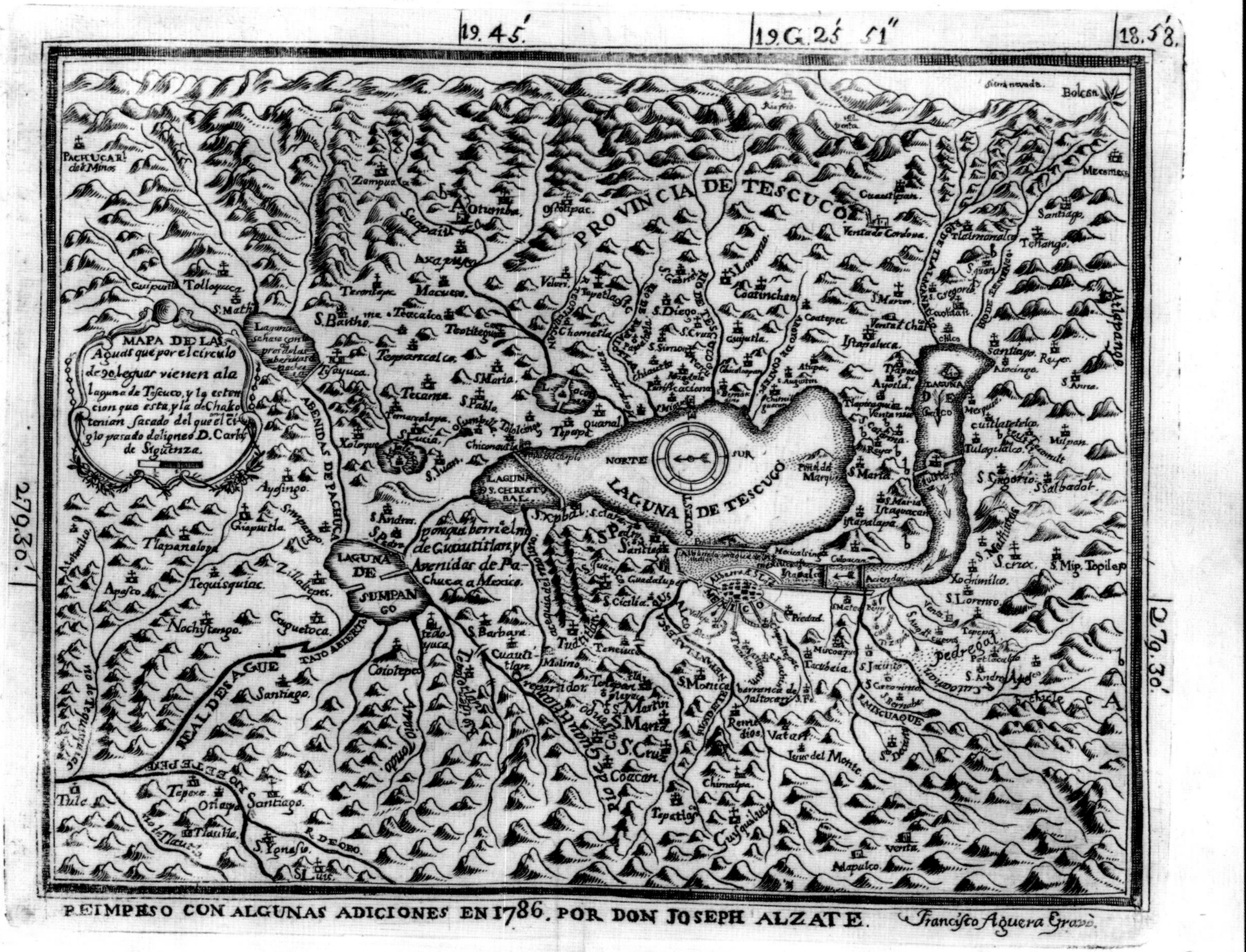

Map of the waters that come through the circle of 90 leagues to the lake of Tescuco. José Antonio Alzate y Ramírez was a scientist interested in the pre-Hispanic past of New Spain, his homeland. *La Gazeta de literatura de México*, founded by Alzate in 1788, was a periodical the purpose of which was the dissemination of science and literature to illustrate the subjects. This figure shows a map of the relief and hydrography of the region around the Lake of Texcoco. This map was traced by Carlos Sigüenza y Góngora and later modified by Álzate himselfIt was published until 1795.*

eminent Criollo scientist José Antonio Alzate y Ramírez (1737-1799). One of the most important cartographers of the Age of Enlightenment, Alzate acknowledged the importance of Sigüenza's work in his essay "Estado de la geografía de la Nueva España y modo de perfeccionarla", which he published in 1772 in his scientific journal *Asuntos varios sobre ciencias y artes*, where he stated: "The general [map] of the entire kingdom, set out by that wise man, pride of the nation, Don Carlos de Ziguensa [*sic*], is a good demonstration of what that great genius was capable of. His major achievements describing such vast parts of America make one forget the mistakes observed in it."[19] Continuing his praise of Sigüenza, Alzate pointed out that the latitudes and longitudes indicated by Sigüenza for several places in the New Spain were more exact that those of any European authority to that date. After establishing the superiority of Sigüenza's map, Alzate revealed his own debt with the Criollo wise man: "This general map by Don Carlos Ziguensa is the main support of the one I made in 1766, whose copies are in the hands of several persons who have wanted to favor me ascribing some merit to it. I just consider it an attempt, very far from perfection."[20] Alzate's commentaries and the several manuscript and printed versions of his New Spain map that circulated in Mexico and Europe until the end of the viceroyalty ensured the posthumous fame of Sigüenza's contributions to New Spain cartography.

The most known and copied map by Sigüenza was his map of the Valley of Mexico, perhaps prepared in 1691 when the viceroy consulted him about the never-ending project for the Valley's drainage. This map was printed for the first time in 1748 in a report about Mexico City's drainage and identified with the title "Map of the waters that through the 90 league circle flow into the Tescuco lake and of the former extension of this lake and the one of Chalco, taken from the one drawn by Don Carlos de Siguenza the previous century."[21] It was again Alzate who popularized the map of the Valley of Mexico by Sigüenza through manuscript adaptations and printed versions of it. In 1786 Alzate printed the map at his expense, crediting Sigüenza for his creation in the title and praising the wise Criollo in the accompanying text. From the 1780's until the mid-19th century, Sigüenza's map of the Valley of Mexico produced plenty of copies. The Spanish cartographer Tomás López copied it to accompany the *Historia de la conquista de México* by Antonio de Sólos y Rivadeneira, printed in Madrid in 1783, and his son Juan López printed a loose-leaf revised version of the map in 1785. Alzate printed it again without the text in 1790 in his journal *Gazeta de literatura de México* to accompany his essay "Descripción topográfica de México", and an adaptation of Sigüenza's map by Manuel Mascaró accompanied the *Calendario mannual y guía de forasteros en México* printed by Manuel Zúñiga y Ontiveros from 1794 until 1821.[22]

When the next generations of Criollo scholars and patriots looked back into the past for their precursors and to validate their cause, they found in Sigüenza and his work their most illustrious ancestor. This impression was based on the knowledge they had about his

BIBLIOTHECA
MEXICANA
SIVE
ERUDITORUM HISTORIA VIRORUM,
qui in America Boreali nati, vel alibi geniti, in ipſam Domicilio aut Studijs aſciti, quavis linguâ ſcripto aliquid tradiderunt:
Eorum præſertim qui pro Fide Catholicâ & Pietate ampliandâ fovendâque, egregiè factis & quibuſvis Scriptis floruere editis aut ineditis.
FERDINANDO VI
HISPANIARUM REGI CATHOLICO
NUNCUPATA.
AUTHORE
D. JOANNE JOSEPHO DE EGUIARA ET EGUREN, Mexicano, electo Epiſcopo Jucatanenſi, Metropol. Eccleſiæ patriæ Canonico Magiſtrali, Regiæ et Pontificiæ Univerſitatis Mexicanenſis Primario et Emerito Theologiæ Anteceſſore, quondamque Rectore, apud Sanctæ Inquiſitionis Officium Cenſore, Illmi. Archiepiſcopi Mexicani Conſultore, et Diœceſis Examinatore Synodali, Capucinarum Virginum à Confeſſionibus et alijs ſacris.
TOMUS PRIMUS
Exhibens Litteras A B C.
MEXICI:
Ex novâ Typographiâ in Ædibus Authoris editioni ejuſdem Bibliothecæ deſtinatâ. Anno Domini
MDCCLV.

life and works, as much as on his works that circulated printed or manuscript. In *Bibliotheca mexicana* (1755), one of the peaks of 18th century Criollo erudition, Juan José de Eguiara y Eguren celebrated Sigüenza as the most distinguished son of the Mexican homeland.[23] For the revisionist historians at that time, like Lorenzo Boturini Benaducci (1702-1755), Francisco Javier Clavigero (1731-1787) and Mariano Veytia (1718-1780), Sigüenza's researches on indigenous civilizations, always welcomed within the context of his legendary collection of manuscripts and codices, provide them with a model for research methodology and also a fundamental resource for their own investigations while they struggled to claim Mexico's ancient past.

In a time when Criollos had not yet found a common voice to express their cultural autonomy, Sigüenza played the roles of architect, promoter and champion of the new culture. Like no other Criollo scholar of the 17th century New Spain, Sigüenza defined and articulated the concerns that gave rise to Criollo consciousness: the struggle against Old World prejudices, the search for the acknowledgment of their intellectual equity, and, above all, the search for autonomous cultural and religious identities. Sigüenza was the first to synthesize the several manifestations of Criollo patriotism, uniting the cultural heritages of Indians and Criollos. Sigüenza's legacy to his Mexican homeland was an original history recreated in an image that would be equal to those of Spain and the Old World.

Juan José de Eguiara y Eguren was one of the great defenders of the intellectual integrity of Spanish America. In his *Bibliotheca Mexicana*, he reflects on the history of New Spainn and the brightness of its minds, besides being a collection of the distinguished works of local scholars in an attempt to publicize the scientific and literary production of the viceroyalty. [CAT. 128]

NOTES

1. Jacques Lafaye, *Quetzalcóatl y Guadalupe: La formación de la conciencia nacional en México,* trans. by Ida Vitale, Mexico City: Fondo de Cultura Económica, 1977, p. 114.

2. Alberto María Carreño, "El Archivo Municipal de la capital de Nueva España y su salvador don Carlos de Sigüenza y Góngora," *Memorias de la Academia Mexicana de la Historia,* Mexico City: 1949, vol. 8, p. 324, facsimile between pp. 332-333.

3. Francisco de Florencia, *La estrella de el norte*, Madrid: Lorenzo de San Martín, 1785, p. 698.

4. Carreño, *op. cit.*, p. 324.

5. Carlos de Sigüenza y Góngora, *Seis obras*, Caracas: Biblioteca Ayacucho, 1984, p. 187.

6. Carlos de Sigüenza y Góngora, *Piedad heroyca de don Fernando Cortés*, Jaime Delgado (ed.), Madrid: José Porrúa Turranzas, 1960, p. 65.

7. Ernesto de la Torre Villar and Ramiro Navarro de Anda (eds.), *Testimonios históricos guadalupanos*, Mexico City: Fondo de Cultura Económica, 1982, p. 26.

8. Ernest J. Burrus, SJ, *The oldest copy of the Nican Mopohua*, CARA Studies on Popular Devotion 4, Guadalupan Studies 4, Washington DC: Center for Applied Research in the Apostolate, 1981.

9. Carlos de Sigüenza y Góngora, *Poemas*, Irving A. Leonard (ed.), Madrid: Galo Saez, 1931, p. 77 ["air's embarrassment/from Querétaro noble suspensions/without begging for Europe's perfections / or distrusting from time any rejections"].

10. Lafaye, *op. cit.*, p. 116.

11. Sigüenza, *Seis obras*, p. 172.

12. Francisco de la Maza, *El guadalupanismo mexicano*, Mexico City: Fondo de Cultura Económica, 1984, p. 61 ["an arch well erected / the city without interest / had it here made, / though praising it polite / was still Indian-like"].

13. Alonso Ramírez de Vargas, *Zodiaco illvstre de blasones heroycos*, Mexico City: Juan Joseph Guillena Carrascoso, 1696, p. [Bv].

14. D. A. Brading, *The First America: The Spanish Monarchy, Creole Patriots, and the Liberal State 1492-1867*, Cambridge: Cambridge University Press, 1991, pp. 371-372.

15. Sigüenza, *Seis obras*, pp. 312-313.

16. Pedro Torres Lanzas, *Relación descriptiva de los mapas, planos, &, de México y Floridas existentes en el Archivo General de Indias*, vol. 1, Madrid: Ministerio de Cultura, Dirección General de Bellas Artes y Archivos, 1985, pp. 66-68.

17. Irving A. Leonard, *The Spanish Approach to Pensacola*, 1689-1693, Albuquerque: The Quivira Society, 1939, p. 324.

18. Carlos de Sigüenza y Góngora, *Documentos inéditos*, Irving A. Leonard (ed.), Mexico City: Centro Bibliográfico de Juan José de Eguiara y Eguren, 1963, p. 17; Irving A. Leonard, *Don Carlos de Sigüenza y Góngora: Un sabio mexicano del siglo XVII*, trans. by Juan José Utrilla, Mexico City: Fondo de Cultura Económica, 1984, p. 147.

19. José Antonio Alzate y Ramírez, "Estado de la geografía en la Nueva España y modo de perfeccionarla," *Asuntos varios sobre ciencias y artes*, núm. 7, Mexico City, 1772, p. 51.

20. Ibid., p. 52.

21. José Francisco de Cuevas Aguirre y Espinosa, *Extracto de los autos de diligencias, y reconocimientos de los rios, lagunas, vertientes, y desagues de la capital Mexico, y su valle*, Mexico City: Viuda de D. Joseph Bernardo de Hogal, 1748, map inserted between pp. 42-43.

22. Mitchell A. Codding, "Perfecting the Geography of New Spain: Alzate and the Cartographic Legacy of Sigüenza y Góngora," *Colonial Latin American Review*, vol. 3, 1994, pp. 211-213.

23. Juan José de Eguiara y Eguren, *Bibliotheca mexicana*, Mexico City: Imprenta de la Bibliotheca Mexicana, 1755, p. 470.

VI

Rinda en vez del
aroma nabateo]
sonoros cultos
mi terrestre labio,]
aunque a tan noble
majestuoso empleo]
querúbicos acentos
son agravios.]

Los números (modelo
del deseo)]
sean de tanto empeño
desagravio,]
mientras al orbe
en armoniosa suma]
mi voz cadencias,
rasgos da mi pluma.

The Criollo consciousness

Religious orders and their role in the identity construction in New Spain

Antonio Rubial García

Since the arrival of the first religious orders to the New Spain, in the decade that followed Tenochtitlán's conquest, Franciscan, Dominican and Augustinian friars became a central part of the social landscape, both in rural and urban environments. The strong bonds they established first with the Indian nobility and then with the aristocratic element in the cities, from which many of their own came, made it possible that monasteries became powerful centers of social, economical and cultural action. And when this "ancient" orders were already established, another four arrived into the New Spain: Carmelites, Mercedarians, Brothers of Saint James (*dieguinos*) and Jesuits, orders which soon developed their own bonds with the urban elites. After 1600 two hospitalarian orders made their arrival: the Brothers Hospitallers of St. John of God and the Bethlehemites. All of them experienced a progressive diminution in the number of people that were sent to the New Spain towards the end of the 16th century and during the 18th century. Monasteries, however, continued to grow, because of the entrance of Criollos in their midst. This brought a more intense relationship with the established society.

This process of "*criollización*" (or the process of becoming more criollo) is also seen in female convents. These convents were subjected either to a bishop or to the orders. Many women of the urban elite made these spaces centers of important socioeconomic and cultural activities.

The religious orders acting environments

In two different environments the orders developed their activities: a local and a territorial one. Locally, the monasteries established themselves as structural elements both of "pueblos de indios" and of the cities founded by the Spaniards. In the second case, the religious provinces, as territorial corporations, laid the foundations for regional unities.

Due to the work done by Franciscans, Dominicans and Augustinians, the autochthonous communities of Mesoamerica were integrated as subjects of the Spanish Crown. With the help of the Indian nobility, from the "encomenderos" and viceroys, bishops and other agents of the Crown, these orders congregated the ancient pre-Hispanic fiefdoms around their monasteries. These became seats of doctrine. They were centers of Christian teaching providing a space where the Indians would be able to assimilate and integrate elements of Western culture.

The Franciscan guardian, the Dominican vicar or the Augustinian prior were,

The Spaniards held numerous battles against the Mesoamerican indigenous population: among the most prominent are those of Zempoala and Cholula, two towns that, being densely populated, placed particular challenges for the Spaniards loyal to Cortés. It is said that in these two cities the brutality of the Europeans became apparent, prefiguring the horrors experienced in Mexico during the siege of Tenochtitlán. [CAT. 67]

BATALLA DE SEMPUALA
A. Acude Cortes con la Caballeria contra Acamapich que benia con sus Exersitos. B. Acamapich. C. Maxtlaton Capp.n
D. Acechan los Españo.s del puente ha los Yndios q. estorban El passo. E. Encuentro de Espa.s con Acultuage S.r de Tepanco. F. Untersio de Alcabuseria de Paphilo Narbaez. G. Arcos de Sempuala

Reverse of the **Folding screen of the Conquest**. In this Mexico City landscape, the main buildings, gardens and squares of the Most Nobel and Great City—founded in 1521 by the Spaniards—appear related and identified with numbers. [CAT. 24]

besides being the head of a small community of five or six friars, parish priests and political leaders of these towns and the scattered visits assigned to them. They also had their say in the authorities elections, counseled the neighbors in dictating their wills and were judges in minor matters and family quarrels. The friars devoted themselves in organizing hospitals, confraternities and "cajas de comunidad" (savings banks). They introduced many fruits and the foundations of Western culture among the noble children gathered in their schools. These children would later become their active collaborators.

Amongst the nomadic and semi-nomadic peoples of the North, this activity was undertook by Franciscans and Jesuits, with the help of the Crown, interested in the rich silver veins in those areas. With their missions, these men were important factors in the colonization. With the support of the military, they penetrated mountains and deserts, and became the explorers, cartographers and reporters of the geographical and human reality of those regions.

Christianity, notwithstanding the fact that by the 17th century many of the religious foundings were already consolidated, had not yet penetrated the most profound roots of Indian communities. Secretly they continued celebrating the rites taught to them by their ancestors. They kept their pilgrimages to the sanctuaries of their old gods. Therefore, many clergymen noticed the necessity of substituting the ancient divinities with images of Christ and the Virgin, as a more efficient way for Christian penetration. There was a cult to this series of images, whose miraculous appearance showed divine favor. This cult founded sanctuaries, which began to attract innumerable pilgrims. Our Lord of Chalma, near the Augustinian monastery of Malinalco, was an icon created to substitute the ancient cult of the cave-god Oztotéotl. The Lord of Sacromonte was associated by the Dominicans of Amecameca with the cult to the relics of Friar Martín de Valencia and placed near them to supplant a water related divinity; Our Lady of Izamal became the center of a Franciscan sanctuary erected near an ancient Mayan ceremonial center.

A similar, no less important, role had the monasteries in the shaping and consolidation of Spaniards' cities. They were founded more or less at the same time the city was founded; and were naturally supported by the Spanish neighbors and councils. Mexico City, Puebla, Valladolid, Oaxaca, Guadalajara, Guatemala are examples of this. Thus, Franciscans, Dominicans and Augustinians introduced themselves in the urban social milieu from their very beginning, even before this cities became bishopric sees. Soon enough they founded houses in the "reales" (mining centers) like Zacatecas and San Luis Potosí and in agricultural villages like Querétaro, Atlixco, Celaya or Salvatierra. In all these cities and villages the friars very soon undertook the religious care of the Indian quarters, like happened in the capital, where the Franciscans monopolized the sacraments in Santiago Tlatelolco and San Juan Tenochtitlán, although this last site was latter shared with the Augustinians.

Even though, at first, the religious orders monasteries in those urban spaces were only mere logistical centers from which the distribution and maintenance of the missions

Saint Francis Borgia was the third General of the Society of Jesus and was in charge when the Jesuits came to America to fulfill their ministry. He belonged to the nobility and was part of the court of Emperor Charles V. Being part of the court, he was asked to escort the body of the Empress Elizabeth of Portugal to Granada. When the coffin was opened to bury the body, the saint was horrified at the devastation caused by decay in the once beautiful face of Elizabeth of Portugal. From that moment, he decided not to ever serve a lord who might come under such laws, and he devoted his life and resources to the Society. [CAT. 54]

S. Francisco de Borja

was coordinated, little by little they began lodging schools and novitiates since the mid-16th century. The same happened with Mercedarian and Carmelite monasteries in the last decades of that century. Since then, these houses served also as dispensaries for older, sick or demented fathers, and as dependencies destined for provincial chapters or administrative work. Among the hospitalarian orders these only could be carried out in their headquarters in the Viceroyalty's capital since the hospitals granted to them could not have any convent community.

During the last decades of the 16th century and the first decades of the 17th century, the number of members inhabiting these urban houses raised considerably. These houses grew richer and vast because of the support of Spanish neighbors and councils. In contrast to the hospitalarian and mendicant orders, Jesuits founded, in urban centers, colleges for the Criollo sector. This gave the Jesuits a great prestige and allowed them to accumulate land donated by their benefactors, land which provided for their needs.

Nuns had many functions in the urban sphere. Besides being proprietors of tenant houses and capitals to be loaned, convents were protected environments for women and schools were girls were taught and feminine conduct was modeled.

During the day, to the churches next door of these convents and monasteries, people from all social groups came in order to hear mass, receive the sacraments and to participate in liturgical holy days. In the churches, the faithful obtained news through the sermons, aesthetic pleasure from the music and the visual arts and traded gossip about their fellow parishioners.

It was common, in the presbytery, the lateral chapels, naves and sacristies of these churches, to find the gravestones of gentlemen and ladies, who were sometimes buried with the habit of the corresponding order, according to their rank and their donations. There were also chapels were the members of guilds and confraternities gathered and were buried.

But most important, in the churches images and relics were worshiped. Several of them functioned as urban sanctuaries and welcomed the constant flow of pilgrims that

Nun's shield. Female monastic life in New Spain was actively developed since the 16th century. The first order to settle and to found a convent in Mexico City was that of the Conceptionist nuns. The nuns took the veil in a ceremony of profession where they wore and outfit with which many were immortalized in portraits: the habit of the order, the crown of flowers, a palm decorated usually according to the same patterns as the crown, an effigy of the Baby Jesus and a shield, worn on the chest. [CAT. 36]

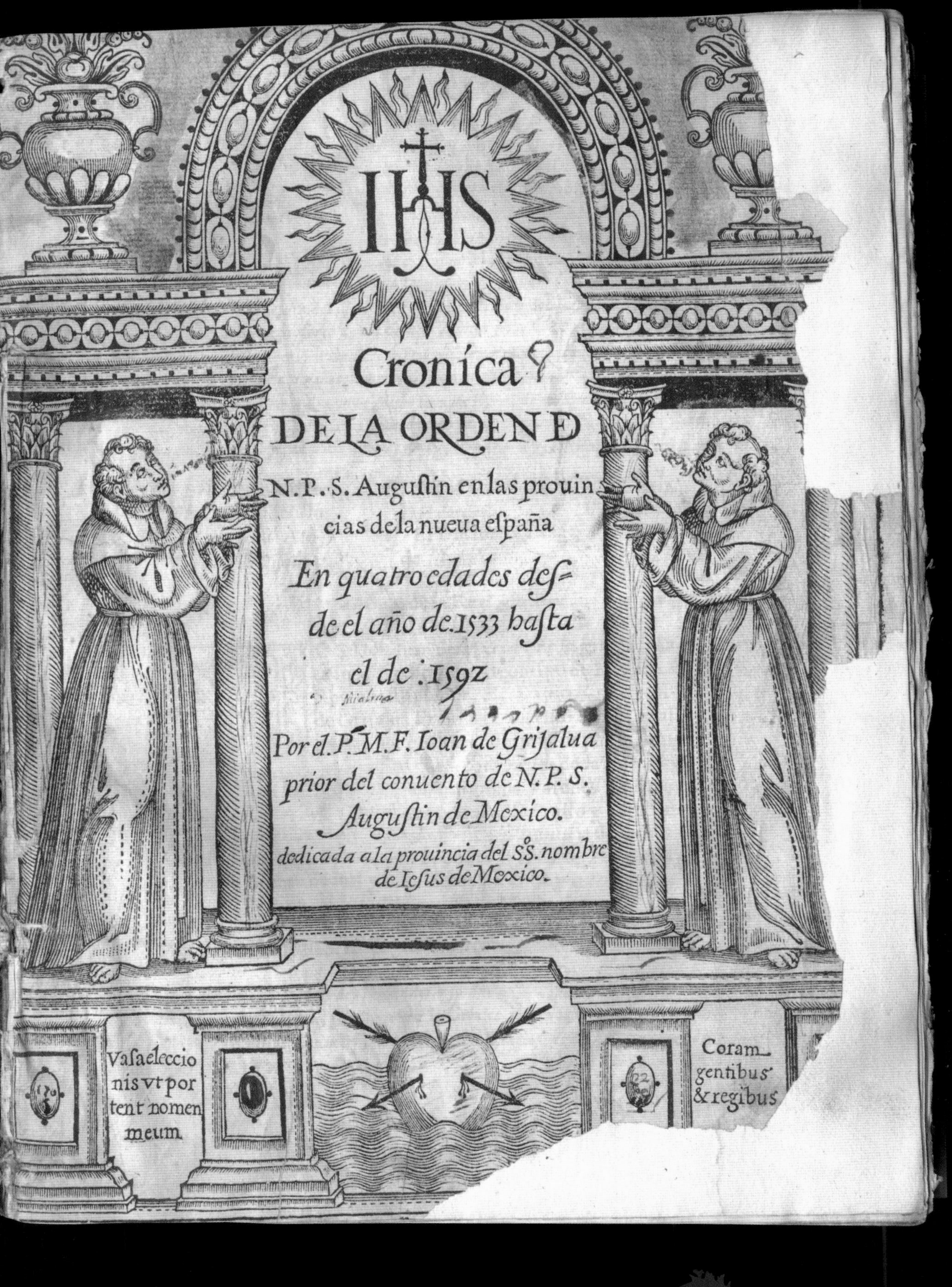
IHS
Cronica
DE LA ORDEN D
N. P. S. Augustin en las prouincias de la nueua españa
En quatro edades desde el año de 1533 hasta el de 1592
Por el P. M. F. Ioan de Grijalua prior del conuento de N. P. S. Augustin de Mexico.
dedicada a la prouincia del SS. nombre de Iesus de Mexico.
Vasa eleccionis vt portent nomen meum
Coram gentibus & regibus

The role played in the spiritual conquest of America by the religious orders was praised by the chroniclers of each of these orders, who focused their attention on the titanic nature of the enterprise undertook by the friars, as well as on how much the Church earned spiritually by converting such a large number of souls. Friar Juan de Grijalva was one of those who wrote the account of the Order of St. Augustine, since their arrival in 1533.*

IHS

MENOLOGIO

de los Varones mas señalados en perfeccion Religiosa De la Provincia de la Compañia de JESUS de Nueva-España.

Escrito por el P. Francisco de Florencia, y aprobado por N. M. R. P. JUAN PAULO OLIVA, Preposito General de la misma Compañia.

Nuevamente añadido â peticion de la Congregacion Provincial, q̄ se celebro en Mexico â principios del mes de Noviembre del año de 1733.

POR EL P.

JUAN ANTONIO DE OVIEDO, Calificador del Santo Officio, y Preposito de la Casa Professa de la misma Compañia de JESUS de Mexico.

Aprobado Por N. M. R. P. Francisco Retz Preposito General año de 17[illegible]

visited them in order to ask for the solution to their needs. The Franciscan church in Puebla sheltered the image of the Conquering Virgin, which, according to one tradition, had been brought by Cortés himself. The Augustinians of Mexico City preserved the miraculous Christ of Totolapan. In Oaxaca, the important sanctuary where Our Lady of Solitude was revered was next to a nuns' convent, as was the chapel of the Holy Christ of Ixmiquilpan, worshipped at the Carmelite nuns' church in the capital. The church of Our Lady of Health in Pátzcuaro was in the keep of Dominican nuns from the 18th century on.

To the thaumaturgical power of the miraculous images it was added that of the relics, which also worked as amulets. Monasteries kept the bodies and all kind of objects belonging to friars and nuns who had died in the odor of sanctity: towels and ribbons with drops of the balsamic sweat their skeletons expelled; fabrics, flowers, sheets that were in contact with the bodies of the venerable: rosaries, scapulars, cilices, wire, rough doublets and other instruments of devotion or penance which had belonged to these ascetic men and women. It was more than often that the faithful begged at the monasteries gate houses to be allowed to touch those relics with their rosary (because their power transmitted itself by mere contact) or to be given a hand of the earth in which the venerable were buried.

The presence of these "miraculous" dead bodies confirmed the central role of members of these orders in urban social and political life. In Mexico City, for instance, friars and Jesuits, as members of the wealthy Criollo families, attended the public acts offered by the court, the university, the cathedral and the monasteries. Several friars and clergymen revalidated the titles obtained in their own orders for university grades and held chairs at the Royal and Pontifical University; and some of them became rectors. At the beginning of the 18th century some Criollo friars were appointed for bishoprics in the New Spain, South America and the Philippines. Many had an influence in political life, as confessors or chaplains of the Viceroyalty authorities, as well as *calificadores* and consultants of the Holy Office of the Inquisition, as orators acknowledged by the viceregal courts or as writers. Notwithstanding an explicit prohibition, some members of the orders belonged to confraternities or brotherhoods or acted as godfathers in baptism; this made for stronger bonds and better businesses. The orders had, besides their political and cultural influence, strong economic interests. Some of the friars made very good deals with private people, even being they were forbidden to them; they also practiced the loan of capital from the alms they received: most convents and monasteries administered rich haciendas and orchards.

Along with these local activities, religious orders were organized in corporations called provinces. In each province existed a variable number of monasteries erected in cities, towns or villages across the territory. Each province had a central, independent government, independent from the other provinces and from the diocese, although in theory they all depended in a direct manner from the general of each order, living in Rome, and, through him, from the Holy Father. Each province was judicially organized

The menologies are compendia coming from the tradition of the Orthodox Church consisting of accounts of the martyrdom of early Christians persecuted, tortured and murdered by the Romans in the ancient Byzantine Empire. The menologies multiplied in the West, as collections of stories of lives of men distinguished by their moral virtues. Each religious order, in each province, had its own list of righteous men. This work bears testimony of the derivations of a scriptural tradition of the Orthodox Church and its adaptation to the context of New Spain.
[CAT. 95]

under constitutions, had the possibility of electing their rector bodies in the provincial chapters were all the heads of the monasteries in the province congregated, and had its own saints, emblems, escutcheons, habits and symbols of identity that were exhibited in processions and civil and religious festivities. This enacted a corporate consciousness that went beyond the city were the headquarters were established (Mexico City, Puebla, Valladolid de Michoacán, Antequera de Oaxaca, Guadalajara, Guatemala or Mérida). The distribution of the three original orders in each of the missionary territories had brought the building of a network of rural monasteries in Indian towns. Each one was not too far from the other and they grouped together around the provincial capital. The Franciscans had six provinces in the New Spain, the Dominicans four and the Augustinians two. The later orders, even having foundations in practically all Spanish cities, only created one province each.

Monasteries as centers of Criollo identity

Since the end of the 16th century, and throughout the next centuries, the New Spain lived through the building of a series of sentiments of belonging and identity that have been denominated with the term "*criollismo*". Today we know that these features were not unique to Criollos; identified with their postulates was also the Indian nobility, many of the so-called Mestizos and even some mainland Spaniards that adopted this land as their homeland. The first "symptoms" of this Criollo sentiment expressed themselves in the extolling of the beauty and fertility of their land (even compared with that of the Garden of Eden), in an idyllic description of its cities (often assimilated with Jerusalem and Rome) and in an apology of the wit and ingenuity of its inhabitants. This optimistic vision responded at first to the contemptuous attitude of the Peninsulares, who considered America to be a degraded continent. This degradation determined that their inhabitants, including those of Spanish descent, were soft, and lazy, incapable of any kind of civility: they had received the vices of the Indians because of the milk of their wet nurses.

To this rhetorical exaltation of space, to which moral depths were bestowed, the reconstruction of a glorious past was soon added. This reconstruction was structured around three thematic lines, all related to the historical memory; the Indian past (basically the Nahuatl past), the foundational facts of the New Spain (the Conquest and the Evangelization) and the prodigious events around the miraculous images and "saints" of their own. These three lines had a simultaneous development, had a mutual influence during the three centuries of viceregal rule and, in their making, orders, monasteries, convents and colleges had a fundamental role.

These centers were not just convivial places: they were structured as spaces that forged the norms of sociability and civility and as guardians of a historical memory stored in their archives and passed, in an oral or visual way, to the new generations. All of them

This image of the Our Lady of the Rosary has a border made up of scenes from the life of the Virgin Mary, beginning with the Annunciation, and following, in a counter clockwise direction, with the Visitation, the birth of Jesus, the Presentation in the Temple, to arrive at the scene of the Virgin in glory, crowned by the Holy Trinity. [CAT. 98]

had this sense of historicity, manifest in the fact that there was a chronicler of each corporation, who had the job of amassing all information, for as good part of the privileges could be defended by the use of this documentary memory. Chronicles, and the paintings filling their walls, reminded those in the monasteries, their illustrious (because of their wisdom or their sanctity) men or women, even though Rome only beatified two of them, the Franciscans Felipe de Jesús and Sebastián de Aparicio. On the other hand, Orders that had administrative powers over Indians, in addition to their missionary activities, engaged in gathering information about the languages and customs of their converts, in order to eradicate the survival of the ancient rites they called idolatry. This is how the first interest in the recovery of the Indian past and the knowledge of the Indian languages emerged.

To face the communication problem that arose from the linguistic diversity and because of the difficulties implied in the use of interpreters, those members of the orders who had most talent for learning languages or those who had come to the New Spain very young and had learned them in their childhood, decided to codify the more widely used languages. With great patience they compiled all the words they learned from the children and searched the grammar that ruled those linguistic constructions. Regardless of the difficulty to reduce the sounds of those languages (some of them tonal) to the Latin alphabet, by the end of the 16th century a corpus of texts that allowed friars and Indians to understand each other already existed. Dictionaries, vocabularies and grammars; collections of sermons (*sermonarios*) and guides for confessors (*confesionarios*) to help those friars who experienced difficulties in their learning; catechisms, lives of saints and biblical passages translated for the use of catechists and literate Indians, short religious plays (*autos sacramentales*) and songs for the propagation of their teachings. The Jesuits in their missions among the northern tribes accomplished a similar work during the 17th and 18th centuries.

In Mesoamerica, some friars and Jesuits thought that, beside languages, it was necessary to know the customs, rites and beliefs that their faithful had before the Conquest, in order to discover the idolater survivals and to be able to transmit the Gospel in a more effective way. To that end, Friar Bernardino de Sahagún, helped by his pupils from the Colegio de Santa Cruz, compiled by means of inquiries made to the elders of Tepeapulco, Tlatelolco and Tenochtitlán, an impressive amount of information about the pre-Hispanic Nahuatl world of the Mexican plateau. His contemporary the Dominican Friar Diego Durán did a similar work; and before them, the Franciscans Friar Andrés de Olmos and Friar Jerónimo de Alcalá had made important contributions to the study of the Nahuas and Purepechas.

All this texts remained unpublished, but they were known and disseminated when the monumental work of another Franciscan, the *Monarquía indiana* (Indian Monarchy) by Friar Juan de Torquemada, was published in Seville in 1615. Endowed with a universalistic

St. Jerome was one of the Fathers of the Church and is known as a deep student of the Holy Bible. Born in Damatia in the fourth century AD, he was named presbyter. He devoted himself to the ascetic life, and undertook the task of translating the Bible into Latin version which was known as the *Vulgate*. In his iconography usually goes a great book—the Holy Scripture—, a skull and a crucifix, symbol of his study and meditation, but also often a trumpet, evoking the Last Judgement. He may appear as the ascetic, that is, naked and in a rough, or dressed as a cardinal. [CAT. 56]

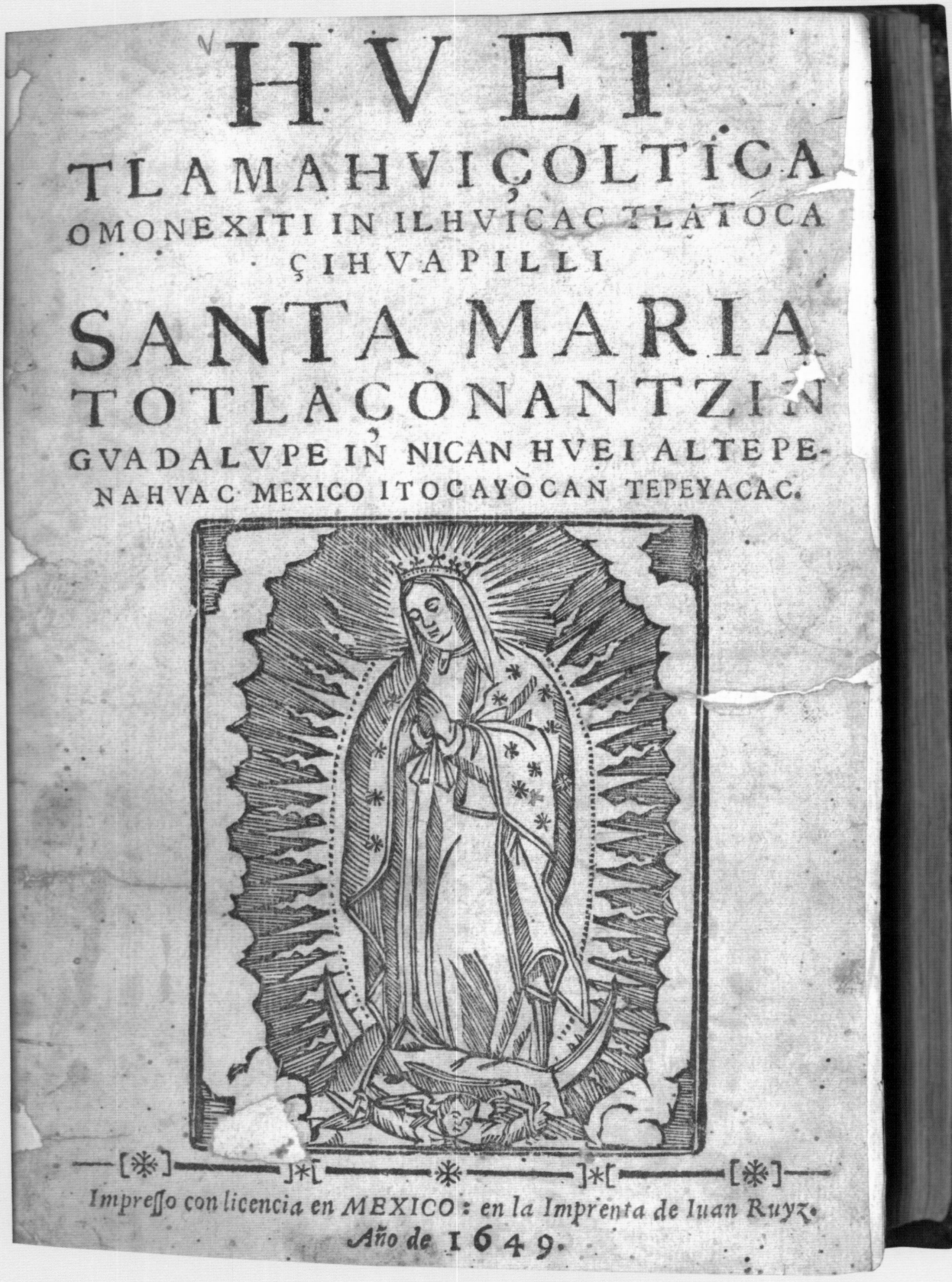
HVEI
TLAMAHVIÇOLTICA
OMONEXITI IN ILHVICAC TLATOCA
ÇIHVAPILLI
SANTA MARIA
TOTLAÇÒNANTZIN
GVADALVPE IN NICAN HVEI ALTEPE-
NAHVAC MEXICO ITOCAYÒCAN TEPEYACAC.
Impresso con licencia en MEXICO: en la Imprenta de Iuan Ruyz.
Año de 1649.

Becerra Tanco was aware of the previously published *Image of the Virgin of God of Guadalupe* (1648) and *Haei Tlamahuizoltica* (1649), published by Miguel Sánchez and Luis Lasso de la Vega. Becerra was based on scientific basis for proving the Virgin aparition and satated that the image was stamped according to Juan Diego to keep it original.*

vision, this work compiled unpublished materials about the Indian world, including those of the friars (Las Casas, Olmos, Motolinía and Sahagún) and those from the Indian and Mestizo nobility (Pomar, Muñoz Camargo, Chimalpáhin, Ixtlilxóchitl and Tezozómoc). In Torquemada's vision the parallels between the Nahuas and the civilizations of the Old World were evident, inserting them in the context of a universal civilization, equal to Greece, Rome or Egypt. This allowed explaining the "fast achievements" of Christianity among them. Furthermore, the arrival of the Gospel had been announced in these parts during their heathenism.

This same interest in directing profane history themes towards a religious vision is observed when Torquemada deals with the subject of Conquest. Hernán Cortés is compared with Moses, because he took the Indians out from the captivity of idolatry to bring them to the Promised Land of true faith. The fall of Tenochtitlán is seen in the guise of the fall of Jerusalem, an idolatrous and sinful city; it is an eschatological view of the end of times. In his interpretation of the prophecy of Daniel that speaks about the fall of the great empires, the Aztec Empire would be the fifth monarchy to fall before the end of the world. This process of the final destruction of Tenochtitlán was proclaimed by presages and prophecies that showed the providential announcement of its redemption according to the divine plan. War, hunger and disease were the just punishment that their idolatry and immorality deserved.

But in fact the military conquest was seen only as a necessity for the spreading of the Gospel. Therefore, the principal function of Torquemada's work was to show the actions of the first missionaries, the protagonists around whom history revolves. They founded the New Jerusalem born into a Golden Age (an idea that Torquemada took from Friar Jerónimo de Mendieta), and this could be because of the activity of these first friars in the New Spain. In that age, Indians and Spaniards lived apart, and that was the reason that the Indian Church could keep itself pure and uncontaminated, directed as it was by apostholic men of standing that lead an irreproachable life and who had the primitive Church as their model. It is clear that Mendieta and Torquemada were writing from an assailing position to the new episcopal policies that tried to displace the friars from their leading role in the Indian communities. The political use that had the defense of the Indians in the 16th century, with authors like Friar Bartolomé de las Casas, changed its course, and became a defense of the friars.

This Franciscan tradition had been born with Friar Toribio de Motolinía in the mid-16th century, and was then completed by Friar Jerónimo de Mendieta and Friar Juan de Torquemada. It generated a universal vision of Novohispanic history in which both the Aztec empire and the Spanish Conquest were seen as a prelude to evangelization. By the end of the 17th century, another Franciscan, Friar Agustín de Vetancurt, would give it a profound Criollo sense in his work entitled *Teatro mexicano*. This monumental work, printed in Mexico in 1698, was divided into four sections that gave news about the geography, the pre-Hispanic Mexica history, the conquest of Mexico-Tenochtitlán, the Franciscan evangelization framed by the biographies of its protagonists, the state of the Franciscan monasteries in the 17th century and the description of the cities of Puebla and Mexico, with their climate, their squares, streets, churches and convents. For him the New Spain was not only the most prosperous part of the world, because from its metals other lands nourished (a metaphor that brings to memory some verses by Sor Juana Inés de la Cruz); it was also a prodigal land in virtuous and intelligent men.

Even if Vetancurt's work possessed an exceptional character, some chroniclers, his contemporaries, like the Dieguino friar Baltasar de Medina and the Dominican Friar Francisco de Burgoa, had a very similar approach. They were Criollos proud of their history and their country, worried about protecting them from oblivion. The literature they produced (almost all miscellaneous even when the central theme was religious) was not only a compendium of past events: it included geographical news and descriptions of present things. The main subject of these chronicles was, however, the description of the lives of friars, lives filled with virtue, piety, sacrifice and devotion, as well as revelations and superhuman feats. Because of the facts compiled in them, these chronicles were also used to complete the general histories of each order in Europe, and through them they had an influence in the conception of the New World in learned circles of the Old World.

Not only the chronicles: to the exaltation of these men and women contributed the funeral sermons, the edifying letters, the inquests about virtues and miracles, particular biographies and the biographies that accompanied a text about a sanctuary. All these texts had a double intention: to give an example of virtue to the generations of young friars of how spirituality had to be practiced in order to mitigate the moral relaxation of the times; but also to justify the rights of the orders over the "doctrinas de indios" or about the right they had that their haciendas were exempted from the tithe, issues that became acrimonious disputes with the bishops.

These texts and chronicles were also important instruments of institutional cohesion; this would explain why all religious provinces had the official post of chronicler. However, these works can be considered as collective, because the corporate tradition allowed that, unpublished chronicles from the orders, jealously guarded in the monasteries archives, could be inserted in others so that would see the light when they were published, influencing the identity discourse of other corporations. Religious authors were the only ones in this period that could print their work.

Something similar happened with the life of the nuns, more often than not included in the chronicles of the friars, or in eulogies or biographies based on unpublished material, that the same nuns wrote and kept in their archives. For a society so obsessed by the fear of the Lord's justice, the nuns, wives of Christ, were intercessors to lessen divine rage bent on annihilating sinners. Their main role was to beg their husband not to send plagues, floods, earthquakes. On their behalf cities were sheltered, less exposed to catastrophes. But the saintly nuns were not only protectors, but also a source of pride for the cities. Most of them were Criollo women who had practiced their virtues and developed a miraculous activity in the place where they were born. So, local oligarchies paid clergymen, in Mexico City, Oaxaca, Puebla, Valladolid and Guadalajara so they would write and publish the lives of these women cloistered behind the walls of their urban convents.

Contrary to those nuns, who belonged to specific urban environments, friars and Jesuits published their works to extol more universal instances such as their religious provinces. The territoriality of these corporations made that their discourse centered not in one city, but in a more ample environment. Their interest was in praising the identity of a corporation that had several foundations in a territory, besides being formed by friars who in turn came from many cities. This corporate sense of the provinces had created, since relatively early dates, an almost homogenous vision of New Spain's territoriality; we might say that the friars wrote the first regional histories, such as the *Historia de Yucatán* by Franciscan Friar Diego López de Cogolludo (Madrid, 1688), the Michoacán chronicles by Augustinian Friar Diego de Basalenque (Mexico, 1673) and Franciscan Friar Alonso de la Rea (Mexico, 1643); the two books about Oaxaca written by the Dominican Friar Francisco de Burgoa (published in Mexico in 1670 and 1674), or the histories of Zacatecas from Friar José Arlegui (Mexico, 1737) and Nueva Galicia by Friar Antonio Tello (unpublished during the viceregal era).

From this regional sense an identity sentiment that encompassed the whole of America opened its way, and in this the religious orders played a fundamental part. From the 16th century on, the mendicant chroniclers spoke already of the kingdom of New Spain or Mexico as an entity where their orders toiled in their missionary, saving undertaking. This can be seen in the titles of the chronicles: those by Franciscan Friar Toribio de Motolinía (unpublished in its own time) and by the Augustinian from Colima Friar Juan de Grijalva (Mexico, 1624) include in its enunciation the words New Spain; the one by the capital born Dominican Friar Agustín Dávila Padilla (printed in Madrid in 1596), speaks about Mexico.

The territoriality issue was consolidated at the end of the 17th century by Criollo authors like the already mentioned Friar Agustín de Vetancurt (with his *Teatro mexicano*) or the Jesuit born in Florida Francisco de Florencia (author of a Jesuit chronicle published unfinished in Mexico City in 1694). By means of this literature, that united time and space with encyclopedic zeal, the Novohispanic memory rooted itself generating a territorial consciousness that went beyond urban localisms.

In the 18th century the Society of Jesus and the Franciscan Propaganda Fide colleges held the central role in this process. The active participation that both institutions had in the frontier expansion because of their missionary activities, resulted in a kind of chronicle that reflected this "Novohispanic territoriality," brought to the far North. The Jesuits made surveys that constituted a real visual appropriation of those territories. Due to them,

PP. 146-147. The Great dimension Chorus books were placed on a huge lectern of fair faces called "facsitol" at the center of a space aroud which the singings were acomodated. Chorus books were made for all the festivities of the Liturgical calendar. [CAT. 62]

Accipe quod offerimus
Recivame Señora mi corazon

Hriſtû
Regem
adoremus domi-
nantem gentibus
*Quiſe manducâ-
tibus datſpiritus

people in the center of the New Spain became aware that the lands of Nueva Galicia, Nueva Vizcaya, Nuevo León, Nuevo México, Texas and California were also a part of this Northern America. Many of the chroniclers belonging to these orders came from the province, like Friar Isidro Félix de Espinosa from Querétaro, or came from other parts of the Americas, like the Jesuit José Antonio de Oviedo, from Bogotá. From the second half of the 18th century on, this sense of America was reinforced by the expelled Jesuits. To those driven out to Italy by Charles III the word "country" began to have a meaning that went beyond the city of their birth and that comprised all of the Americas.

A fundamental part in the construction of this vision was the feeling of living in a land chosen by the divinity to manifest itself. It is because of this that the rich apparitionist Novohispanic tradition became one of the pillars of an identity that we might call "proto-national."

This conception was the creation of Francisco de Florencia, a Jesuit, who had visited the most important Marian European sanctuaries after a voyage to Spain and Italy as procurator for his order between 1669 and 1678. When he returned to the New Spain, he consecrated to gather material to promote, by means of accounting their miraculous events, the local sanctuaries of the New Spain giving them the universal character they had in Europe. His voyage had provided him with ideas to globalize the Novohispanic religious life. His first task was to gather all related material concerning the sanctuaries of the Virgin of Guadalupe, Los Remedios, Zapopan and San Juan de los Lagos, Our Lord Christ of Chalma and the sanctuary of San Miguel del Milagro in Tlaxcala. In his varied production, Florencia insisted that the foremost argument endorsing the devotion for the images was the continuing historical tradition that referred to them. Besides the existence of an uninterrupted devotion, was the bishops authority that had sponsored the sanctuaries, the dissemination and multiplication of the images in domestic shrines, and the abundance of alms given by the rich, alms used in the erection of their temples. Florencia himself was one of the most decided impeller of *novenarios*, little prayer books printed as an addition to apparitionist literature and important instruments in the spreading of cult. In his works, the Jesuit author gave the image a character of visual document that had never had before: the use of indigenous pictograms and votive tablets to prove the authenticity of the stories about the images and point out to the hieroglyphic character of some icons, is significant.

The monumental work by Florencia, which allowed him to cross-reference the images, was not only a propaganda work to promote devotion among the faithful. For him, these icons were a proof of the divine favor granted to these parts, a statement concerning the unity of the faith that existed in the New Spain and its character as a chosen people. Over New Spains's map, Florencia created, for the first time, a cartography of all miraculous apparitions: his vision was far more totalized and global than the partial vision of those who had written about this subjects beforehand.

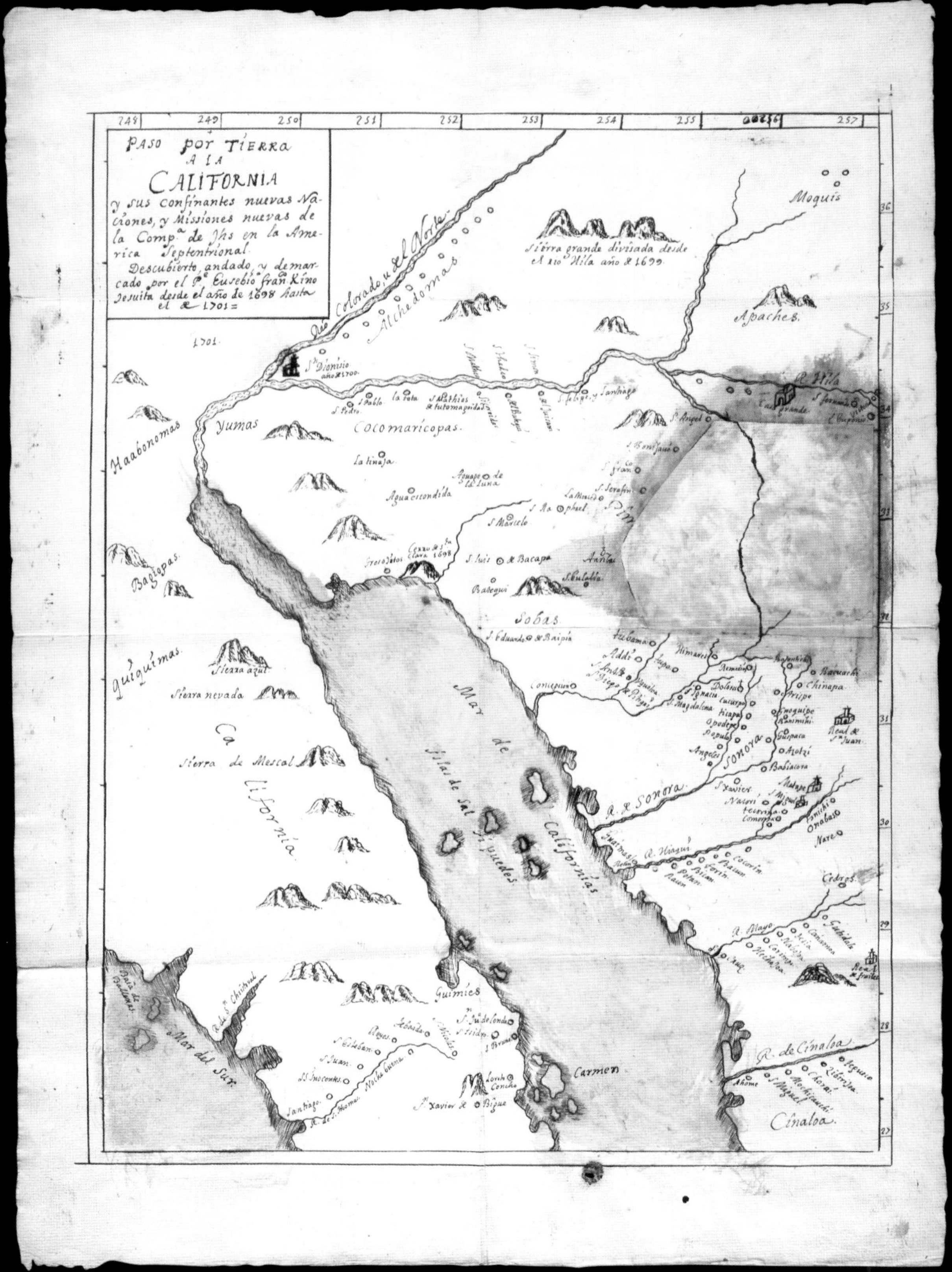

Land passage to California. Eusebio Francisco Kino was a missionary of the Society of Jesus, who stood out in cartography, geography and knowledge of the indigenous languages and cultures of the northwest of the Viceroyalty. Still at the end of the 17th century, exploration on the north of the territory had failed to discover that California was a peninsula. From the 16th century it had been taken for an island. The discovery of the land passage opened the eyes of the explorers about hydrography, cultures and resources that were still unknown. Kino did not change his insular vision of California until exploring further north in the territory known at the time as the Pimería Alta, around 1699-1701. [CAT. 91]

Arellano. F. Año. de 1691

This same spirit inspired him into writing an encompassing work about the Virgin apparitions in the New Spain: the *Zodiaco mariano*, which he did not complete. The work was finished and published in 1755 by another Jesuit, Juan Antonio de Oviedo, to whom we owe the inclusion of the materials about Guatemala and Ocotlán, the foreword and the thematic organization by dioceses. For Florencia and for Oviedo images were a token of divine favor, a manifestation of the unity of faith in America and of their character of chosen people. It is significant that this work was conceived by two Jesuits, members of a Society that maintained colleges and missions all over New Spain's territory and therefore stood as the only corporation able to produce a unifying perception of a kingdom in terms of a Marian celestial choosing.

All these messages arrive to the masses by the numerous resources the new pastoral of the Counterreformation used in the process of re-evangelization of laymen. The religious orders had a vital role in this. On one hand were the sermons, spoken not only from the pulpit, but also in squares, in public ceremonies and in every event where a moral teaching could be learned, including places of capital punishment. In these activities the Jesuits excelled as with the promotion of a urban evangelical kind of theatre, the auto sacramental. In platforms put in strategic places, especially during the *Corpus Christi* feast, pupils of Jesuit colleges would act short plays of a didactic nature, written by their priests. This same feast, as happened with all the other solemnities, with its visual and symbolic apparatus, became an instrument to dramatize religion, making it more accessible to people, turning it into a spectacular living sermon.

Together with the sermons, the theatre and the solemnities, the Counterreformation used the printing press in a exhaustive way as a means to spread its message. At first they printed mainly catechisms (some in indigenous languages) but during the 17th and 18th centuries guides for prayer (novenas, *Via crucis*) and brief texts that included lives of the saints stood out. What they tried to do, with this promotion of an outward devotion, was to conduct practices to a more intimate moralization by anchoring the belief. This printed matter disseminated because of the continuous effort of the Jesuits: sermons, confessions, spiritual direction, public readings in confraternities, in convents and monasteries, family gatherings, spiritual retreats

However, books, reading, talks with the confessor were not enough: a variety of objects worked as mediators, being relics and images the most important. Amongst them were also the already mentioned local miraculous images, that had appeared in hills and caves, and which were promoted by dioceses and orders. These images were offered by the Novohispanic Church as a fountain of spiritual and material wellbeing for collectivities and individuals alike and as a remedy against fires, droughts, plagues or floods. And together with these special icons, other images, either sculpted or painted, in altarpieces and walls of temples and monasteries were used as visual sermons to spread the message of virtue and sanctity, of salvation or damnation.

This image shows the young Saint Aloysius Gonzaga teaching the children of Rome. Saint Aloysius belonged to the Society of Jesus and was characterized by his devotion to the care of patients during the epidemic of plague that struck Rome in 1591. He died at an early age, as a result of having contracted the disease while caring for patients in the hospital improvised adjoining the church of Il Gesú in Rome. Benedict XIII canonized him in 1726 and gave him the title of patron of youth. [CAT. 11]

Images were not only didactic instruments and objects of public worshipping; they were also devotional images in the private sphere: paintings, sculptures and engravings (etchings, novenas, and grants, contracts and the summaries of the indulgences of confraternities) allowed even the more modest people access to this objects of veneration. And, with them, various objects with images embedded that had also healing powers: medals, rosaries, blessed bread, *Agnus Dei* made of wax, scapulars (remnants of fabrics to be wore over the chest and back with the embroidered image of the Virgin or some saint). Among these objects with magical properties, relics (parts of a saint or possessions of a saint bestowed with healing powers) were the most important ones. From the 16th century on, the Church in New Spain promoted the import of these objects from Europe. Their fragmentation meant the multiplying of miracles and, at the same time, encouraged the veneration of local relics.

The members of religious orders not only built and diseeminated the identity symbols that would work in the entire territory, they were also the first that rooted a feeling of belonging to this country that, in time, would become a source of pride and in a clearer consciousness that they lived in an entity which was very different than the Spanish one. This feeling was strongly influenced by the quarrels between Criollos and Peninsulares in the midst of the religious orders in the first decades of the 17th century. These struggles were a breeding ground to prop the sense of difference. The religious environment was the first in which the mainland prejudices against the Criollos were faced, and this happened because of the imposition of the alternatives in the mendicant provinces.

In 1614 and 1629 the Papacy, prompted by the king of Spain and some Spanish friars, issued apostolic briefs that imposed the rule that the provincial positions of the American mendicants had to alternate between those born in the Indies and those born in Spain. As a result, the Spaniards (a minority in most of the provinces) would govern the province in a triennial basis: the Criollo majority would thus be deprived of expressing its will. The apostolic brief unleashed a strong reaction in all Criollo spheres, because of the strong bonds friars had with the most active sectors of society: their right to form self-governing bodies appeared to be violated. For them, religious orders were not only environments of political and economic power, but also one of the few spheres in which Criollos elected their own representatives. The fact that a Spanish minority dominated in a triennial basis a province by the Kings decree, notwithstanding the will of the Criollo majority, seemed to the elite in the New Spain an attack against their rights. The problems that these alternatives brought created a strong social tension between Criollos and Peninsulares that lasted for many years in all of Hispanic America, but they also helped to generate a particular consciousness of belonging by exacerbating the antagonistic positions between these two groups, and by producing abundant discourses of Criollo exaltation. Those were the basis of the pride and the demands of equality between Europeans and Americans.

The Society of Saint Dominic, also known as the Society of Preacher popularized the Mariana advocation. The leyend tells that the Virgin Mary appeared in front of Santo Domingo in a Rosary and she taught him to prade. Her holiday is celebrated on October 7th. [CAT. 61]

A hundred years later, the Spanish Crown would frown upon these Criollo postulates. It was then that the Bourbon policies declared a merciless war against religious orders: they took their parishes away, reduced their incomes and limited the entrance of young people into their novitiates. It is not a surprise that from those monasteries people like Friar Servando Teresa de Mier or Friar Melchor de Talamantes emerged; nor that monasteries and convents became centers for conspiracy. In 1768 the King ordered the authorities in the New Spain to admonish the friars so that they might control "the prophecies and fantastic revelations from some nuns about the return of the Jesuits." The nuns where thus answering to the attempted reforms from the bishoprics, showing their repudiation, shared by many Criollos, to the expulsion of the Jesuits, seen as wise teachers and spiritual directors, the men that stood out in New Spain's intellectuality. By then the Criollo consciousness, born and fostered in monasteries and convents, was already present in ample sectors of society.

Since male and female monasteries are institutions of community life, it was necessary for each order to have a rule. St. Benedict of Nursia (480-527 AD), abbot of Montecassino, issued a rule that served as the axis of community life for many monasteries over time, however, there is no such definition for female monasticism, as it had its origin among women hermits of the 3rd and 4th centuries, but their norms of community life were not as precise as in the case of the rule of the Benedictines. Several female orders in New Spain took as their model the rule given by St. Augustine to the nuns of Santa Mónica in Puebla, including the Hieronymites, to which Sor Juana Inés de la Cruz belonged.*

REGLA DADA POR N. P. S. AVGVSTIN A SVS MONJAS.

CONSTITVCIONES, QVE hàn de guardar las Religiosas Augustinas Recoletas de Santa Monica de la Ciudad de la Puebla, Aprobadas por los M. SS. PP. Paulo V. y Vrbano VIII. y ampliadas por el Illustrissimo Señor D. D. MANVEL FERNANDEZ DE SANTA CRVZ del Consejo de su Magestad, y Obispo de la Puebla; en virtud de Breve que obtuvo de N. M. S. P. Innocencio Vndecimo.

Su Señoria Illustrissima Cõcede quarenta dias de Indulgẽcia à todas las Religiosas por cada vez que leyeren estas Constituciones.

Con licencia, en la Puebla, en la Imprenta de Diego Fernandez de Leon. Año de 1691.

VII

Oh, Tú, que en trono
de diamantes puros,]
pisando estrellas vistes
del sol rayos,]
a cuyo lustre ofrecen
los Coluros]
brillantes luces de
su obsequio ensayos.]

Purifica mi acento,
y mis impuros]
labios se animen
florecientes mayos]
que a tu sombra
mi voz bella María]
triunfa inmortal
del alterable día.

Devotion and identity

Bodily metaphors in Criollo spirituality

Sara Gabriela Baz Sánchez

Catholic body, sacrificial body

In the vastness that shaped the Spanish monarchy between the 16th and 19th centuries, one feature remained as a unifying constant: the role that Catholicism and monarchy played in Christendom expansion. Although worship had regional variants and some devotions were more widespread and promoted than others, every individual under the rule of the Spanish Crown shared a set of values and a series of moral standards that bond him tightly to the congregations and locations that invested him with an identity.

Rather than to expound upon popular devotions in New Spain, this essay expects to establish the relation between the devotional practices and the concept of body. This aspect, still little explored by historians, and even less by theologians, will enable us to cover the scale of how, in practical terms, a world-view manifested itself and lead New Spain society, in its profound diversity, to set itself up and to merge around an idea.

In Catholic thought between the 16th and 18th centuries, the body metaphor was useful to give sense, soundness and eternity to the wording of different ideas, like the very idea of State. Just like every individual owns a body that enables him to act within the world, the whole society was conceived as a sum of congregations that reached their highest unity point within the Monarchy and the Church; both had a head that lead the movements of all the remaining parts, of which, in this concept, even the smallest one was important. As head of the Church, Christ, his suffering and his sacrifice for humankind, were the leading threads of a way of thinking that culminated with the highest appraisal given to every harshness that could be inflicted on the body.[1] "The sacrificial death of Christ symbolized his humanity; while his resurrection was the symbol of his divinity. Even if human condition was not divine at all, Christendom enabled human beings to participate in the sacred world by incorporating them in the process of achieving salvation."[2]

Besides the metaphorical-political character of the body, it was also identified as a "prison of the soul" by some 16th and 17th centuries theologians, starting from a reinterpretation of Plato, through Plotinus. This metaphor made possible a paradox within the Catholic world-view at that time: although the body was seen as a burden, a prison and, finally, as remains, there was a devotional practice that permanently stressed the importance of restraining it and controlling its five senses, since these were, at the same time, the five entrances for sin to corrupt the soul. "The [...] Church taught that the pain caused by the death of the body was compensated by the hope of happiness in life after death. The body was considered impure and imperfect, since it was subject to the earthly passions and expires in time. The soul does not need the body to be saved, since it is the soul that instills life in the body. The soul inhabits the bodily prison, it is confined or embodied by it."[3] However, and here lies again the paradox, the soul could only exist in the world through its embodiment. In the very same mystery of Christ's Incarnation lies this necessary relation between matter and spirit, and since theologians—despite all the flesh's flaws—could not find how to base an existence only on the soul, Catholicism offered all

Through trade with Asia, New Spain knew and consumed fine objects of ivory of an incalculable value. From an ivory tusk, were developed several images that still show the natural curvature of its raw material. Ivory was carved and polychromed to give its final finishes. These pieces embellished above all the houses and domestic chapels of well-off New Spaniards. [CAT. 30]

that was needed, through the liturgical practice and the resort to the sacraments, to restore in the soul the power of grace, but only by means of a punished, temperate and controlled body.

Although this and other metaphorizations of the body were issues shared by the whole Christian world, in the New Spain, as in other domains of the Spanish Crown, it is impossible to speak of a compact society that developed its spirituality orthodoxically according to the canon and regarding the model behaviors proposed by the State. A society as complex as the one that shaped the New Spain was made up of people from quite diverse strata, with ethnic features that provided it with an identity and specific ways to live their religion and to crystallize their beliefs. However, there was a hegemonic discourse that laid down the norms of behavior and how people should act in everyday life in order to keep the legal, social and moral order. In this sense, spirituality had guidelines that should be followed rigorously and, to that end, created a complex machine of publications, rituals and sermons that told parishioners what to believe and how to behave. But apart from this, there were of course many heterodox expressions and some devotions were specifically promoted and their cult attracted large numbers of devotees. One example is the cult to the Virgin of Guadalupe, which became an identity banner.

But, what do we understand for devotion? For historians, it is difficult to venture a definition for terms like this one. The *Diccionario de Autoridades* defines devotion as the "adoration, veneration and cult dedicated to God, the Most Blessed Virgin Mary and the Saints. Comes from Latin *Devotio*, which means offering. It is usually taken for the zeal and reverence with which Church is attended and the Sacraments frequented [...]."[4] Another sense of devotion is: "[...] the attention, meditation, peace and respect with which a religious act is attended".[5] Devotion is, as we see for this last definition, an attitude expressed both by the spirit and the body. It is exercised and reinforced by resorting to the Sacraments, created and established by Jesus Christ for the spiritual renovation of men, "the amendment of habits, the sanctification of souls, a healthy medicine and an effective remedy against spiritual illnesses;

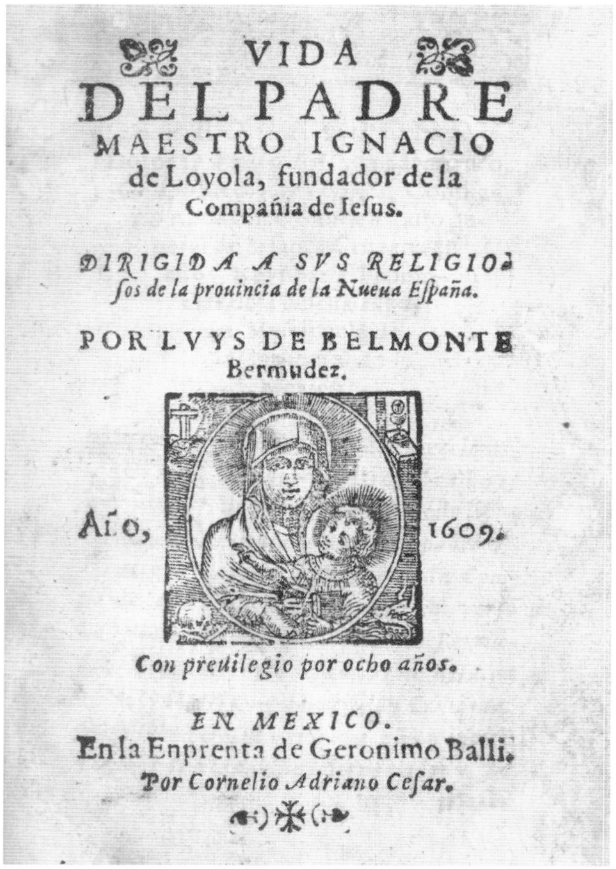
VIDA
DEL PADRE
MAESTRO IGNACIO
de Loyola, fundador de la
Compañia de Iesus.

DIRIGIDA A SVS RELIGIOsos de la prouincia de la Nueua España.

POR LVYS DE BELMONTE
Bermudez.

Año, 1609.

Con preuilegio por ocho años.

EN MEXICO.
En la Enprenta de Geronimo Balli.
Por Cornelio Adriano Cesar.

San Ignacio de Loyola was the founder of the Society of Jesus. By all accounts, was a soldier who was wounded in battle and during his convalescence, he experienced a divine vision that led him to become a religious life and founded and order that essentially fought against the enemies of the Catholic faith. Besides being the author of the *Constitutions of the Society*, he also writes the *Spiritual Exercises*, and approach based on phases that guide the meditation to the importance of saving the sould from the consciousness of bodily death, the possibility of eternal punishment and the sacrifice that Christ made for humanity. [CAT. 132]

for the restoration of grace destroyed by guilt, the increase of charity and, eventually, for its preservation and final persistence in holiness."[6]

Remember the importance of the *Spiritual Exercises*, created by St. Ignatius of Loyola in order to lead the devotee's soul gradually to the vision of God, and to meditate on the sins committed and the offenses made to the Father. The *Exercises* were originally published in 1548[7] and comprise a series of meditations, prayers and advices for those who want to seclude themselves for a one-month period in order to exercise their soul and direct it to salvation by means of contrition and penance.

This work, and this system, starts from the premise that individual prayer is of the highest importance, and, within the framework of Ignatian spirituality—which had a major impact within New Spain society in general—, that the meditation system is to be built on the composition of place (*compositio loci*), resorting to environments created with images, so as to guide the soul to the desired state: the ideal one to size up the sacrifice made by Christ for humankind and, as a consequence, to consider the huge offense made to Him by committing sin. It is in great measure for this reason that religious images acquired a basic role as vehicles of faith.

The *Spiritual Exercises* are the fundamental axis of the constitution of modern subjectivity in the Christian sphere. During the Counter-Reformation, the method set out by Ignatius of Loyola enabled each person a much clearer rapprochement to his own spirituality and to its ultimate aim, that is to say, God, but also was careful to emphasize the importance of the mediator between men and the divine, in other words, the personal confessor, the priest of souls or minister of cult. "The concepts 'I', 'individual', 'subject', 'person', 'personality' are very familiar, and quite often the historian takes them to other eras with the current meaning and tends to look—unsuccessfully—in old biographic texts for that self-knowing being that would be more precisely shaped by René Descartes (1596–1650)."[8] This means that we can not just look for the subjective factor in New Spain spirituality by shifting categories, but we must understand the meaning of this dimension of the subject-individual, immersed in a collectivity assumed as a corporatist society and also in a world-view in which the promise of happiness was always laid in life after death. "The Christian pastoral is organized as morals made of rules that restrain the conducts and the body control that must be imposed universally."[9] The question is that, within this universal imposition, it is necessary to look for distinctive elements or variants that make possible to build, at the same time, identities beyond the belonging to Catholicism. It is necessary to understand how belonging to a religious system opens gaps that can be filled with particular factors that define spirituality and devotion in a geographic environment and the delineation involved by being born in a specific social stratus, subjugated to certain conditions.

PP. 164-165: Don Juan de Palafox y Mendoza was viceroy of New Spain and occupied the archiepiscopal see of Mexico in 1643. He devoted himself to the struggle for the rights of bishops and diocesan clergy against regular orders. He built several schools and convents in New Spain and collected a large quantity of books, which today are preserved in the Biblioteca Palafoxiana in Puebla. [CAT. 126]

PROEMIO
Domine, ante te omne desideriũ meum,
& gemitus meus, á te non est absconditus. Ps.
37

PROLOGO

DOMINE ante te omne desiderium meum: & gemitus meus à te non est absconditus.

Psalm. 37.

GRANDE ES LA FVERÇA que Dios a puesto en los desseos, para inclinar su misericordia a remediar nuestra miseria, no siendo el menor effecto de su benignidad reconociendo la tibieça de nuestras obras, y la flaqueza de nuestro poder; darnos los desseos, con que se pueda suplir lo que obramos, para perficionarlo: y-

lo

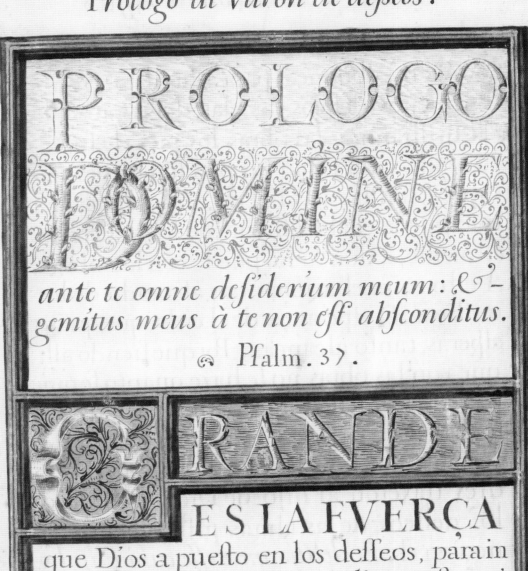

Body and morality

The Ignatian method, masterly set out in the *Spiritual Exercises*, had a huge spreading not only inside the Society of Jesus, but also virtually in the whole Christian sphere. Despite some theologians expressing that the three ways propound by the method —the purgative way, the illuminative way and the unitive way—, as well as the resort to the composition of place, were meant for those believers who were just beginning the path of meditation in order to save their souls, others believed in the extreme efficacy of the method and use it for structuring their moral discourses, whether written or preached. Such is the case of *Varón de deseos en que se declaran las tres vías de la vida espiritual, purgativa, iluminativa y unitiva...* by Juan de Palafox y Mendoza, bishop of Puebla.[10] In this book, the bishop makes the reader imagine a soul that goes through these three phases, and he resorts to the *compositio loci* at the beginning of each chapter to place that principal soul; by example, at the beginning of the first feeling in the purgative way, he poses a setting in which the soul tries to get closer to the light of divine love in a scary night.

As it is usual in this kind of publications, the body is presented in its most corrupt phase, in other words, as a group of bones and putrefaction to be lost in the course of time. In the "Breve exhortación a la vida espiritual", which opens the *Varón de deseos...*, by example, Palafox speaks of the alleged obstacles that stop the Christian in his pursuit of the path of salvation. It is said that ancestors are "piled up bones that only light up our own fragility."[11]

The body is a vehicle but also a cultural representation. Devotional literature makes us face the culturized body that acts, paradoxically, as actantial subject of sin and as what is punished to achieve salvation. To repress thoughts, evil gossip, the view of sinful images, the heeding of foolish words and, of course, to repress the sense of touch, were indispensable factors to keep control over the soul and to prevent its corruption by sin.

Tropology, at least during the 18th century, was closely linked to the sphere of morals.[12] According to the 1739 edition of the *Diccionario de Autoridades*, tropological is the "doctrinal, the moral and directed to the reform or amendment of customs." In the middle of the 17th century a work was published that perhaps could be remembered as the most representative of the genre known as "moral enterprises," the *Idea de un príncipe político cristiano, representada en cien empresas*, written by don Diego Saavedra Fajardo. This work organizes the education of princes through emblems, duly explained, that come mostly from Andrea Alciato's tradition. In the *Idea...*, Saavedra Fajardo resumes his experience as diplomat for the Spanish Crown and synthesizes the maxims of political praxis, essential to conduct the reigns to a happy fate.

Diego Saavedra Fajardo was a notable exponent of this genre, but we must also recall the contribution made by Sebastián de Covarrubias Orozco (Segovia, 1589) and others, whose names were lost among plenty of writers who cultivated the genre until the 18th century. These "moral enterprises" were meant, as was previously mentioned, for the

The archangels correspond to a higher hierarchy of the angelic choirs and are responsible for bringing important messages of divinity. The story relates that Archangel Raphael instructed Tobias to catch a fish, with the viscera of which he would cure the blindness of his father. He is regarded, therefore, as related to medicine. [CAT. 141]

education of princes—and often devised by their own preceptors—; however, their rules, in addition to their political sense, revisit moral issues that must have been valid for large groups of readers and for even larger groups of visual recipients of these codes translated by artists into painting. Spanish art—and hence New Spain art—has many examples of it.

A Criollo example within this tradition of emblematic literature is the *Theatro de virtudes políticas que constituyen a un príncipe*, by Carlos de Sigüenza y Góngora, published in 1680.[13] In this publication, the notable Novohispanic polymath dared to describe the virtues of the Mexica princes, in a triumphal arch, basing his account on the usual lattice of references to the authorities from the Greek and Roman antiquity. Thus, Sigüenza established a narrative thread that linked America's pre-Hispanic past with the classic past that upheld Western tradition; this no only ensures its dignity, but even places it above the ancient Greeks and Romans, since the virtues of the indigenous nobility were praised even more considering that they had not received the light of the Gospel. Far from being a mere account of the line of indigenous kings, seen as savages and foreign, Sigüenza approaches them from Western rhetoric and deals with them with the familiarity of those who recognize their ancestors and their works proudly.

Just as princes' mirrors were used for their own physical, moral and intellectual education, Christian "wake-up calls" were meant for the physical and moral education of the congregation. It is risky to suggest, firsthand, that the body is a relatively important matter in these books. Nonetheless, it is important to point out that if the body is not controlled and appeased, then the soul is at the risk of getting lost in the sinful pleasures and temptations that enter through the five senses.

In a society made of corporations, it is important to understand the role played by religious orders, parishes, the Holy Office and other "arms" of the Catholic Church in spreading and defending a moral code disseminated through images, sermons and publications. The chronicles of male and female orders contribute to strengthen their own role in expanding faith. The menologes and writings that spread the lives of the venerables and blesseds insist on highlighting the virtues that only the most notable Christians could cultivate. Here, it is essential the mediation between the individual and the sacredness, represented both by the confessor and by the devotional images that bring the prayers of the congregation closer to their final recipient.

In the New Spain, religious orders promoted devotions that grew in importance until the 19th century. Such is the case of the devotions introduced by the Society of Jesus and their fondness for relics: the proliferation of works that depict the images of saints such as St. Ignatius of Loyola, St. Francis Borgia, St. Aloysius Gonzaga and St. Stanislaus Kostka, or images of Our Lady of the People, of the Snows or of Light, apart from the expansion of the cult and devotion for Our Lady of Guadalupe during the 17th and 18th centuries. Saint Joseph, putative father of Christ, was well accepted by the New Spain society, which made him patron saint of the Indies, since his adopted parenthood

The iconography of the Virgin of Guadalupe corresponds to that of the Apocalyptic Virgin. According to the vision of John of Patmos in Revelation 12, a sign appeared in the sky: a woman clothed with the sun, crowned with twelve stars and the moon under her feet. Although not exactly identical to the representations of the Virgin of the Apocalypse, the Virgin of Guadalupe has these symbols, in addition to being pregnant. [CAT. 60]

burden could be equated with the adoption of the Indians by the Spanish Crown and the growing vocation of faith. On the other hand, there were also the specific devotions of each religious corporation, like Our Lady of the Rosary for the Dominican Order, Our Lady of Mount Carmel for the Carmelite Order, and many more examples that were depicted in countless images and *novenas*, as well as in paintings done under patronage and engravings in varied formats.

A special feature of the Novohispanic sphere was the devotion professed for the Sacred Heart of Jesus and for the Immaculate Heart of Mary. Miguel Cabrera, a notable painter, author of *Maravilla Americana y conjunto de raras maravillas…*,[14] was one of the main promoters of these images, under the patronage of the Society of Jesus.

Cabrera and his workshop are now famous for the softness of his outlines, his Baroque palette and because, regardless of the Italian Renaissance concept that gives priority to correct drawing in order to achieve naturalism in the pictorial composition, Cabrera knew how to touch the sensitive spots of the heart filled with devotion of the Criollo parishioners and how to enrapture them with his compositions made of diffuse lines and ethereal figures. The *incarnations* worked by Cabrera and other painters, such as José de Ibarra and José de Alcíbar, are made of soft pink tones; the hands and faces of the characters of sacred history, saints and martyrs are chubby and kind; even those depicted during their martyrdom show a sweet expression. The taste of the Criollo society, which commissioned this kind of works, considered vehicles for devotion, has not been sufficiently studied; nonetheless, it is remarkable that these works were so successful within the Novohispanic sphere and that they became so formally distant from the Spanish depictions, much more austere and less colorful, exception made of the work by Bartolomé Esteban Murillo, who exploited that sweetness that conquered the heart of the viewer, especially in his representations of the Immaculate Conception.

This doesn't mean that in New Spain painting there were no dramatic images and a great appreciation for blood: it is enough to take a look at the carved Christs, mainly used for processions during the Holy Week. These figures reached their most dramatic quality during the 18th century, when they were embedded with real bones and dyed glass in order to make the wounds inflicted to Jesus during the Stations of the Cross look more realistic.

Although New Spain painting, in general terms, shifted from a non-contrasted tenebrism to a gradual soothing and the use of a more vivid chromatic range, it is risky to judge the taste of the Criollo society for religious images based only on their formal elements. Of course, there were regional variants, painters and image-makers, who responded to different inspirations, and, certainly, countless factors that affected the production of devotional images. If we focus on the subjects and the recurrence to certain kind of representation over others, we would inevitably be carried to a regionalization of devotions, due to the dominion exerted by a specific religious order over certain locality or to the impulse given to certain images for cult by the secular clergy. In *Theatro ameri-*

cano..., by Villaseñor y Sánchez, for example, some parts of the text are assigned to refer the specific devotions of each diocese. Joseph Antonio de Villaseñor y Sánchez, general accountant of the Royal Treasure for the mercury industry and "cosmographer of this kingdom," gave King Philip V an obedience tribute when he started the research for what would be two broad volumes on jurisdictions, population, occupations, products, climate and geography of North America under Spanish domain: the *Theatro Americano, descripción general de los reynos y provincias de la Nueva España y sus jurisdicciones*.[15]

Absent bodies honored in death

It is relevant to also refer to other sorts of devotion. Despite usually understood as affection towards a certain religious figure, devotion was also experienced as a similar feeling for the king and for the Spanish Crown. The Spanish monarchy developed civil rituals and a complex machine that reinforced the mystery, majesty and parental figure of the king, especially in his overseas domains. Historiography is full with case studies in the devotional sphere and its *public* expressions. However, it is more difficult to study its *private* manifestations, since records and sources are scarcer.

Spirituality differed from devotion in that it was used as term and concept to refer to what derived directly from the Spirit: "It is used also for an effect caused by the spirit, or that is due to and derives from a spiritual thing."[16] The question underlying this essay is if we can sustain that there was a devotion that conferred identity to Criollos, or if they, in terms of spirituality, expressed himself in the same way as any other subjects of the Spanish Crown.

It is worth pointing out that the Criollo elite developed an identitary cultural program over three centuries. Criollos felt linked to the New Spain territory in a very different way than their Spanish parents, since they were born in this part of the world and were raised within the framework of cultural institutions typical of the New Spain: this implies a closeness to the indigenous world—which many felt as their heritage—and the wish to be recognized for their accomplishments, in all spheres—there are many samples that is not worth quoting here. Nonetheless, we must quote as examples the celebrations and the huge amounts of money spent on triumphal arches, for the arrival of a new viceroy, and funeral pyres, when a royal family member passed away.

These festivities and commemorations were done in style, despite the express prohibitions set by the Crown against spending large sums on the erection of ephemeral artworks, on the celebration of too ostentatious liturgies, and on the obligation of wearing mourning, since it was not affordable for most subjects. However, for the accounts of these festivities and commemorations it is clear that it was extremely important to highlight the devotion and commitment that New Spain subjects displayed during them, all this to strengthen their sense of belonging to the grand building of monarchy, and to

PP. 172-173. Mary ascended to heaven, body and soul, as a reward for her holy life and the suffering she endured because of the Passion of her Son. In iconographic terms, the scene that precedes it is the one of dormancy, death of Mary, rare in the iconography of the Western Church and abounding in representations in the Byzantine world. [CAT. 20]

make clear that Novohispanic cities could not be left behind regarding the celebrations and commemorations carried out in mainland Spain.[17]

There is therefore a kind of devotion not felt for the characters of sacred history, but for the monarch as providing father. As I wrote before, the publications known as *relaciones de exequias* (funeral rites accounts) or *libros de honras fúnebres* (last honors books) show that when a monarch died, the commemorations carried out in New Spain cities were so important that the town hall and the city council did not spare any expenses in its production: candles, burial mounds, sermons, Latin prayers, music and mourning clothes to be worn by varied corporations; the whole expenditure was justified if it was enough to demonstrate that the Novohispanic city had done it all with more luxuries and majesty than any city on the Iberian peninsula.

The *relaciones de exequias* shed light on fervor felt, during the rites, for the person of the deceased king. It is worth pointing out that, between the 16th and the 19th centuries, no Spanish monarch ever set foot on his American domains; therefore, the symbolization of the Monarchy's body and of the royal remains was significantly important in terms of generating a cohesion factor, tightening the bonds with other kingdoms belonging to the Spanish Crown and demonstrating the superiority—whilst waiting for recognition—implied by the whole organization of the commemoration.

The body of the absent king—due to his death and to the real distance—became present for his New Spain subjects through several resources: the burial mound erected in order to honor the late monarch was a ephemeral construction made of perishable materials, with a climbing structure, to be placed in the transept of the church where the funeral rites took place. This mound, catafalque, structure, "funerary machine" or *capelardente*, originally conceived—during the 13th and 14th centuries—to publicly exhibit the mortal remains of an important figure within the social hierarchy became, in the New Spain and in the Viceroyalty of Peru, a support for the portrait and the emblems of the late king. The climbing image of this structure was later equated, during the funeral rites, with the king himself; therefore, it didn't matter that his true remains weren't actually there, and it could be considered that a funeral mass was being held, by officiating and preaching at the same structure that constituted the mound, full of names, images and emblems that showed the virtues of the late king and highlighted, above all, his generosity towards his American children and his victory expanding the Christendom. The dead king, as champion of the faith, succeeded also in his task as father, regardless the number of his children or the physical distance between them and their father.

The symbolic body—in the sense Ernst Kantorowicz understands it in his well-known study *The King's Two Bodies*,[18] that is to say, the immortal body—is received by the apparatus built to make him present in an environment that always longed for him. The last honors books, starting from the one published in 1560 after emperor Charles V death, show the devotion with which the subjects attend the funeral rites, cry for the king's

The dogma of the Immaculate Conception of the Virgin Mary dictates that she was conceived without stain and preserved from all sin from the moment of her conception. It was proclaimed in the papal bull "Ineffabilis Deus…" by Pius IX in 1854, but the devotion to this image in the territories belonging to the Spanish Monarchy dates back to earlier centuries. The Immaculate Virgins painted by Bartolomé Esteban Murillo in the 17th century were the model for many images produced by artists from around the world. [CAT. 6]

TOTA PVL
CHRA ES AMICA ME
ET
MACVLA ORIGINALIS
NEST INT

The Wedding at Cana. This scene refers to a New Testament passage which recounts one of the miracles performed by Christ in his public life. It is said that in this city of Galilee, while celebrating a wedding feast the wine was finished. Jesus commanded to fill jars with water, which instantly became wine of the best quality. This helped to reinforce his credibility among his disciples.*

death and make whatever is possible to carry with them at least a small demonstration of their mourning. The thing is to belong, to feel as a participant, to wish for overseas recognition and not to spare whatever is needed to accomplish these results. This is another form of devotion promoted by the Criollo elite and with clear identitary features.

Public cults and private cults

As don Diego de Saavedra Fajardo stated: "luxury authorizes majesty." We can still find many temples decorated with maximum dignity, conceived in the purest style of Baroque luxuries. For Saavedra, luxury was the proper vehicle to honor majesty and to fill the subjects and the congregation with fear. Typical of the apparatus with which both the royal power and the ecclesial power manifested themselves—two large corporations—, luxury is an ingredient of Baroque culture, according to José Antonio Maravall's typification of it. In the New Spain sphere, luxury due to cult was not an exclusive expression of the Criollo elite, although their temples were the radiating focuses of esthetic ideas that were taken up again, with other materials and in different applications, by the Indian towns on the countryside.

In this sense, it's enough to mention some examples of works done with *enconchado*, like the ones that could be appreciated seen in the exhibition subject of the current catalogue. *Enconchado* was a technique privileged in the New Spain, which consisted of applying a ground base on wood, thick enough to inlay, while still fresh, ink-dyed mother -of-pearl fragments to depict different scenes. This Eastern technique—it was early spread in the Viceroyalty of the New Spain due to trade with China and Japan, and to the arrival of Asian artisans at these parts—was typical of several works on wood and folding screens created to decorate the domestic environments of the Criollo elite. These works show images taken from the sacred history, like *The Wedding at Cana*, as well as of Our Lady of Guadalupe. The visual richness of *enconchados* contributed to strengthen Saavedra Fajardo's maxim and to provide the devotional scenes with a brilliant and luxurious appearance.[19]

Thomas Gage, a traveler who went through the New Spain during the 17th century recording his experiences, said that Mexico City was like "another Sodom," and that "even if the city inhabitants tend extremely to pleasures, there is no other country in the world more bent to do well to their Church and ministers. They all do their best to delight friars and nuns, and to enrich the convents. These erect at their own expenses rich altars in the chapels of the saints of their personal devotion; those offer crowns or golden chains to the Virgin images or give them silver lamps; some erect convents or restore them at their own expense; others, finally, send them two or three thousand ducats off the rents. Thus they imagine that by doing good deeds to the churches they will prevent punishment that their sins deserve."[20]

AD
MAIO
REM
DEI
GLORI
AM
Man.l Serna fecit

Gage doesn't take out his anger only on those citizens with reprehensible customs that get rid of their guilty consciences by giving donations to the Church and financing pious works. The Mexican clergy itself seems to him of dubious morality when he writes: "I won't say much against friars and nuns in Mexico, but that they enjoy a greater freedom that the one they would have in Europe, and that the scandals they provoke every day deserve to be punished by Heaven."[21]

Between 1625 and 1627, Gage lived in Mexico City and accounted what he saw; with fervent catholic zeal, he judged harshly the attitudes of New Spain clergy and criticized the lax customs among the members of the religious orders and among laymen, as well as that Mexico City's temples served more as settings for numerous amusements than for solemnly celebrating the cult.[22] Around 1640, back in England, Gage realized that his personal aspirations came in conflict with his Catholicism and he decide to join the Anglican Church; he became a convert in 1642. Six years later, his book *The English American by Sea and Land or a New Survey of the West Indies*,[23] in which he recounts his travels around the West Indies, saw the light in the British presses. Thus, it is understandable that, for a convert like Gage, the dissolute spiritual life of New Spain inhabitants could be so profoundly horrifying. However, New Spain inhabitants clung to the recurrent devotional practice, especially since it implied specific attitudes linked to the celebration of public cult. This leads us to think that norms—pointed out by spiritual literature, meant to save the soul from corruption and sin—, no matter how scarce they were, manifested themselves on numerous situations and were transferred, as a sort of inventory of pious attitudes, into painting and fine arts in general.

Within the urban trace, monasteries and parishes were built to serve the spiritual needs of its Spanish and Indian inhabitants. This division of the congregation equated the split established by the urban grid; ideally, Indians and Spaniards should not mingle, but soon after plotting the terrains for the city in 1521, it was obvious that this ideal could not be fulfilled. Racial mixing, the procedures that Indians often had to deal with at the Palace and the provisional market on the Plaza Mayor (main square), where they traded their products, prevented this from happening.[24]

The surface covered by the Spanish city wasn't very extended; Ajofrín, based on the *Theatro Americano* by Villaseñor, states that: "the terrains taken up by this city could be, roughly, like Madrid. Villaseñor, in his *Moderno teatro americano*, 1st book, chap. 8, says that from North to South it has one league extension, and from East to West three quarters league."[25] If we compare these data with the large number of religious buildings that we will talk about below and the whole surface of Mexico City seems plentiful of them. "In 1697, the Italian Gemelli Careri lists twenty-two convents and twenty-nine monasteries: 'Power, as much as assets, are in the hands of the clergymen.' The annual income of Mexico City's archdiocese amounted then the considerable sum of three hundred thousand pesos. Since those times, Gemelli Careri considered that the city surface was too small to house so many churches and convents!"[26]

The image of the Immaculate Conception was a reminder of purity and chastity for many nuns in New Spain. Therefore, they decided to commission shields for their profession with this Marian advocation, surrounded by saints of their particular devotion, like the parents of the Virgin Mary, St. Joseph and some others promoted by various religious orders. [CAT. 37]

The abundance of religious buildings comprised not only parishes and convents, but also hospitals in the charge of orders such as the Brothers Hospitallers of St. John of God (known as *juaninos*) or the Bethlehemites, as well as colleges run by the fathers of the Society of Jesus. "Mexico is a small city with a circumference of sex miles, a narrow space for so many churches that make scarce the number of rooms."[27]

Unlike the friars, who devoted themselves to the spiritual cure of the Indian population, secular clergymen and the establishment of parishes became necessary since the first moment to serve the Spanish population, living inside the urban grid. The first parish was itinerant, since it was the Sagrario (the Shrine), which lacked a fixed see because it didn't have a worthy building to house it. In 1568, two more parishes were founded: Santa Veracruz and Santa Catarina, for the use of the non-Indian population.[28] Its jurisdiction wasn't limited only to Mexico City, but, as the white population expanded to other areas within the Valley, both the Sagrario and the other two parishes had to broaden their field of action.

In time, five parishes for Indians in the charge of the regular clergy were founded: Santa María la Redonda, San Juan y Santiago Tlatelolco, in the hands of the Franciscans; San Sebastián, "founded in the old district of Atzacoalco"; the parish of San Pablo, and one more founded during the term of the second Audiencia, that was also trusted to the friars of St. Francis.[29]

According to Serge Gruzinski, "during the 17th century, Mexico City became a sacred city."[30] In the section focused on the urban trace, several authors state that during the 17th century the priority was not to broaden the city limits, but to beautify it and to ennoble it with the luxury of its buildings. As more clergymen arrived and had the opportunity to enter the University, and as more religious orders were authorized to settle,[31] Mexico City saw an intense constructive activity and of improvement. This is what made Thomas Gage state that: "there are no more than fifty parish churches, monasteries and churches; but those that can be seen are better than the ones I know. Ceilings and beams are gilded; they decorate most altars with marble columns of different colors, and benches are made of Brazilwood; in a word, tabernacles are so rich that the smallest one is worth twenty thousand ducats."[32]

Used to set the price of everything he saw, Gage expresses in his testimony some of his dissatisfaction with Mexican clergy and with the attitudes developed by the population to silence their guilty consciences. For Gage, all this embellishment of the religious buildings, as well as the luxury inside them,[33] were only due to the heavy moral burden that Mexico's inhabitants tried to get rid of.

Whether it be to get rid of guilt, or about the sense of belonging (which results in the construction of identity) or the whish to spare no expense in order to express their faith and devotion, the New Spain found its special features in the way it created its spaces of cult, both public and private. Its inhabitants were guided on this path by countless

de ALvarado el Badajoz
la Conquista de Mex.
Fue a 12 de agosto de 1521
A de bosion de Dn. hipolito Caci
Ayotzi. Hernz. Se hizo este
lienzo a 10 de agosto
Aqui estando
enterrando polita
no los guesos de Sn.
lorenzo en un llano

Hippolytus is a martyr of the Christian church, who died in 235 AC. His feast is celebrated on August 13, day of the surrender of the city of Tenochtitlán and the delivery of its command to Cortés and his Spanish soldiers. Hippolytus became therefore a figure of great importance for Mexico City. His feast commemorated every year having won for Christianity and the Spanish Monarchy one of the most noble and beautiful cities. [CAT. 55]

printed and preached works that uphold their doing and suggested them ways to distinguish themselves form the mainland Spaniards in the expression of their affections, whether for a providing father on Earth, the king; for their most distinguished authorities, such as bishops and viceroys, or for the maximum authority and head of all the bodies, God himself, thanks to whose message America became the most precious jewel of the Crown, the indisputable proof that the Spanish Crown was blessed by fortune, the opportunity for the Roman Church to regain, both in quantity and in quality, the congregation lost with the Lutheran Reform; the scenario for the miracle where the Virgin Mary did what as she never did for any other nation.

NOTES

1. "The modern State adopted from the Church the idea of society as a political body, a republic or a community of men for men. This structure gave good results to the ecclesiastical State in terms of concentrating power, prestige and privileges for its members. Furthermore, it entailed not only strength and security, but also the quality of eternal. Thus, in the 14th and 15th centuries, civil European governments undertook a secularization process in order to benefit the courts' bureaucracy and the increasingly dynamic trade. The new large body, the nation-State, corresponded to a new lifestyle, urbanism, a solidarity network, new loyalties and ambitions." Marialba Pastor, *Cuerpos sociales, cuerpos sacrificiales...*, p. 55.
2. Marialba Pastor, *Cuerpos sociales, cuerpos sacrificiales...*, p. 45.
3. Id.
4. *Nuevo Tesoro Lexicográfico de la Lengua Española* (NTLLE), Real Academia Española (RAE), 1732, p. 249, 2.
5. Idem.
6. Francisco de Lárraga, *Prontuario de la teología moral, first treaty*: "De sacramentis in genere."
7. *Exercitia spiritualia*, Rome: Antonio Bladio, 1548.
8. Norma Durán, *Retórica de la santidad*, p. 134.
9. *Ibid.*, p. 141.
10. For this essay the edition printed by Benito Cano in Madrid in 1786 was consulted.
11. Juan de Palafox y Mendoza, *Varón de deseos...*, "Breve exhortación a la vida espiritual."
12. Today, the term tropology refers to figurative language or to the one conferred with an allegorical sense. Specifically, tropology deals with the use of tropos or language figures like metaphor, metonymy, synecdoche and irony. In historical theory, stands out the study by Hayden WHITE, *Metahistory: The Historical Imagination in Nineteenth-Century Europe*, 1st edition, Baltimore: The Johns Hopkins University Press, and the one by the Dutchman Franklin Rudolf ANKERSMIT, *History and Tropology: The Rise and Fall of Metaphor*, 1st edition, The Regents of the University of California, 1994.
13. *...advertidas en los monarcas antiguos del Mexicano Imperio, con cuyas efigies se hermoseó el Arco*, Mexico City: Viuda de Bernardo Calderón, 1680.
14. *Maravilla americana...* was written by the painter Miguel Cabrera and referes to the divine origin of the Guadalupan canvas. It is a study about the Tepeyac's *tilma*, which concludes that this work could not have been painted by human hands. *Maravilla americana y conjunto de raras maravillas observadas con la direccion de las reglas de el arte de la pintura en la prodigiosa imagen de Nuestra Sra. de Guadalupe de Mexico* by Miguel Cabrera, Mexico City: Imprenta Real y más antiguo Colegio de San Ildefonso, 1756. Miguel Cabrera, along with other painters, submitted to the Court a plan to create an art academy in order to systematize Novohispanic artistic production. His motion had no repercussions in his time; it was necessary to wait until 1785 for the creation of the Real Academia de las Tres Nobles Artes de San Carlos (Royal Academy of the Three Noble Arts of St. Charles), founded by the engraver and minter Gerónimo Antonio Gil.
15. In his *Biblioteca Hispanoamericana Septentrional,* Beristáin y Souza states that this work was ordered by Philip V in a royal grant issued at the Buen Retiro on June 19, 1741, "addressed to the Viceroy of Mexico, Count of Fuenclara, who, informed of the talents, knowledge and dedication of our author [Villaseñor], commissioned him its creation." Beristáin y Souza, *Bibliotheca Hispanoamericana Septentrional,* vol. 3, p. 320.
16. *Nuevo Tesoro Lexicográfico de la Lengua Española* (NTLLE), Real Academia Española (RAE), 1732, p. 609, 1.
17. On March 22, 1693, a royal pragmatic sanction was issued to forbid excessive expenses on funeral rites. In the account of Louis I funeral rites, José de Villerías states that, as soon as the viceroy knew about the king's death: "His affection was already meditating, to relief his sadness, on celebrating the most ostentatious and solemn funeral rites and mourning that magnificence had seen dedicated to a late Monarch; then he noticed that along with the first royal decree came a second one, which read as follows: ...concerning mourning, must be precisely and punctually applied what the decree of March twenty-two, one thousand ninety-three, and the pragmatic there quoted order; and concerning burial mounds, these should be moderated, and all non-necessary expenses must be excused; for this purpose, you must notify this order to all parts affected and to account for its execution." José de Villerías, *Llanto de las estrellas al ocaso del sol anochecido en el Oriente. Solemnes exequias que a la augusta memoria del serenissimo y potentíssimo señor don Luis I celebró el Excmo. Sr. D. Juan de Acuña,* Mexico City: Imprenta de Joseph Bernardo de Hogal, 1727.
18. *The King's Two Bodies. A Study in Mediaeval Political Theology*, Princeton University Press, 1997. The first edition dates from 1957. Kantorowicz's thesis demonstrates that medieval kings from the royal houses of England and France possessed two bodies: the symbolic and immortal one, which guaranteed the continuity of the monarchy as institution, and the physical one, which really died.

19. This technique wasn't used only for religious images, for instance stands out the *Biombo de la conquista* (Conquest folding screen) kept at the Museo Nacional del Virreinato, in Tepotzotlán (INAH, CNCA).
20. Thomas Gage, *Viajes en la Nueva España*, edited by Roberto Román Velazco, note for the reader by Salvador Bueno, Havana: Casa de las Américas, 1980, p. 65.
21. Gage, *op. cit.*, p. 66. A few lines below, Gage wrote: "it is a custom that friars pay a visit to nuns of their same order, and that they spend part of the day hearing their music and eating their candies."
22. Chapter 21 of the Travels in the New Spain is lavish with descriptions that prove this argument. Mentioning only the colophon, I will quote Gage when he says that "everything what amuses and delights the senses abounds in Mexico City, even the temples, that should be devoted to God's service and not dedicated to men's pleasure." Gage, *op. cit.*, p. 67.
23. *Ibid.*, p. 11.
24. Solange Alberro, on chapter IV of her essay *Del gachupín al criollo*, speaks at length about the early confusion between both population spheres, the Indian and the Spanish, despite the fact that the urban grid had left the Indians outside for political as well as for practical reasons: labor and indoctrination. According to Alberro, from very early dates on, all social strata took advantage of the confusion caused when the merchant Indians and the plaintiffs to the Audiencia arrived in Mexico City; soon, the domestic staff had to dress in a fashion that nobody knew to which caste they belonged, and Indians were taken to the parishes (and not to their doctrinas) to receive spiritual care. See Solange Alberro, chap. IV, "Las mutaciones profundas" in *Del gachupín al criollo, o de cómo los españoles de México dejaron de serlo*, Mexico City: El Colegio de México (Serie Jornadas, no. 122), 1992.
25. Friar Francisco de Ajofrín, *Diario de viaje que hizo a la América en el siglo XVIII el padre...*, Mexico City: Instituto Cultural Hispano Mexicano, 1964, p. 59.
26 Serge Gruzinski, *La ciudad de México...*, p. 139.
27. Gemelli, *Viaje a la Nueva España*, Libro I, p. 22.
28. Manuel Ramos Medina,"La Iglesia y la ciudad de México en el virreinato," in Tovar de Arechederra, *La muy noble y leal ciudad de México...*, p. 118.
29. Idem.
30. Gruzinski, *La ciudad de México...*, pp. 139-140.
31. Manuel Ramos Medina states the arrival of other orders. Besides Franciscans (1524), Dominicans (1526) and Augustinians (1533) during the first phase, Jesuits arrived in 1572, "Discalced Carmelites in 1585; Mercedarians in 1593; Benedictines in 1602; Augustinians Recollects in 1606; hermits of St. Anthony the Great in 1628; hospitalarian orders: Hyppolites in 1604, Brothers of St. John of God in 1604 and Bethlhemites in 1674." Ramos Medina, "La Iglesia y la ciudad...," p. 120. This as far as the male orders is concerned, but it is necessary to add the nine convents founded by the Conceptionists, "the sole case in a city of the Spanish Empire": La Concepción (1541), Nuestra Señora de Balvanera (1573), Regina Coelli (1573), Jesús María (1581), Nuestra Señora de la Encarnación (1593), Santa Inés (1595), San José de Gracia (1610) and Nuestra Señora de Guadalupe y San Bernardo (1636)". To them we must add the six convents founded by the Poor Clares, one by Hyeronimites, Augustinian Sisters and Dominicans, two by the Discalced Carmelites, one by the Bridgettines (Order of the Holy Savior) and two by the Company of Mary. Ramos Medina, p. 126. Gemelli, while describing his describe adventures in Mexico City, visits several nuns' convents: "I spend Thursday 7 in St. Bernard's convent, inhabited by nuns of the same order. It was big, and the church was adorned with the most sumptuous altars. Also magnificent and wealthy is the one of Our Lady of Balvanera; as I entered the church on Friday 8, I saw it served by venerable priests, and the upper and lower choirs by noble nuns." GEMELLI, *Viaje a la Nueva España*, Book I, p. 20. His description is not substantially different from the ones about male monasteries, also by Gemelli or even by Gage, since both merely admire the luxury of the buildings and inner decorations, although from different perspectives.
32. Gage, *op. cit.*, p. 66.
33. "Besides the beauty of the buildings, it's infinite the number of gems and treasures that belong to the altars, like chasubles, jewels, chalices, golden and silver crowns, and the monstrances of gold and glass, treasures that are worth a silver mine and that could make rich the nation that could own them.". *Ibid.*, p. 66.

VIII

A la cuarta estación,
que señorea]
del frígido Aquilón,
nieve volante,]
corría el año,
mientras clamorea]
lánguida Clisie
al fugitivo amante.]

Comunicando
liberal Astrea]
escarchas al
invierno reiterante]
y haciendo en
desiguales horizontes]
selvas del hielo,
de la nieve montes.

Criollo taste and the Mestizo nation

Alfonso Alfaro

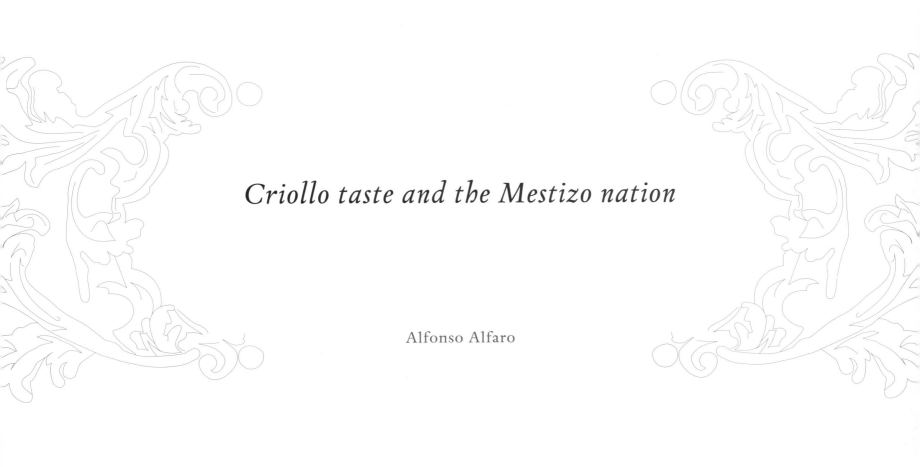

If we were writing this dissertation moved by any passion or interest, then we had rather embarked on the defense of the Criollos, since in addition to being much easier, we should be more concerned. We were born to Spanish parents and have no affinity or consanguinity with the Indians, nor can we expect any reward from their misery. And thus no other reason than love of truth and zeal for humanity make us to abandon one's cause to defend the others with less danger of erring.

Francisco Javier Clavijero
Ancient History of Mexico

A society as fragile as the Mexican one has, however, among its main resources, a painfully assembled network, whose existence is infrequent even in more ancient and consolidated countries.

The bonds that organically unite individuals and groups from different ideologies and skin colors, that makes possible to the powerful and the destitute to merge into one only "us," is the common consciousness of belonging to the same society.

The number of people that define themselves as Mexicans, a category that prevails over other ones with regional or ethnical character, is extremely large. This situation is the outcome of the arduous construction of a symbolic structure that serves as common focus of reference. The unifying agent, the meeting point for such unequal groups and individuals, comprises elements provided by the different populations that make up the country. These signs integrate an irregular and polymorphous whole, by which most Mexicans have felt represented. This system is due to integrating models, to which racial mixing belongs. That notion, of cultural character, goes well beyond the limits of biology and enables us to differentiate those societies that find inspiration in it, like the Mexican society—which has attempted to minimize ethnic peculiarities and strives to build common focus of reference—, from those whose founding pattern is multicultural. In a society like the American one, provided with very efficient mechanisms of economic and social integration, the phenotypic or cultural peculiarities that distinguish its members can be explicit. In Mexico, on the contrary, to make less flagrant and tense the deep differences between us, we have made an effort to create a broad zone of irresolution in which to blur those distinctive features.

On this land, while men and women from Europe, Asia and Africa mixed with those from America in conflict, rivalry, indifference, friendship, passion or love, cultural *métissage* became the founding principle of the new society due to a continued process in which signs came closer, juxtaposed, slowly integrated until merging into a group of symbolic systems that serve as shared references. The poles that magnetize the compass of the inhabitants of this homeland are made of images, values and affections identified as their own by the different dwellers of this extremely unequal country. What so many inhabitants of these parts recognize as close and enjoyable, what they consider honorable

The watches that the Lady uses as part of her dressing, were a sign of distinction of the Criollo society, a very important detail that must had been considered by the painters. [CAT. 142]

and real, is the result of a long building process in which chance and will have intervened in equal proportions and nothing in it has been atavistic or predetermined. Due to this slow building labor, Mexicans have accomplished, to an amazingly large extent, to limit step by step the scope of blood or color skin barriers (certainly still too broad).

What images do the several populations and families that consider themselves Mexicans share? What values do they evoke? What verbal and visual languages do they use to express themselves? These questions necessarily arouse a new one: in which way have the different constituents of its population contributed in creating these common signs? In the context of a reflection devoted to the Criollos, it is worth highlighting the fact that these New Spaniards contributed decisively to the sensitivities and esthetic forms in this building of common cultural references.

Diversity

Europe

To this day, in some rural populations in Mexico, those who are native to a place, those who were raised there are still called Criollo to differentiate them from the origin of their lineage or of their parents. The children of Spaniards born in America experienced the ambiguous situation in which they were placed by the status of this territory: a kingdom, but without courts—enjoyed only by mainland people under the Castile Crown—that eventually, under the Bourbon dynasty, became a real colony. Criollos were undoubtedly part of the upper layer of a population separated by emphatic ethnic, profession and social divisions, but were excluded from access to the top of that system. Towards the end of the Spanish tutelage, the need to solve this problem became more and more pressing, but the advanced state of decay of the imperial order—which received its coup de grace with the Napoleonic invasion—prevented a solution that would have enabled an evolutionary and bloodless transition towards political independence and would have provided the new countries with a more favorable geopolitical frame.

Europeans born in the New World had acquired, along with their genealogy, a referential background that was already diverse. The first generations of Criollos were born into an atmosphere that still kept intense Byzantine and Medieval traces, in which Hebrew and Mudejar influxes were a living heritage and where the Renaissance impulse was at its height—the fall of Constantinople was an open wound in European consciousness; the Jews were expelled less than 30 years before the conquest of Tenochtitlán, and the expulsion of the Moriscos would begin only in 1609. Thus, the first Criollos received from their grandparents from Castile or Extremadura, still living in their lands of origin, a sense of vassalage that allowed high levels of autonomy, made up for the demands of loyalty to the Sovereign that chivalrous pride imposed and for a refined conceptual and

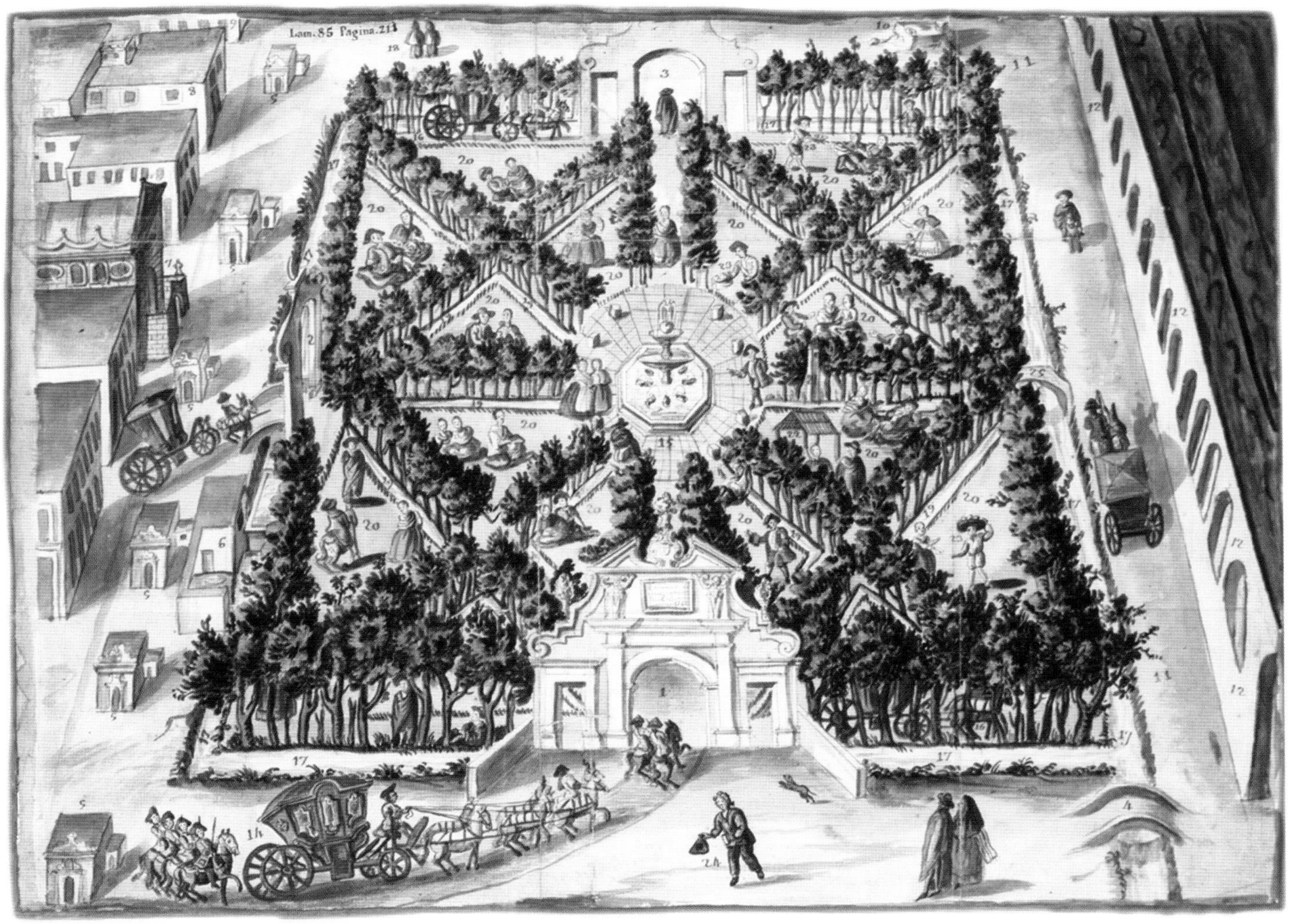

literary system. They also inherited an identity awareness defined in terms of religious lineage, in tense confrontation with other religious families—Judaism and Islam—, as well as an immediate familiarity with materials whose shine and texture flattered both the senses of touch and sight, stirred to look for the rapture promised by the infinite interweaving of the arabesques. From their own times, on the other hand, Criollos received the infinite horizons, the conviction that man is the measure of all things, the will to transform the Globe through their ambitions, the dream of utopias, the passion for an unlimited knowledge and also the certainty that there was a rule of human perfection, traced by Homer, Plato and Aristotle, extended by Seneca and Cicero, transformed into living wisdom by St. Augustine, St. Basil the Great and St. Thomas Aquinas, and renewed by the Fathers of the Council of Florence. Thus, the first New Spaniards lived surrounded by the massive walls of fortress-like monasteries, were in constant sensory contact with the opulent Mudejar heritage, and had, at the same time, an existence framed by the balance

The book *Origin, customs and present state of Mexicans and Filipinas* by Joaquín Antonio Basarás, captures everyday life scenes of the New Spain with many persons belonging to different castes and social hierachies. [CAT. 112]

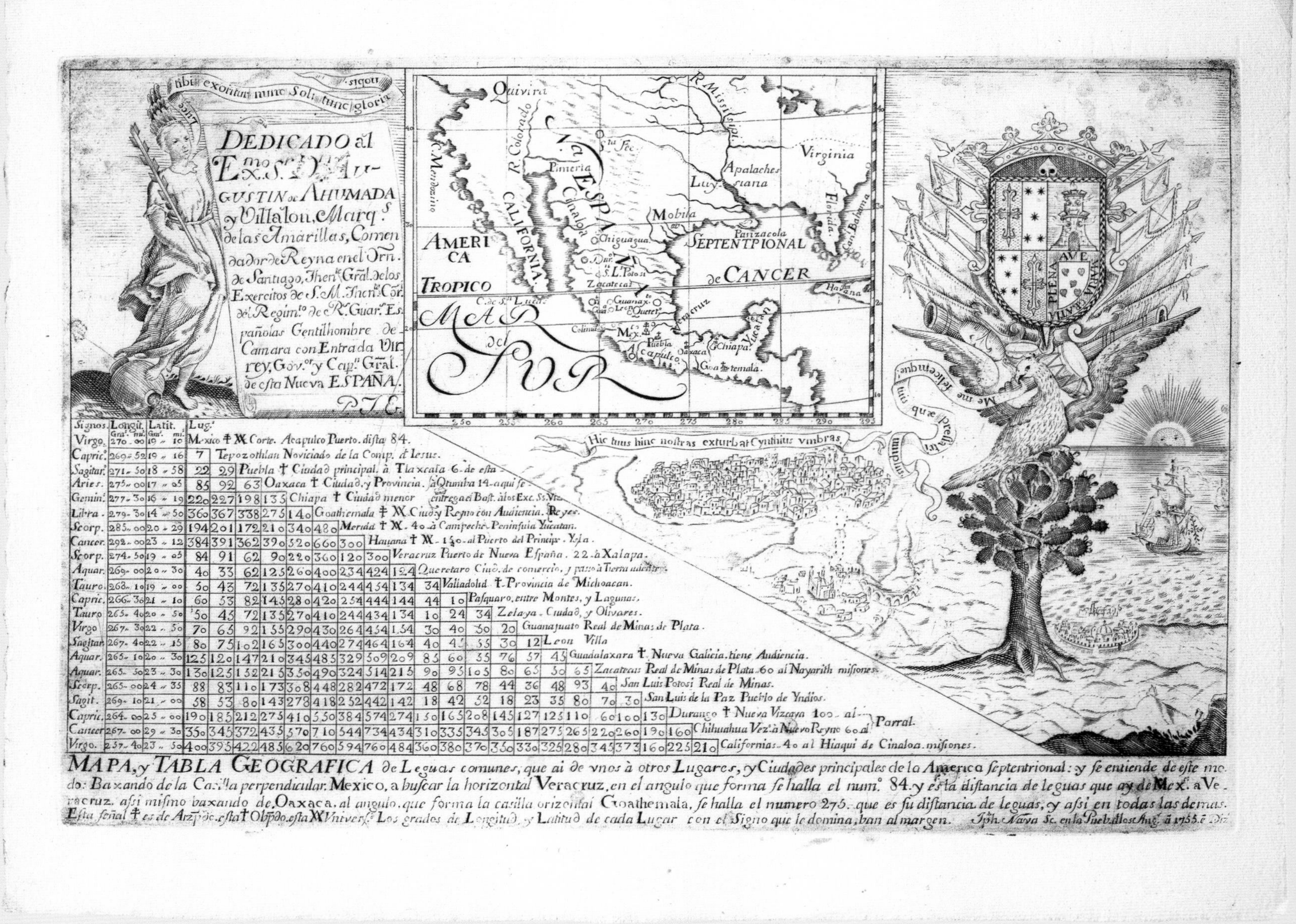

Map and geographical table of common leguas in some to other places, and mayor cities of North America. The geographical tables have information related with the necessary distances and references to give the territorial dimensions and to calculate arrival times from one city to the other. These tables were very help ful to make statistics and to program comercial routes through the open and traveled paths. [CAT. 123]

and harmony of columns with capitals, but also by frescos in the grotesque atmosphere of which were visible the traces of nymphs and fauns. Medieval and Byzantine, Jewish and Morisco, enthusiastic child of the Renaissance, was their first sensitivity.

As subjects of a supranational monarchy with universal plans, Criollos had from the first moment on a cosmopolitan gaze. Flanders and Italy, as much as Germany, Hungary and Bohemia, all under the tutelage of the same family, exerted a visible presence in the vast and different territories that shaped the space of the Habsburg crowns. The intense cultural comings and goings in which the Spanish monarchy was immersed went beyond the dynastic frontiers to include other powers, whether remote, hostile or expected to join an impossible fraternity, like Denmark, England, France, the Ottoman Empire or Portugal. All these influxes were part of the first family heritage of New Spain lords.

America

The native landscape imposed a strong imprint on the Spaniards native to the Anahuac. Criollos were marked by their homeland, the only one they knew, because the hills used to wheat and vine, the fields planted with ancient olive trees, the fertile mists that descend from the Pyrenees or Mediterranean light shades, were only familiar through tales and fables. Not even art, devoted to heaven's things, could evoke for the Criollos the far-off continent—an almost inaccessible planet—that their parents had left behind and where most of their relatives dwelled. When Catholic painters from those centuries wanted to show nature, that timeless geography where the inhabitants of heaven encountered those of earth, resorted to idealize vegetation inspired by Flanders or Tuscany, in whose atmosphere the academic canon placed the episodes from the tale of origin of Christianity. For those generations, history was above all the one of salvation. Thus, the infinite oceans barely glimpsed, the steep ravines, the snow at the peaks, the suffocating heat or the implausible vegetation were, for Criollos, as much as the bright silence of the deserts, part of a vital experience that practically had no channels to manifest itself into the sphere of artistic forms; but there it was, nesting in their eyes, indelible in their skin, transformed into the raw material of their memory.

The close contact with men and women of different skin types, the daily and domestic familiarity from the cradle on with children whose faces multiplied their shades and whose languages learned without meaning to, filled their fantasy with genies that mingled with those living in the legends of their grandmothers from Asturias and Navarre who they never met.

From the very beginning, their palate was receptive to maize—in the infinite variations of a plant that gave birth to an entire civilization and that, adapted to the plow, was living a second life. Even if wheat was occupying growing extensions of land, maize was still, together with silver, the soul of the kingdom and it never abandoned its

function as supporting pillar of Novo-Hispanic demography. Maize soon went into the pots and *comales* in the kitchens of noble houses until it definitely settled in the taste buds of the Europeans born under the tutelary shade of the volcanoes. Together with maize, of course, tomatoes, avocados, countless chili peppers, nopal cactuses and *huauzontles* participated creating a new culinary art that resorted at the same time to local turkeys and chickens of Castile, or lambs, cows and goats. Cheese, wine and olive oil, but also chocolate, vanilla and even *pulque* were included in Criollo tables. This refined core of a vernacular cuisine owes a lot to convents and haciendas were selected and varied products were abundantly enjoyed, and where numerous people had all the time in the world to experiment new dishes and to digest complicated and not at all light makings, as the European tradition imposed in those times. Since the top political authorities were mostly temporary, there was never a stable court like the ones in the Old World, which served as reference for table pleasures. This task rested on the grand Criollo families and, of course, on women's convents, especially on those in which observance was less strict. (The attempts to reform convents in the 18th century and, later, the almost disappearance of these institutions, together with the subsequent decline of the haciendas at the beginning of the 20th century and of rural economy at the end of the same century, would considerably limit the evolution of Mexican gastronomy.) Criollos, nurtured with the produces of this land, assimilated their substance and turned their aromas and shades into their own flesh. Thus, the taste sensitivity of these Europeans of Cantabrian skin or Andalusian look became more and more alike to the one of their countrymen of different descent—while the entire world made American native products their own.

Among the most impressive presences surrounding the Criollos were the rasping breaths of the pre-Hispanic cities, the vertiginous collapse of which was witnessed by the first generations. Their traces were always within view, although the historic implications of the death of a lacustrine civilization were not understood, nor the reason why, within a cultural catastrophe without plan or strategy, cattle was facing *chinampas* and terraces, and leading a thousand-year-old technological infrastructure to succumb in a few years.

Cosmogony, science, the memory of the pre-Hispanic world protected by the ethnographers-missionaries at the Colegio de Tlatelolco—and their counterparts and successors—were also part of the cultural view of Criollos, and would become, in a process already noticeable in the 17th century and clearly fast at the end of the 18th century, the founding reference of the heart of patriotic consciousness.

The influence of the european art was notorius in the everyday life of the New Spain and influenced even the furniture manufacture, as shown in this Wastepaper basket from Pátzcuaro. [CAT. 46]

Africa

Besides European and American heritages, Criollos received other more indirect influences, but not less important. Quite early, in Veracruz, men and women from Africa, walking unsteadily because of the shackles, hungering and grieving, disembarked to replace the more than decimated Indians at the mine-works. They brought a different light on the skin, other spirits, other words. Their uprooting, so different from the one suffered by Europeans, hid in a memory without letters of glyphs, without canvases or murals where to find shelter. The voice of such homesickness became gradually opaque until it encysted itself in one of those imperceptible but always present zones tied behind consciousness. Their music stayed, of course, and their vocabulary and phonetics, and, above all, countless spirits that swarm around our mines and orchards, but also in our kitchens, bedrooms and living rooms. Today, this heritage is more alive than we usually acknowledge, in that secret refuge for ghosts that traditional arts are, especially in the coastal enclaves of Guerrero, Oaxaca and Veracruz.

Asia

Also the sea, a different sea, the one that made the Earth a space without limits, brought streams that transformed the appearance of this land and its inhabitants. Japan, India and, of course, China had been the founding spirit of these kingdoms, the spur that drove Europeans to the Atlantic adventure. The continent of spices, the homeland of silk, porcelain and lacquer—not yet mastered by European craftsmen—was the envy of the Christian courts. China was, in addition, the greatest of all empires, the see of a monarchy that dazzled princes and philosophers—the key to such a power, according to what Europeans thought to have discovered later, was a meritocracy that made nobility unnecessary and a deism that turned every religion superfluous. From the first moment, the existence of the Viceroyalty became part of a geo-strategic realm, which had the Pacific and Indian Oceans as essential references. The Catholic monarchy was certain that by imposing its hegemony all over the globe would contribute to the triumph of God's Kingdom. The conquering spirit that inspired it joined its missionaries in an impulse that took them to explore lands and seas attempting to cover the entire planet.

The first promising attempts to infiltrate into Japan were brutally ended. The martyrdom of St. Philip of Jesus, a Franciscan friar raised to the altars, accounts for a tropism that attracted Criollos and made them think that Asia was part of their natural space for expansion. The debates about the relevance and feasibility of conquering China, which Serge Gruzinski has analyzed, are also part of the same phenomenon. The routes opened to navigation from Barra de Navidad and the subsequent establishment of a regular link through the port of Acapulco turned the New Spain, for several generations, into the privileged way of communication between Europe and Asia. Some of the rich goods for

These mugs or cups for drinking chocolate were widely used by the noble families of New Spain. They were obtained by carving with decorative motifs the hard dry shell of a coconut and mounting it, after carving, on a silver foot with handles. These coconuts for drinking chocolate are documented in many inventories of New Spain noble families, all of which are evidence of the syncretism that marked everyday life in New Spain. [CAT. 29]

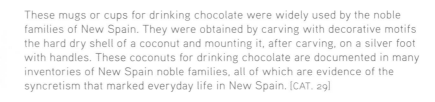

the merchants on the Guadalquivir were dropped behind while on pack mule's route towards Veracruz. The capital and Puebla, chiefly, benefited from this constant dripping that lent Criollo salons with an eclectic, opulent and cosmopolitan air. On the other hand, local craftsmen begun to create for their Criollo customers objects that aimed to be compared with the pieces arriving from the Philippines. The quality of Asian merchandises was a constant motivation and nurtured the longing for perfection of the most outstanding guild members. Their influence left a definitely oriental air on much of our ceramics. The Parian of Manila—the market after which also those of Mexico City and Puebla were named—was a vital part of New Spain economy. Asian aromas penetrated through Criollo skins: new spices and fruits broadened the range of delights, and American eyes turned into the tools for a new view, now global. The amazement caused by the Japanese traveling to the Peninsula, and the progressive settlement of Indians and Filipinos—whose emblem was Catalina de San Juan, the "China Poblana," who would contribute to fabricate one of the symbolic landmarks in New Spain's imaginary—, allow us to weigh up the importance of the various Asian influxes on the shaping of a Criollo taste. This taste was modeled by the translucent delicacy of porcelain, the gleams of nacre, the crispy caress of silk, the infinite superposition of subtle layers on lacquers and the thaumaturgical effectiveness of ivory, which allowed to represent divine flesh.

Integration: profusion and emptiness

Criollo taste owned a wide and diverse horizon, since New Spaniards revolved in a whirl of images and experiences that were the sign and result of the first globalization in history, the first time humankind achieved the unity of the species.

But how did this society avoid turning into a total chaos, a trivial cacophony of languages and cultures? How did so conflicting heritages and contributions—medieval, Byzantine, Jewish, Islamic, Renaissance, pre-Hispanic, African, Asian...—join to build an articulated system? How could such a wide range of knowledge, nuances, flavors, merge into a coherent esthetic language, into a sensitivity shared by so diverse individuals? In the sea of signs that united the four parts of the world into a single planet waved some currents visible from the surface: the unifying project of the Catholic monarchy with its centralizing institutions, its hubs of integration (economy, the Crown, languages: Spanish, Latin, Nahuatl), its expansion drive, its world project... But in the deep waters of signs and representations, an esthetic program, which had in spirituality and theology its integrating principle, shaped the bottom streams that bound the continents.

The pre-Hispanic cosmos, with its imposing forces of nature and its dramatic regeneration cycles, had been replaced by an alliance pact and a linear sense of history, inherited from the people of Israel. At first, Franciscan missionaries maintained that the era of prodigies had passed and that miracles were no longer necessary. Educated in the Erasmian atmosphere that preceded the fracture of Latin Christendom, and driven by the wish to found

These ceramic vessels were used for storing grains, and of course among these grains were cocoa beans, basic for elaborating chocolate. Cocoa beans were so coveted that the jars had lids or locks of iron to protect them, which sometimes were kept under the bed of the mistress of the house so that she could administer them for the daily production of the precious drink. The shape and decoration of these vases is based on the taste aroused by Chinese porcelain in its infinite variations, among New Spain society. [CAT. 58]

a purified kingdom from a portion of humankind that seemed to have remained in an almost Adamic state waiting for the light of the Gospels, the friars tended to clearly distinguish the territory of idolatry from the one of a profound and discerning faith. But Criollos, actually, only achieved a consistent presence in demographic terms in the following decades, when the broken Church made of its failed reconciliation synod the starting point for the renewal of a now globalized catholicity.

The spirit of Trento revolutionized the taste and sensitivity of all the territories that received its influence. It is true that its decrees on the cult called for order and discipline, without tracing more ambitious guidelines, but the concerns that had driven the Church since the purifying projects of Cisneros and Erasmus became, after Luther's break, a movement aiming to revitalize the role of the ecclesiastical institution in every sphere.

The intellectual climate in those times received its impulse from the Aristotelianism of the scholastics, the Florentine Neo-Platonism and the emphasis on Ciceronian rhetoric of the humanistic movement. In the hands of the Church, these streams turned into means for redefining its place in the world.

In a clear affirmation movement of what had been rejected by Protestants, the Eucharist and the cult of the Virgin and the saints received a frank drive from the post-Tridentine Church. To Reform iconoclasm, the Church responded with an emphatic and triumphant iconodulism, with which revived the climate of the Byzantine dispute that had been solved by the Second Council of Nicaea. The Renaissance Church resolutely stated the possibility of representing the corporealness of heavenly persons for their cult. This issue, raised to the foremost dignity by the Incarnation of the Son of God, well deserved the exploring efforts of the artists of the time, inspired by the forms and volumes of classical antiquity. For Renaissance art, the attempt to understand the body's plastic reality became a clamor, in a rising effort to reach the truth of the divinized flesh that had been the price for the redemption of humankind. The represented body of heavenly persons could be—besides the scale with which desires climbed looking for the absolute—a channel through which divine grace flowed in response.

Religious painting received from its Byzantine inheritance the status of vehicle for hierophany, although strongly tempered by the exceptional position achieved by the Eucharist cult in the Latin Church after the Fourth Lateran Council. Compared with the almost intangible whiteness of the consecrated host, from its monstrance sparkling solid gold, painting and sculpture saw their role as acting intermediaries of sacredness attenuated, although it was not reduced to merely evoking history, nature or everyday life, as did happen in the figurative arts of Protestant regions. An art that was not afraid of representing the body for its cult and which spoke to the viewers' senses, and a moral theology that emphasized the infinite generosity of divine mercy and encouraged individuals to be part of their own salvation through their acts, and which excluded any possibility of predestination, joined the climate of enthusiasm that accompanied the geographic expansion to model an ardent sensitivity that was eager for excess. Even if, of course, the dark counterpart could possess the same kind of ardor, especially since the early stagnation of the imperial system. The accessible heaven made equally probable the tragedy of hell. Redeemed flesh could also, if it persisted in denying the overabundant help of grace, burn in flames, the fierceness of which artists showed no mercy while evoking them.

Renaissance figurative art could achieve its peaks because it was part of a whole with the extraordinary formal device that marked the art of the time: perspective. Due to it, it was possible to give room on flat surfaces to three-dimensional reality, and thus to integrate in the same pictorial space a wide range of realities arranged with a system, in which the visible disposition could involve an underlying structure. The representation of emptiness, that trace of the spirit, in its double presence: as air filling the gaps between the drawn bodies or where the rising and suspended figures float, and as vanishing point to where the lines that provide the complete structure converge—the founding elements of the pictorial system developed from the vital drive emanated from a Rome anxious of purification. A spirituality stirring to open the senses to the infinite variety of creation, to integrate its elements in guidelines that converged in an intangible vanishing point, and a figurative art of perspective, the principal exploration subjects of which were human body and space, could nothing but to merge into an art seeking to stimulate the emotions through chromatic intensity and contrast. The will to gather every possible language (verbal, visual, spatial, dramatic, sound) in a rhetoric of seduction stimulated this encounter, and thus a spirituality, a theology and an esthetic project articulated in a large cultural system that prepared to enter into dialogue with all cultures around the world. That was the model that allowed to structure in a coherent system the unrelated variety of signs and forms that had the New Spain for scene.

The studies of Marc Fumaroli from the point of view of cultural history, and of father Heinrich Pfeiffer, S.J., from the angle of esthetics and spirituality, allow us to understand the intense and fruitful bonds established between the Society of Jesus and the evangelization project carried out by the Tridentine Church. The spiritual and esthetic program of Catholicism, renewed by the Council of Trento, uses as one of its main resources the stimulus of sensorial and figurative imagination (the Ignatian composition of place), and it is open to all expressions of reality (following the invitation made in the last exercise of the homonymous book) and is able to structure them in an organic system along some very clear guidelines (the vanishing lines of "principle and fundament" that open the spiritual experience preconized by St. Ignatius).

The art of those Tridentine centuries was able to integrate into the same pictorial representation all possible levels of reality, from the putrefying horror of supreme death to the translucent corporealness of divinized flesh, which occupied the ultimate vertex of perspective. This art made room for the limitless profusion of every form, because its lines are structured to guide the viewer's eyes and affections to the intangible emptiness,

The Annunciation is a scene depicted thousands of times in the New Spain art. It is the moment when the archangel Gabriel announced to the Virgin Mary that she would conceive and be the mother of the Savior, Jesus. The assenting attitude of the Virgin Mary was an example for the nuns. [CAT. 116]

which is a metaphor of the divine. An esthetic theologically sustained from the Byzantine tradition by the Oratorian Baronius and the Jesuit Richeome, sketched by Correggio and turn into a program by Rubens and Pozzo, was the language by which the various legacies and influences enriching New Spain culture could be structured in a coherent system, which was able to provide each one of these features with a place of their own and to turn them into useful elements for the whole.

Thus, an art made of absorption and mix, looking for irresolution—since it does not attempt to distinguish elements according to their origins—, an art built to incorporate and integrate all esthetic forms and all inheritances, was the instrument of contact between Roman Catholicism and world cultures—the first esthetic language of universal

These kind of silver Lectern was an important characteristic of the New Spain liturgy. One of the most popular images in them is the Agnus Dei or the image of the Lamb of God, as shown in this example. [CAT. 26]

scope—that found in this American Spain a space for contact and mixture, a very frutiful land for its development.

That was the esthetic horizon of the Criollos, the one that Villalpando and Cabrera made possible, the one that allowed incorporating golden mines into the sceneries destined to evoke and invoke heavens, framing the everyday miracle of transubstantiation, strengthening thus the awareness of senses fallibility. It is not surprising that from an atmosphere of which that art was a vital sign, Guadalupan fervor would blossom. Criollos began to claim for a place of their own within Providence's plan of salvation. The spaces marked by the influence of that culture, like colleges, convents and the entourage of the viceroy, provided a home for spirits like Sor Juana or Sigüenza, who were able to become part in a natural way of the intellectual elites of the empire without renouncing the numerous inheritances offered by their native land.

The esthetic and intellectual system that provided Catholicism with new air was the structure were diverse cultures could be gradually articulated according to a formula that belongs to the sphere of mixed races. The program of Tridentine synthesis—with its magnificence, its exuberance, its eclecticism, its sensorial intensity, its drive for the integration of collective spaces, which can become gregarious—, together with a clear notion of the existence of irreducible zones, perhaps minuscule, where the exercise of individual freedom takes shelter, could only but mark Criollo sensitivity. That formula, omnivorous but inclusive, had allowed to incorporate in a sole variegated but coherent system a wide range of languages and cultures without forcing them to homogenize. However, that esthetic magnet, which equally attracted Europeans and castes bringing closer all the viceroyalty's ethnic groups—and also allowed the populations of other continents to communicate—, was the object of a violent offensive by the elites that from Madrid ruled the destinies of an empire as heterogeneous as disperse.

The Neoclassical offensive: perplexity and forgetfulness

In the 18th century, the cultural project of Catholicism—once the geo-political order that uphold it had disappeared and with the intellectual model that inspired it undergoing a serious crisis—undertook its scientific and stylistic renewal, but time was short to carry out its adaptation to the new airs of history. In Spain, the empire's ruling elites, urged by a cultural and geo-political context that made them extremely vulnerable—the cultural rise of enlightened French-like regalism, the British predominance in economy and politics—, eagerly embarked upon the destruction of the system that allowed the heterogeneous populations that composed the Catholic king's states to communicate with each other and to be organically related.

The Society of Jesus had been decisive to build the cultural order that structured the empire, and within it abounded agents advocating for its renewal. Once the Society of

Jesus was expelled—and later suppressed—, the enlightened leaders who managed the interests of the Spanish branch of the Bourbon dynasty devoted themselves to dismantle what was left of the existing order. Their purpose was to replace it with a cultural system that had already proved to be efficient in France and which was the expression of a highly homogeneous society, centralized around the State—therefore radically different from the Spanish monarchy.

Neoclassical art would be a key instrument for this authoritarian and statist modernization. The system that enlightened officials wanted to impose on behalf of the king was the complete opposite of the one here en vigor, which had allowed a minimum—although unstable—balance between institutions.

Within the new order designed in Madrid, inspired on Anglicanism and French regalism, the interplay of power between Church and State, which had been so fruitful, solved quickly with the altar's clear submission to the throne, setting up an absolutist power system. The dynamics between transcendence and immanence was overruled, and the first became a mere mechanical projection of the later.

If the once unfading divinity had to reduce its scope and confine itself within the narrow boundaries of human reason—which would be henceforth the only and final measure of all things—, then the esthetic exploration of boundless affections became unnecessary and its expression, dysfunctional.

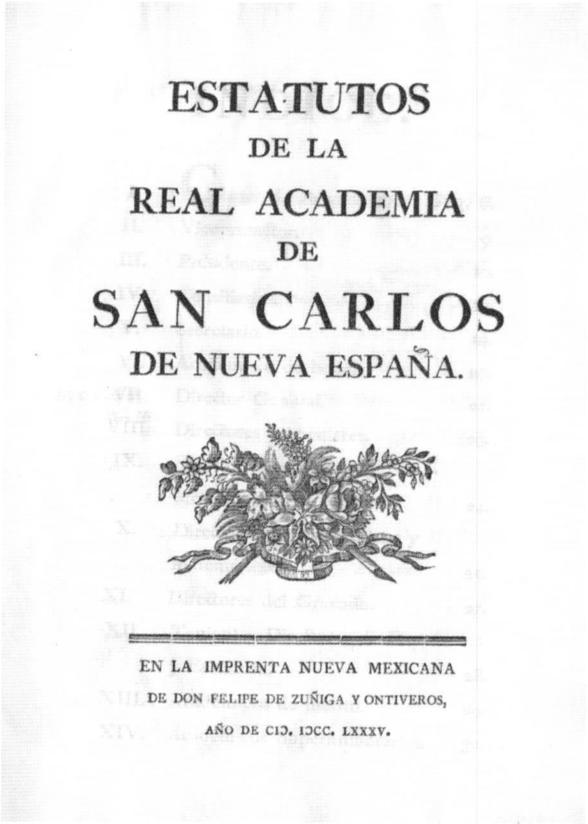

ESTATUTOS
DE LA
REAL ACADEMIA
DE
SAN CARLOS
DE NUEVA ESPAÑA.

EN LA IMPRENTA NUEVA MEXICANA
DE DON FELIPE DE ZUÑIGA Y ONTIVEROS,
AÑO DE CIↃ. IↃCC. LXXXV.

The signs serving as cultural crossroads, as convergence point where refined and coarse languages could meet, where European and indigenous voices and looks coincide united around one same object—altarpieces, processions, public festivities of chivalrous origin, para-liturgical dramatizations...—, became the target of the modernizing fervor of the most radical ministers of the Crown, who strived for its eradication. The bonds between the social pyramid's vertex and its base were broken or obstructed. The elite cultures (enlightened, rationalistic, deistic) and those that later would be called popular (effusive, exuberant, open to transcendence) were thus restructured separately, growingly distant.

The agents sent to impose the new taste arrived directly from Madrid. Manuel Tolsá would be their emblematic figure.

The Royal Academy of the Three Noble Arts of San Carlos was founded in 1781 and received its statutes in 1785. Its intention was to systematize the production of art in the Viceroyalty of New Spain and to ensure that painters, sculptors, engravers and architects developed works of sufficient quality to compete with the production from other parts of the Spanish monarchy. It began teaching engraving, entrusted to Don Jerónimo Antonio Gil. [CAT. 2]

REAL ACADEMIA DE SAN CARLOS DE NUEVA ESPA

To replace the dismantled educative system of the Jesuits, which had covered every level—from Indian schools to university level colleges—, the State created two main institutions: a large technological training center (the Colegio de Minería) and an academy that should serve as training and standardization center for the artistic disciplines, which would have also among its aims to hasten the end of the guild system. The university was isolated and only its summit survived, without the natural nurture from the network of schools that once covered the entire viceroyalty, until it completely vanished in the 19th century.

Some of the figureheads of the neoclassical offensive, artists of undoubted skill and true talent, were able to create more than once, using the esthetic vocabulary they had come to impose for the totalitarian will of the Crown, works of remarkable value, and they knew on occasion how to effectively integrate them within the esthetic program of the works they intervened. But many of their followers took to the letter the modernizing program guidelines and were responsible for the greatest destruction of the artistic heritage that had been carried out in these parts since the fall of the pre-Hispanic cultures.

The God who had made himself heard through the brushes of Rubens and Pozzo, the one whose flesh had been evoked by Michelangelo, Bernini and in Guatemalan *estofados*, the one who whispered into the heart of St. Teresa and whose golden voice flowed in torrents from the top of the helical and *estípite* columns to console literate and illiterate, and to whom Indians pleaded with their dances, eclipsed, hidden by a small, reasonable deity speaking in a flatten plaster and painted wood language. Indians and *Mestizos* tried to revive the interiors of their churches—which had muted when losing the polyphonic choir of their golden and varnished altarpieces—with scallops of shiny fabrics and garlands of paper, with bunches of baby's breath flowers, cockscomb flowers or marigold flowers. Certainly, there were artists and patrons who maintained the rhythm of their lives or who interpreted the new formal vocabulary in the light of the old schemes, but both were being isolated to the margins of the new mainstream.

The Rome-Antwerp-Seville axis of cultural influence had already died when the French Revolution made its death public. Most of the Criollos, mired in confusion, lost their compass and no longer knew what they liked. Of course, they wanted to be at the same time zone than the Villa and Court—which already was the Versailles meridian—, and those who could afford it were quickly portrayed with French coat and powdered wig, and their wives, later, in costumes inspired by Pompeian taste, but more likely is that almost no one was sure of the reasons why what they had enjoyed and admired, and had built with so much effort, suddenly had become excessive, overelaborated, "tasteless." As unfortunately the riches in their coffers were plentiful, many, and among them many members of the clergy, applied themselves to hand over to the ax the same artworks they had just finished paying for the day before.

The most radical enlightened Criollos were becoming isolated in their salons, newly furnished to the empire fashion, decorated with bronze pieces "à la Egyptian." Communi-

cation with their countrymen of different social groups was becoming less fluent, and also, paradoxically, their cultural and geo-political perspective became increasingly provincial—exception made of some cases, which began testing new tropisms, particularly in the direction of England. The most acute phase of Bourbon modernization brought serious consequences for the Criollos: it tore the intellectual network that due to their friends and relatives—now exiled in Italy by Charles III—allowed them to have a deep memory—through the knowledge of history and ancient languages. The vital link with classical and Renaissance humanism faded into extinction. They also lost consciousness of a geo-political horizon, which they had begun to acquire through the transcontinental nature of the institution that served as their social reference: the global network of correspondence that the Jesuits had implemented was for the Criollos a continuously open window to the realities of the world. This situation would be dramatically visible

These vessels, usually made of glazed terracotta, were used in housework, like washing clothes and for bathing. They came in various sizes, including some of about one meter in diameter. [CAT. 43]

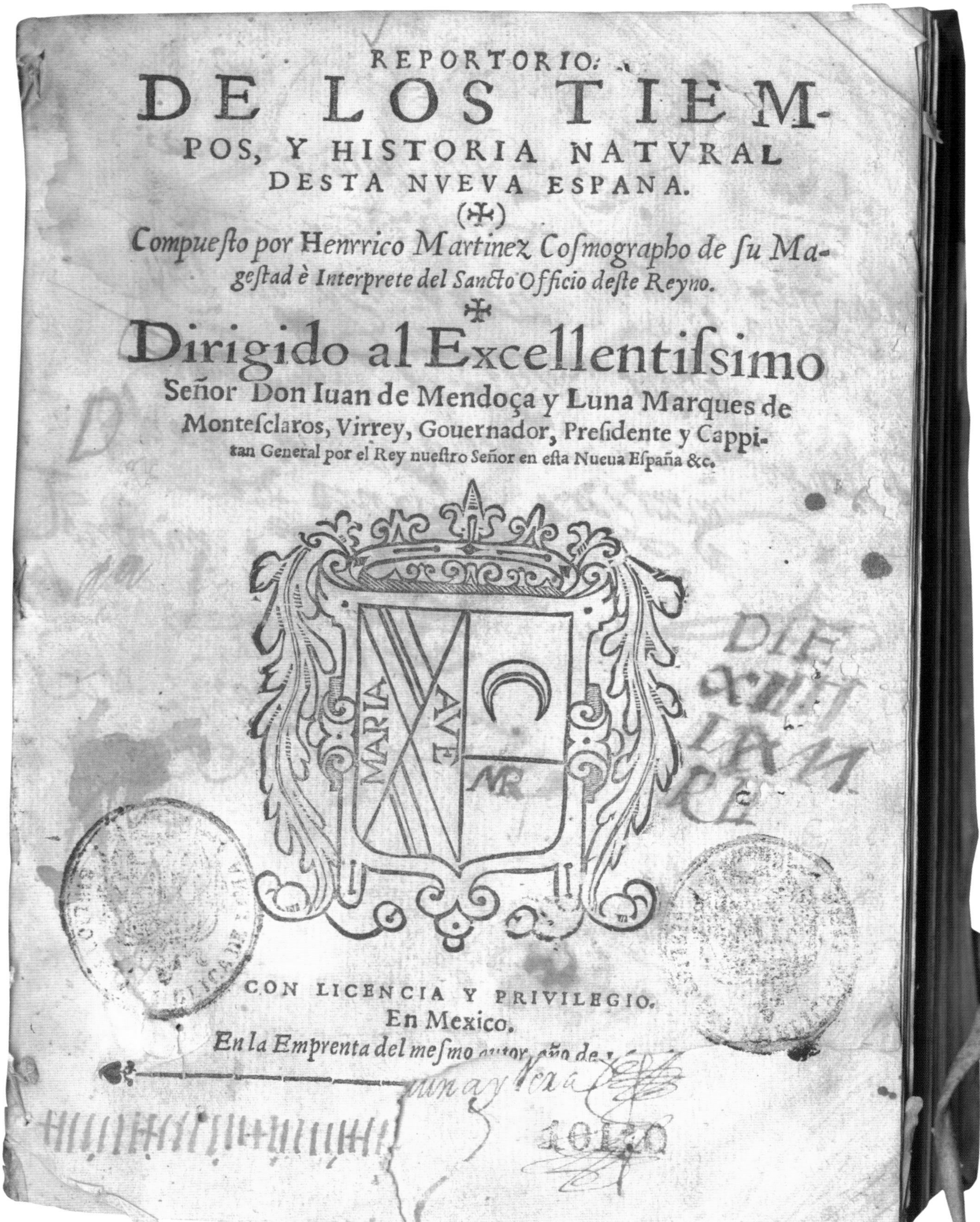

REPORTORIO

DE LOS TIEMPOS, Y HISTORIA NATVRAL DESTA NVEVA ESPANA.

Compuesto por Henrrico Martinez Cosmographo de su Magestad è Interprete del Sancto Officio deste Reyno.

Dirigido al Excellentissimo Señor Don Iuan de Mendoça y Luna Marques de Montesclaros, Virrey, Gouernador, Presidente y Cappitan General por el Rey nuestro Señor en esta Nueua España &c.

CON LICENCIA Y PRIVILEGIO.

En Mexico.

En la Emprenta del mesmo autor, año de

Enrico Martínez was of German origin and bore the name of Heinrich Martin. Born in Hamburg, he was a prominent scientist and a scholar in various disciplines. He served as royal cosmographer in the court of Philip II and he took care of the drainage works to prevent flooding in Mexico City. [CAT. 90]

at the time that the newly independent Criollos were unable to devise coherent economic and political alliances, which would have allowed them to defend the interests of their country in the world. In addition, as a result of the Bourbon attempt to limit the use of indigenous languages, and expatriated the "tongues" that had been their teachers, for New Spain Criollos became increasingly difficult to fulfill their role as ruling elite of a society, since their communication channels with most of their countrymen hopelessly atrophied.

The violent eradication of the Jesuits was a milestone in Criollo history, since almost all native-born exiles belonged to this social category and constituted the core of the intellectual elite of the viceroyalty. The leadership of New Spain had been educated in their schools and the Society had members of many important family clans. Moreover, the network of sociability that the institution had implemented—in particular through associations such as the Marian congregations—had been the setting where the New Spain elite had been built.

Criollos experienced a dramatic shock as a result of Bourbon modernization, the scope of which they do not seem to have understood at the time: they lost their organic links (family, friendship) with their intellectual elite, and the aesthetic system that had been their frame of reference and vital means of expression, and which was also the vehicle of communication with their countrymen and the world, had been reduced to smithereens. It is not surprising that their taste had been affected: the elites of New Spain became insecure, forgetful, provincial, disposed to the destruction of their artistic heritage.

The loss of a very considerable cultural capital by their owners or guardians and, of course, the collapse of the imperial system itself, and, later, the inability of the Criollos to take the reins of the country effectively—the political independence of which they had just won in an almost accidental fashion—are eloquent proof of the disintegrating effect that 18th century modernizations had for New Spain society. It is clear that political leaders never anticipated effects of that nature. The empire did not become more prosperous and better able to confront the big powers and, when it had to face a major continental crisis—the Napoleonic wars—, it ended dissolving.

Criollos resented this situation directly and the effects of their vulnerability affected all their countrymen. Because the heavy burden that the young nation had to charge, forced to face its independent life without a clear awareness of its historical path—and, therefore, of its real potential and limitations—, lacking the slightest hint of a geopolitical project and devoid of functional systems of communication between its towns, was largely the result of the recent disruption of its elites, the breakdown of its embryonic ruling class.

It is clear that the reform of taste advocated by the introduction of Neoclassical aesthetics—coated with the character of official art to face, with purposes of eradication, the Iberian Baroque program, organically linked to the cultural matrix of Tridentine Catholicism—was only one facet of the regalist impulse, which aimed to increase state

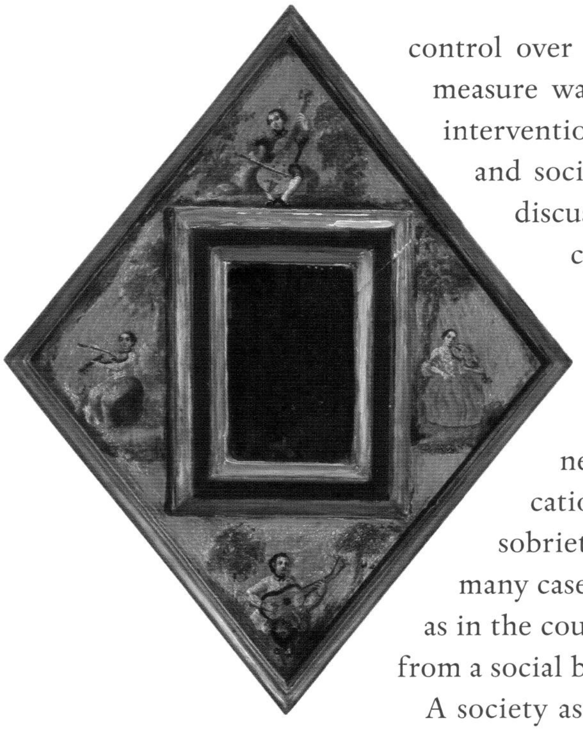

control over a group of poorly structured societies. This measure was part of a strategy involving homogenizing interventions in the administrative, political, economic and social fields. But focusing on the subject of our discussion, we can now weigh up the ruptures caused by the attempts to replace in an accelerated and authoritarian manner a culture of inclusiveness—although certainly profuse and hyperbolic—with another based on balance and symmetry but lacking effectiveness as instrument of expression and communication of a transcontinental political space. The sobriety of an imposed Neoclassical style became in many cases forced and superficial, since it did not arise, as in the countries that were cradle of the Enlightenment, from a social base of which it were a living expression.

A society as diverse and in full shaping process, through efforts to bring closer and mix the various cultures that stirred inside it, could not, without serious detriment, try to use abruptly as a means of expression and communication system an aesthetic language located at the antipodes of the one that was its own. The aim of Neoclassical culture was to level and depurate, and was based on a semiological system of which the founding principles were the rejection of paradoxes and to be repelled by contrasts. The greatest feat of this art was to elude the tragic dimensions of reality.

If the oxymoron, which brings together opposites, is the rhetorical figure that could represent the vehemence contained, the profusion structured into an emptiness that is the mark of Baroque centuries, then litotes, which minimize, which imply, relegating beyond the explicit limits of language complex realities, would represent the more delicate forms of neoclassical sensitivity. But in the case of an imposed esthetic program, these shades were erased; nothing remained but the exclusion and harsh denial of reality, the disappearance by decree of everything for which the less subtle rationalizations offered no immediate explanation.

In the daytime clarity of Port Royal or the Trianon (not in the early mornings of Restif de la Bretonne or those of Sade), the measured and almost crystal-clear discourse, carefully refined and polished, which the French call classical, is relevant and useful. The wish to implement an approximate version of that language as a communication system capable of organically integrating a multitude of European, Asian and American cultures, might seem an expression of unbridled delirium if it were not exactly what the brilliant modernizers expected; trying to strengthen the empire, they precipitated its collapse.

In the doors of this cabinet are depicted scenes of musicians playing various instruments such as harps, guitars, flutes, etc., including a singer. The musicians are not related to an ensemble, like in modern times, but separate, in an open air area, as playing popular tunes for relaxation and enjoyment of the spirit. [CAT. 17]

As Marc Fumaroli has shown, the precepts of taste that would later become the soul of Neoclassical aesthetics had been formulated by the first Jansenist generations, having opposite as catalyst the publication by Flemish Jesuits of *Imago primi saeculi* (1640), a paradigmatic work of the taste and sensitivity in Tridentine culture. Their aim was to build an autonomous space for the national reason and the reason of State facing a language that defined itself as the voice without borders of a Catholic (i.e., universal) institution. But the difference that in Champaigne or Poussin brushes compared with those of Rubens appears as an enriching emphasis, as a complementary shade, ends up becoming, in the works of Perrault and Soufflot compared to those of Bernini, an irreducible branch.

In New Spain, and more than a century after Arnauld and Pascal, turned Neoclassicism into an instrument of the so called Spanish Jansenism, and in the hands of medium scale officials and artists who were sometimes talented but hardly geniuses, the results of the imposition of the aesthetics of the reason of State became very different from those expected.

As we know, Neoclassical culture immediately generated its indispensable complement: the Romantic movement, where all those dimensions of reality peremptorily evacuated from Western consciousness because of the Enlightenment took shelter. In our country, the destruction of Baroque altarpieces by regalist reformers—and their liberal followers—brought an unexpected consequence: the disappearance of the representations of heaven and the survival of the images of hell, with the consequent detriment of Criollo reputation. The joyous evocations of paradise occupied the vast majority of the spaces carved and painted in Tridentine churches, while for the allusions to the first three of the Four Last Things (death, judgment, hell) a circumscribed space was reserved, which was, in any case, neutralized by the splendor covered in gold leaf that announced the glorious victory over all death. The aesthetics of Romanticism, in appropriate reaction to the narrowness of the Neoclassical taste view, which had evacuated from its field of vision all agonies but also all ecstasies, and devoid of a horizon that would allow it to legitimately evoke jubilant dimensions of reality, focused its gaze on the depths (of nature, war, passion...), keeping for the vehement chromatisms, daring compositions and vivid sensuality inherited from Rubens tradition the exploration of the joyful mysteries of earthly life.

The only facet of the Baroque legacy that was attractive to the Romantic view—like later for the Surrealist one—was precisely the one referring to anxieties and nightmares, which influenced not a little the evaluation and protection of paintings and sculptures of painful tonic. In this context, the selective survival of many works of the Baroque era, the dark theme of which made reference to sin and its consequences: the passion of Christ, hell, contributed to create a skewed picture of the spiritual atmosphere of the Tridentine centuries. Once eliminated the echoes of an accessible heaven, for the convulsive generations of the 19th and 20th centuries only remained the representation of an imaginary Criollo past marked by anxiety, guilt and the repression of the senses.

The Mestizo answer of the Criollos

As a result of Bourbon modernizations, Criollos saw their possibilities to establish themselves as a central part of the social and political leadership that New Spain needed strongly diminished. This situation would worsen during the civil war that erupted in 1810, the ethnic violence of which would lastingly deepen the gap between American Spaniards and their mainland relatives, with the subsequent blocking of the formation processes for consistent elites and for the design of a viable geopolitical project. However, Criollos constructively confronted the challenges of a history that was so adverse and strived to restore the communication channels damaged by the reforms.

Particularly, a group of men of science and letters, with the only weapons at their disposal, research and writing, stood out, contributing to the formulation of a new patriotic imaginary and helping shape a sensitivity and a taste that would later prove effective as tools for social integration. In that proposal, they merged the legacy of the past with the scientific and aesthetic horizons of their time. The symbolic references the construction of which they promoted have been valid since the country achieved independence; the multiple regime changes have not affected that process, one of the few that maintain continuity in a history as spasmodic as the Mexican one.

Of the Enlightenment modernity and its main aesthetic branch, Neoclassicism, Criollos were only surprised by its authoritarianism. With other aspects, more constructive, they were quite familiar and we can say that in good measure because they already owned them. They were fully immersed in the great social, intellectual and stylistic movements stirring European life. As we know from the researches by Bernabé Navarro, Elías Trabulse, Álvaro Matute, Conrado Ulloa and Arturo Reynoso, their youngest and brightest minds had followed with great interest the renewal movement that advocated to overcome the boundaries of the old scientific paradigms, to expand the territories of the experimental method, and to refine the verbal and visual languages of the sterile convolutions in which the less subtle expressions of Baroque esthetics could incur.

The preference for the decorative arts and the fine objects was extended to other places of the New Spain, as this Two-handled rase from Tonalá of the 18th century shows. [CAT. 64]

In Jesuit colleges, almost all professors who trained their students in the skills of a conceptual fencing based on syllogisms—which were the declared target for the enlightened reformers—used to be speakers of indigenous languages—and also classical and modern—and had personal experience of pastoral and educational work with indigenous and illiterate people. But, in addition, many of them were fully aware of the latest scientific advances both in the fields of philosophy as in physics, astronomy and mathematics, and had passionate controversies with their more conservative colleagues for whom Aristotelianism and the Ptolemaic system were immutable references. The long training period they had undergone, with the duty to perform a wide variety of tasks, and the frequent rotation of functions characteristic of the institution to which they belonged, meant that many members of the order had first hand experience not only as teachers but also as explorers and cartographers, and that natural sciences and ethnographic work (essential functions of missionary work) were not foreign to them. We know, moreover, that the productive activities of the order, the *haciendas*, forced some members to gain a broad experience in technological, administrative and economic issues. For all these reasons, Criollo intellectuals—at least the Jesuits and their numerous disciples throughout the viceroyalty, but not only them—had not waited for the rise of Societies of friends of the country, founded by the enlightened—they rather had preceded them—, to outline programs of agricultural improvement and technological development proposals based on their own experience and to care for the material welfare of their countrymen.

Expelled the Jesuits and immersed the elite of New Spain in the bewildering turmoil of enlightened reformism, a select group of Criollos on both sides of the ocean—in Italy and Mexico—continued seeking ways of reconciliation between systems and cultures, despite all difficulties. The route had been drawn since the time of Sigüenza and the generations of the last third of the 18th century remained faithful to a project that was the result of the cultural model that was their own. To evaluate the legacy of the great indigenous civilizations as fundamental element of New Spain memory turning it into the founding pole of a shared imaginary; to recognize the role that language and culture provided by Spain had played to structure the country's diverse populations into a new set: these would be the fundamental principles of the program proposed by the Criollos. The formula reinforced the symbolic links that bound them to their countrymen without fracturing—although distending—what connected them to their European relatives. Other two devices of great symbolic importance came to reinforce the scene: the exaltation of the native landscape, a clearly distinctive element that brought together all natives of these parts, regardless of their ethnic origin—and which followed in the footsteps of Cervantes de Salazar and Bernardo de Balbuena—, and the postulation of the Guadalupan image as identifying sign of the new common social space that before being a nation was already a homeland—as shown by the researches by Francisco de la Maza, David Brading, Jacques Lafaye and Jaime Cuadriello.

The figures in this process deserve an illustrious place in the memory of their countrymen. They built a symbolic paradigm that allowed the children of these territories to elude their particularities in order to create common references, which were not in principle mutually exclusive, since they did not nullify the operation of other signs of belonging shared with other members of the Church, Hispanity and the human race. Criollos did not erect the symbolic model of the new society around themselves but they displaced what would become to be the cultural center of gravity—on which the future country would be built—into the Mestizo sector. Cultural mixing had overflowed widely the biological one. These American-born Spaniards were already culturally mixed and as such they behaved when they had to define themselves, although in the proposals of these early generations there is no incompatibility between both belongings. The Criollos who turned the *métissage* into the backbone of the new society were the main builders of the tale of origin, the producers of their common imaginary—telluric rooting, symbolic connection with pre-Hispanic civilizations, belonging to the family of peoples of Spanish language and culture.

It is worth noting that this founding tale was gradually taking shape with the various contributions of each and every one but has its place unequivocally in the scientific and stylistic territories of enlightened modernity. Both the language and the epistemological paradigms that these Criollos used were definitely already part of the cultural fields of the Age of Enlightenment. The syntax was sober; the arguments, inductive, based on empirical references, and the axiological proposals were those of common use in enlightened modernity: the love of truth, philanthropy, and their key concepts were culture, civilization, humanity, although of course the radically deistic positions were foreign to them. This is most obvious in the case of the exiles, marked by an intense spiritual experience and a filial affection to the ecclesiastical institution.

The character of these works shows, therefore, that there was no essential incompatibility between the more constructive values of enlightened sensitivity and the groups that from within the Tridentine culture strived to achieve (also in this field) a conciliation of interests and a convergence of views. We do not know what might have been that possible synthesis: enlightened modernity and then the French Revolution and the end of the Ancien Régime heighten the tension between the different positions and durably closed the harmonious roads between reality and dreams, between a memory of their own and the aspirations of mimicry.

Although we might indeed have some clue about this hypothetical solution that could have renewed without violence the social ties painstakingly built over the viceregal centuries. Despite its 18th century enlightened tone, the Criollo formula, as presented for instance by Clavijero, is perhaps less according to Parisian sensitivity than it might seem at first sight. Because it internal structure, which seeks to amalgamate and merge different elements: Indian heritage, Spanish legacy—even at the expense of incurring paradoxes—is more akin to the "way to proceed" of late Renaissance than to a Neoclassical culture that strives to distinguish and refine—even at the expense of incurring simplifications.

The cultural mixing built by the Criollos would perhaps be the last product of a sensitivity and a taste anchored in the atmosphere of the Council of Trent, a victory for the oxymoron that repaired, at least in part, the effects of the enlightened modernizers splitting operation.

Non-Jesuit intellectuals (Alzate, León y Gama, Díaz de Gamarra...) put their talent into practice for the development of sciences and their researches were used by exiles as the basis for some essays with which they were trying to present the realities of this country in European scientific debates. The wise men from the "inland," which were on occasions well-known voices outside their homeland, warmly welcomed, despite the great difficulties of communication, the works of exiles and found in them an incentive both for their research tasks and for the consolidation of their incipient patriotism.

The exiles, in their dedications to the University or to Mexico City, emphatically expressed their affective bond with this land and claimed their character as Mexican—sometimes from the very frontispieces of their volumes. Members of that generation contributed to a high degree to turn the name of a particular people—the Mexica—into the common adjective for all inhabitants of the new country, regardless of their ethnic origin.

By exalting the greatness of the homeland (Landívar and Clavijero), by placing pre-Hispanic people in a universal perspective following an enlightened paradigm the standard of which was the concept of civilization (Clavijero and Márquez), the exiles consolidated as never before the role of foundational core that the pre-Columbian past would play in national memory.

By arguing the aesthetic dignity of the ancient art of Anahuac—which far from appearing as the testimony of an evil influence, was presented as an expression of the human spirit that should be evaluated with the same parameters applied to the legacies of Egypt or Rome—, these scientists, both from the inland as expatriates, made a major contribution to build an already Mestizo taste.

By raising the problem of the painful condition of the living Indians (Clavijero) and by clearly advocating the intensification of biological mixing (Clavijero and Cavo), these intellectuals tried to prevent the occurrence of the disconnection—which unfortunately carried out the next generations—between the admired dead Indians and their despised living descendants.

The other column of cultural mixing, the Hispanic one, was also built by all: Clavijero, with his history of the evangelization of California, Cavo with the one of the viceroyalty, and Alegre, with the one of his religious family and his theological writings.

Interestingly, some of the works that today seem more surprising are the Latin poems (Abad), the Roman archaeological researches (Márquez) or the translations from

La *Storia Antica of Messico* was written by Francisco Xavier Clavijero during his years of exile, after the decree of expulsion of the Society of Jesus in all areas dominated by the Spanish monarchy. As the friars—many of them born in the Viceroyalty—had to leave New Spain in 1767, they used their experience to ponder their historical heritage and being, shaped by a range of cultural influences from the close coexistence with Indians, Africans and Asians. [CAT. 101]

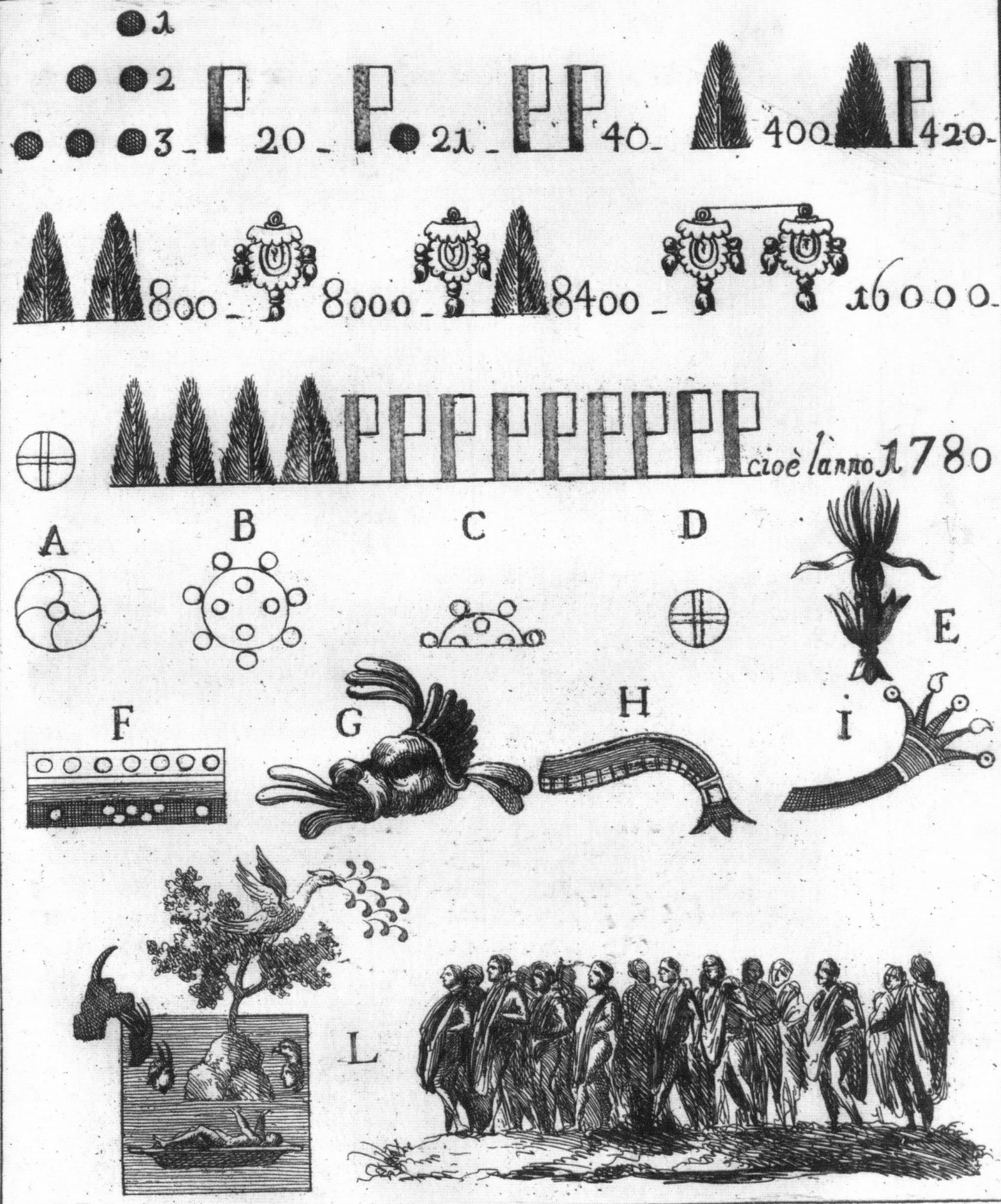

A il giorno. B la notte. C la mezza notte. D l'anno.
E il secolo. F il cielo. G l'aria. H la terra. I l'acqua.
L il diluvio, e la confusion delle lingue.

In *La Storia Antico del Messico*, Clavijero values the antique history of the New Spain and gives importance and dignity to the Indians in comparision to Greeks and Romans from antiquity. [CAT. 101]

Greek into Latin (Alegre). These works pointed out the humanist horizon of universality, depth and refinement in which this new culture that was already fully Mestizo should be included.

The history of these New Spaniards—perhaps the first to consider themselves decisively Mexicans, several decades before independence—can teach us a lot about the turbulent reality of this nation. Criollos, despite their privileged position, were unable to ever become a consistent elite, and a strong and active national leadership still has not been built by their descendants nor by any other group despite the time passed.

However, by passing the baton of cultural and symbolic leadership, manufacturing and making available for the Mestizo majority the model that was to turn it into the backbone of the independent country, the next to last Criollo generations made an invaluable contribution to the harmony among our populations.

The weak and vacillating social harmony we still enjoy today in Mexico rests, largely, on the legacy of these American-born Spaniards, who knew how to articulate the symbolic links that we still use when trying to communicate among ourselves and with the world, and which enable us to still strive to build a common destiny.

IX

Al tiempo, pues,
que la veloz saeta]
remontado blasón
de Sagitario]
a expensas de la luz
del gran planeta]
es del Olimpo luminoso
erario.]

Cuando a Cibeles,
[próvida y discreta]
comunica cristal
la urna de Acuario,]
vegetó sin influjos
de sus giros]
flores la tierra,
envidia a sus zafiros.

“Primavera indiana. Poema sacrohistórico, idea de María Santíssima de Gvadalvpe de México, copiada de flores” (fragment).

"Primavera indiana", is a poem dedicated to the Virgin of Guadalupe by Carlos de Sigüenza y Góngora. This poem is inclued in the book *Glorias de Guerrero*, published in 1680 in the New Spain by the Viuda de Bernardo Calderón.

I

Si merecí Calíope tu acento
de divino furor mi mente inspira,
y en acorde compás da a mi instrumento,
que de marfil canoro, a trompa aspira.
Tu dictamen: atienda a mi concento
cuanto con luces de sus rayos gira
ardiente Febo sin temer fracaso
del chino oriente, al mexicano ocaso.

II

Oiga del septentrión la armoniosa
sonante lira mi armonioso canto
correspondiendo a su atención gloriosa
del clima austral el estrellado manto.
Alto desvelo pompa generosa
del cielo gloria, del Leteo espanto
que con voz de metal canta Talía
o nazca niño el sol, o muera el día.

III

Rompa mi voz al diáfano elemento
los líquidos obstáculos, y errante
encomiendo a sus alas el concento,
que aspira heroico a persistir diamante.
Plausible empresa, soberano intento,
que al eco del clarín siempre triunfante
de la fama veloz monstruo de pluma,
sonará por el polvo y por la espuma.

IV

Si indigna copa a metros raudales
la atención se recata, temerosa
de investigar con números mortales
la inmortal primavera de una rosa.
Al acorde murmullo de cristales,
que Hipocrene dispende vagarosa,
afecte dulce el de Libetra coro
la voz de plata, las cadencias de oro.

V

Matiz mendigue de la primavera,
que afectuoso venero, humilde canto
de Amaltea la copia lisonjera
el de Fabonio colorido manto.
Mientras clarín de superior esfera,
en fijos polos, el florido espanto,
publica del invierno, que volantes
copos, anima en flores rozagantes.

VI

Rinda en vez del aroma nabateo
sonoros cultos mi terrestre labio,
aunque a tan noble majestuoso empleo
querúbicos acentos son agravios.
Los números (modelo del deseo)
sean de tanto empeño desagravio,
mientras al orbe en armoniosa suma
mi voz cadencias, rasgos da mi pluma.

VII

Oh, Tú, que en trono de diamantes puros,
pisando estrellas vistes del sol rayos,
a cuyo lustre ofrecen los Coluros
brillantes luces de su obsequio ensayos.
Purifica mi acento, y mis impuros
labios se animen florecientes mayos
que a tu sombra mi voz bella María
triunfa inmortal del alterable día.

VIII

A la cuarta estación, que señorea
del frígido Aquilón, nieve volante,
corría el año, mientras clamorea
lánguida Clisie al fugitivo amante.
Comunicando liberal Astrea
escarchas al invierno reiterante
y haciendo en desiguales horizontes
selvas del hielo, de la nieve montes.

IX

Al tiempo, pues, que la veloz saeta
remontado blasón de Sagitario
a expensas de la luz del gran planeta
es del Olimpo luminoso erario.
Cuando a Cibeles, próvida y discreta
comunica cristal la urna de Acuario,
vegetó sin influjos de sus giros
flores la tierra, envidia a sus zafiros.

LA AMERICA
Dispuesta segun el Sistema de Mr.
HASIUS Profesor de Mathematicas en
la Vniversidad de Witembergo, añadidos
los ultimos descubrimientos por M. DE LISLE.
DEDICADO
A Exmo Sr Conde de Povolide
Señor de las Villas de Castro
Verde, paradela, y otras
Gentil hombre de Camara
de sua Altesa el Sr Infan
te D. Antonio de Portugal.
Por Pedro Gendron.
Año 1754.
MAR DEL SVR
O PACIFICO
OCCE
AN
TROPICO DE CANCER
EQVADOR O LINEA
GOLFO DE MEXICO
I. de Roca Partida
I. de S. Thomas
Cº de S. Lucar
Puerto de Año bueno
Golfo de S. Martin
I. de Chiperton
I. de Cocos
I. del Galego
Islas de los Galapas
Islas Nuevas descubiertas por los Españoles
I. del Diabolo
I. de Mascarin
I. Malatia
I. de S. Isabel
ISLAS DE SALOMON
I. de Guadalcanal
I. de S. Pablo
Tierra descubierta por David Ingles, Año 1687.
I. de Pasqua
I. de S. Ambrosio
I. de S. Felix
Islas de Juan Fernandez
I. de Afuera
I. Fiera
Mexico
Acapulco
la Havana
CUBA
I. de Jamaica
ANTILLAS MAIORES
Cartagena
Panama
Lima
Callao
Arequipa
Arica
Coquimbo
Valparaiso
Santiago
la Concepcion
Baldivia
I. de Chiloe
Estrecho de Magellan
Tierra del Fuego
C. de Horn
I. de Barnevel
MAGVEL
CHILE
Tucuman
PAR
Guamanga
Cuzco
Potosi
Truxillo
Quito
Popayan
Santa Fee de Bogota
Virginea
Carolina
ISLAS LUCAIAS
Yucatan
Campeche
Veracruz
Guatemala
Golfo de Honduras
Provincia de Campana
Prov. de Sonora
I. de Cedros
I. de Hateras
C. de Gracias a Dios
240
245
250
255
260
265
270
275
280
285
290
295
300

Fomento Cultural Grupo Salinas

Fomento Cultural Grupo Salinas was created in 2001. It emerged because of the interest and commitment of Ricardo B. Salinas Pliego for participating in the support and promotion of culture as a fundamental value of the Mexicans.

Therefore, since then, it is dedicated to promoting the preservation of Mexico's cultural heritage though projects that spread mexican traditions and costums. It also promotes and dissenate artistic creation, and buils national and international parthership with mesums and cultral institutions in Mexico and abroad. Fomento Cultural Grupo Salinas carries out projects of great vitaly for our heritage that trascend national borders and establish links with other people.

Among its programs of action, there are publications, contests and exhibitions, and provides support for various cultural and artistic projects and for the dissemination of kwonledge. Fomento Cultural Grupo Salinas has gathered important colletions, especially in the field of the old Mexican photographs of 19th century, books, maps, documents and drawings on the history of Mexico, and silver pieces made by Mexican artisans and artists. It also publishes books on tipics of national, artistic and cultural interest. Thus the core areas of Fomento Cultural Grupo Salinas are: to editing, contests, exhibitions, partnerships and carries out corporate projects of Grupo Salinas it self.

The Hispanic Society of America

Known as the *Hispanic Museum*, The Hispanic Society of America was founded in May 1904 in New York. It owes its origin to Archer Milton Huntington (1870–1955), an erudite philanthropist who devoted his life and resources to strengthen and inherit the world his passion for Hispanic culture. In 1908 Huntington opened a library and a museum that offer researchers and visitors the opportunity to investigate and promote the study of the arts and cultures of the Iberian Peninsula and Latin America, and a collection of works of art and Spanish painting from the Middle Ages to the present, including real treasures of the Golden Age and the 18th, 19th and early-20th centuries. Since its inception, The Hispanic Society of America has published over 200 monographs by the curators of the Society and other internationally renowned researchers on various facets of Hispanic culture. This has contributed to the development and reassessment of the studies on this subject held in the United States.

The unique vocation of collector developed by Archer Milton Huntington consolidated with his desire and commitment to share and spread knowledge of Hispanic culture not only in the United States but also around the world. This vocation has been extensively enhanced over the years by subsequent directors of The Hispanic Society of America, who continue to support the implementation of major exhibitions and the publication of hundreds of books around the world—all with the purpose of disseminating cultural and intellectual projects related to Spain and its culture. Painting, decorative objects, manuscripts, rare books, are some of the Hispanic treasures preserved in the collection of The Hispanic Society of America, which is unique and important for the value of its contents and the pieces it houses.

Museo Franz Mayer

The Museo Franz Mayer is recognized internationally for the quality of its exhibitions and for its extraordinary collection of decorative arts, which comprises pieces from various sources, materials and styles from the 16th to the 19th century.

Result of the collector and philanthropic vocation of the Mexican citizen of German origin Franz Mayer, after whom the museum is named, the collection consists of silver, lacquered, ivory, tortoiseshell, glass and enameled objects, as well as ceramics, furniture, textiles, sculpture, painting, feather art, engravings, among others.

Opened in 1986, the Museo Franz Mayer has helped to foster research and spreading of decorative arts and design in Mexico, offering visitors a huge variety of activities and exhibitions.

The Museo Franz Mayer is located in the Plaza de la Santa Veracruz, facing the Alameda Central, in a building of mid-17th century in Mexico City. This is a place with four centuries of history that initially functioned as a public hospital.

In the upper cloister of this building is the Library Rogerio Casas Alatriste H., which specializes in decorative arts and has over 14 thousand volumes, among them old and rare books, historical documents and some 800 editions in 18 languages of *The Ingenious Hidalgo Don Quijote of La Mancha*.

About the authors

Alfonso Alfaro
He has a PhD in Anthropology from the University of Paris and is the Director of the Research Institute of Artes de Mexico. He is the author, among other books, of *Voces de tinta dormida. Itinerarios espirituales de Luis Barragán* and *Corpus Aureum. Escultura religiosa*.

Sara Gabriela Baz Sánchez
She has a Master in History from El Colegio de Mexico and is Technical Assistant Director of the National Museum of Art in Mexico City. In 2005, she received the Edmundo O'Gorman award for Best Master's Thesis confered by the National Institute of Anthropology and History.

Mitchell A. Codding
He is Executive Director of The Hispanic Society of America in New York, where he has worked for over 25 years. He is an expert in rare books and manuscripts. In 2006 he received from King Juan Carlos of Spain the Gold Medal for Merit in Fine Arts, awarded by the Ministry of Culture of that country.

Manuel Ramos Medina
Historian. He has authored *Imagen de santidad en un mundo profano: historia de una fundación, Manifestaciones religiosas en el mundo colonial americano* and *Místicas y descalzas: fundaciones femeninas carmelitas en la Nueva España*.

Antonio Rubial García
He has a PhD in Philosophy from the University of Seville and a PhD in History from the UNAM, where he teaches full time. He is the author, among other books, of *Memorias de conquista, Monjas, cortesanos y plebeyos: la vida cotidiana en la época de Sor Juana* and *La santidad controvertida*.

Salvador Rueda Smithers
Historian and Director of the National Museum of History in the Castillo de Chapultepec. He is the author, among other books, of *El paraíso de la caña: historia de una construcción imaginaria, Pinceles mexicanos: tres mil años de pintura* and *El diablo de Semana Santa*.

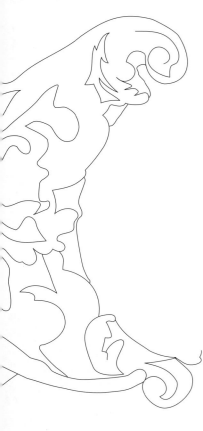

List of Works

* Works not exhibited

1. Abraham Ortelius
Hispaniae Novae sivae magnae, recens et vera descriptio
1579
Print on paper
Ricardo B. Salinas Pliego/Fomento Cultural
Col. Grupo Salinas

2. Real Academia de San Carlos [Royal Academy of San Carlos]
Estatutos de la Real academia de San Carlos de Nueva España [Statutes of the Royal Academy of San Carlos of New Spain], Mexico City, Felipe de Jesús Zúñiga y Ontiveros, 1785. Binding dedicated to the Viceroy Juan Ruiz de Apodaca
Col. The Hispanic Society of America, NY

3. Agustín Dávila y Padilla
(Mexico City, 1562–1604)
Historia de la fundación y discurso de la provincia de Santiago de México [History of the foundation and discourse of the province of Santiago de México], Brussels: Juan de Meerbeque, 1625
Col. The Hispanic Society of America, NY

4. Agustín del Pino
Virgen de Guadalupe [Virgin of Guadalupe]
20th century
Polychrome wood inlaid with shell
Col. Museo Franz Mayer

5. Agustín de Vetancurt
Teatro mexicano [Mexican Theatre]
Mexico City, María de Benavides viuda de Juan de Ribera, 1698
Col. The Hispanic Society of America, NY

6. Alonso López de Herrera
(Mexico, born in Spain, ca. 1580–1675)
Virgen de la Inmaculada Concepción [Virgin of the Immaculate Conception]
Mexico
Signed and dated in 1640
Engraved on the back with 55 images of saints and theological symbols
Oil on copper plate
Col. The Hispanic Society of America, NY

7. Alonso Muñoz
Carta al rey Felipe II sobre la rebelion de Martín Cortés [Letter to the King Philip II on the revolt of Martín Cortés]
Mexico, January 28, 1568
Manuscript on paper
Col. The Hispanic Society of America, NY

8. Alonso Muñoz, royal commissioner
Carta al rey Felipe II sobre la rebelion de Martín Cortés [Letter to the King Philip II on the revolt of Martín Cortés]
Mexico, January 28, 1568
Manuscript on paper
Col. The Hispanic Society of America, NY

9. Antonio de León Pinelo
Questión moral si el chocolate quebranta el ayuno eclesiástico [Moral question whether the chocolate brakes the ecclesiastical fast]
Madrid, Viuda de Juan González, 1636
Col. The Hispanic Society of America, NY

10. Antonio Fernández
Silver frame mirror
Puebla, 1752
Molten silver, engraved and embossed
83 x 38 x 9 cm
Col. Museo Franz Mayer

11. Arellano
San Luis Gonzaga enseñando a los niños de Roma [San Luis Gonzaga teaching the children of Rome]
Mexico, 1691
Oil on canvas
220 x 174 x 8 cm
Col. Museo Franz Mayer

12. Unknown author
Cushion
Pátzcuaro, Michoacán
First half of the 19th century
Lacquered wood with painted decoration
13.5 x 42.1 x 13.7 cm
Col. The Hispanic Society of America, NY

13. Unknown author
Large Oaxacan chest
Mexico, 17th century
Carved wood inlaid with dark wood and wrought iron adornments, engraved and fret-worked
50 x 58.5 x 34 cm
Col. Museo Franz Mayer

14. Unknown author
Large chest
Mexico, 17th century
Carved wood inlaid with shell and pale wood ornamental lines
58.5 x 111 x 53 cm
Col. Museo Franz Mayer

15. Unknown author
Small chest
Mexico, 17th century
Tecali stone with velvet and gilded wrought iron appliqués
10 x 13 x 10 cm
Col. Museo Franz Mayer

16. Unknown author
Wardrobe
Mexico, 18th century
White cedar wood inlaid with different woods and carved bone
293 x 138 x 70 cm
Col. Museo Franz Mayer

17. Unknown author
Wardrobe
Mexico, 18th century
Carved and lacquered wood
224 x 148 x 49 cm
Col. Museo Franz Mayer

18. Unknown author
Oaxacan chest
Oaxaca, 17th century
Sgraffited wood
54 x 40 x 29 cm
Col. Museo Franz Mayer

19. Unknown author
Oaxacan arquilla
Oaxaca, 17th century
Sgraffited sumac wood
32 x 43 x 23 cm
Col. Museo Franz Mayer

20. Unknown author
Asunción de la Virgen María [The Asumption of the Virgin Mary]
Mexico, 17th century
Enconchado (Shell inlay)
72 x 94 cm
Col. Museo Franz Mayer

21. Unknown author
Tray
Peribán, Michoacán
17th century
Lacquered wood inlaid with lacquer decoration
Col. The Hispanic Society of America, NY

22. Unknown author
Tray
Peribán, Michoacán
17th century
Lacquered wood inlaid with lacquer decoration
Col. The Hispanic Society of America, NY

23. Unknown author
Tray
Pátzcuaro, Michoacán
18th century
Lacquered wood with painted decoration
Col. The Hispanic Society of America, NY

24. Unknown author
Folding screen of the conquest
Mexico, 17th century
Oil on canvas
231 x 563 cm
Col. Museo Franz Mayer

25. Unknown author
Folding screen of the nations
Mexico, 18th century
Wooden frame with oil painting
220 x 408 cm
Col. Museo Franz Mayer

26. Unknown author
Lectern
Guanajuato, *ca.* 1760
Silver partially gilded, cast, forged, carved and embossed
46 x 36 x 36 cm
Col. Museo Franz Mayer

27. Unknown author
Bottle
Puebla or Mexico City, 17th century
Glazed ceramic
29 x 12 x 12 cm
Col. Museo Franz Mayer

28. Unknown author
Small boxes
Guadalajara, 17th century
Wood with tortoiseshell appliqués, decorated with silver studs
8 x 7 x 5 cm, 14 x 9 x 7 cm, 14 x 10 x 8 cm, 18 x 14 x 10 cm
Col. Museo Franz Mayer

29. Unknown author
Coconuts for drinking chocolate
Mexico, 17th century
Coconuts mounted on silver base
12 x 10 cm, 13 x 11 cm, 15 x 7 cm
Col. Museo Franz Mayer

30. Unknown author
Christ
17th century
Carved ivory, golden and polychromed
80 x 77 x 15 cm
Col. Museo Franz Mayer

31. Unknown author
Description of the village and lands of San Jacinto de las Milpas, jurisdiction of the Marquessate of Oaxaca
18th century
Oil on canvas
52 x 42 cm
Ricardo B. Salinas Pliego/Fomento Cultural
Col. Grupo Salinas

32. Unknown author
Drawing of the city of Durango, capital of Nueva Vizcaya
18th century
Sepia ink on paper
30 x 22 cm
Ricardo B. Salinas Pliego/Fomento Cultural
Col. Grupo Salinas

33. Unknown author
Writing desk
Puebla, 17th century
Wood marquetry inlaid with wood and sgraffited bone
63 x 71 x 36 cm
Col. Museo Franz Mayer

34. Unknown author
Writing desk
Lacquered wood inlaid with lacquer decoration
54 x 96.3 x 44.4 cm
Peribán, Michoacán
17th century
Col. The Hispanic Society of America, NY

35. Unknown author
Writing service
Mexico, 1823-1843
Silver in its color, embossed, engraved and lost wax cast
13 x 27 x 15 cm
Col. Museo Franz Mayer

36. Unknown author
Nun's shield with the Immaculate Conception and saints
Mexico, 18th century
Embroidered with silk, metallic threads and sequins; painted faces
17.5 cm in diameter
Col. The Hispanic Society of America, NY

37. Unknown author
Nun's shield with the Immaculate Conception and saints
Mexico, 19th century
Oil on copper plate
21 x 14.2 cm
Col. The Hispanic Society of America, NY

38. Unknown author
Silver frame mirror
Mexico, 18th century
Laminated silver, embossed and engraved with gilded appliqués
55 x 95 x 10 cm
Col. Museo Franz Mayer

39. Unknown author
Turkey
Tonalá, Jalisco
17th century
Black ceramic with mica
18.5 x 23.6 x 18.5 cm
Col. The Hispanic Society of America, NY

40. Unknown author
Jar
Mexico, 19th century
Glass with floral decoration in gold
19 x 14 x 11 cm
Col. Museo Franz Mayer

41. Unknown author
Spur set with Mexican star
Mexico, 18th century
Wrought iron
10 x 20 x 10 cm, 6 x 19 x 10 cm
Col. Museo Franz Mayer

42. Unknown author
La nobilissima y muy leal ciudad de los Ángeles (Puebla) [The most noble and loyal city of Los Angeles (Puebla)]
Ca. 1740-1750
Chalcography on paper
Ricardo B. Salinas Pliego/Fomento Cultural
Col. Grupo Salinas

43. Unknown author
Basin
Manises, Valencia, Spain, 18th century
Glazed ceramic with metallic luster decoration. Pink series
38 cm in diameter
Col. Museo Franz Mayer

44. Unknown author
Keys with animal motifs
Mexico City, 17th-18th centuries
Wrought iron engraved and fret-worked
50 x 3 cm
Col. Museo Franz Mayer

45. Unknown author
Keys with animal motifs
Mexico City, 17th-18th centuries
Wrought iron engraved and fret-worked
13 x 8 cm
Col. Museo Franz Mayer

46. Unknown author
Wastepaper basket
Pátzcuaro, Michoacán, 18th century
Lacquered pine wood with wrought iron appliqués
72 x 99 x 56.5 cm
Col. Museo Franz Mayer

47. Unknown author
Leather and pita fiber bag
Mexico, 17th-18th centuries
Strips of bamboo, leather embroidered with pita, wrought iron fittings, engraved and fret-worked
47 x 73 x 55 cm
Col. Museo Franz Mayer

48. Unknown author
Villages of San Martín Tuzamapan, San Juan Nonotla and surroundings. Puebla
18th century
Watercolor on paper
60 x 40 cm
Ricardo B. Salinas Pliego/Fomento Cultural
Col. Grupo Salinas

49. Unknown author
Two-handled bowl
Tonalá, Jalisco
Ca. 1675-1725
Polished ceramic with white slip, decorated with polychrome slips
36.8 x 37 cm
Col. The Hispanic Society of America, NY

50. Unknown author
Two-handled bowl with turkey
Tonalá, Jalisco, 17th century
Black ceramic with mica
14.8 x 7 cm
Col. The Hispanic Society of America, NY

51. Unknown author
Retrato de María Josefa Tobio y Estrada [Portrait of María Josefa Tobio y Estrada]
Mexico, 1788
Oil on canvas
96.5 x 72.5 cm
Col. Museo Franz Mayer

52. Unknown author
Wardrobe
Mexico, 18th century
Polychrome carved wood inlaid with wood and engraved bone
227 x 123 x 43 cm
Col. Museo Franz Mayer

53. Unknown author
Salver
Ca. 1600-1625
Glazed earthenware
Talavera de la Reina, Toledo
Col. The Hispanic Society of America, NY

54. Unknown author
San Francisco de Borja [Saint Francis Borgia]
Mexico, 18th century
Oil on canvas
125 x 65 cm
Col. Museo Franz Mayer

55. Unknown author
San Hipólito y las armas mexicanas [Saint Hippolytus and the Mexican coat of arms]
Mexico, 1764
Oil on canvas
167 x 120 cm
Col. Museo Franz Mayer

56. Unknown author
San Jerónimo [Saint Jerome]
Mexico, 19th century
Enconchado (shell inlay)
84 x 65 cm
Col. Museo Franz Mayer

57. Unknown author
Soup tureen
Alcora, Castellón de la Plana, Spain, 1749–1786
White glaze ceramic with polychrome decoration.
Rocaille series, second period
20 x 33 x 22 cm
Col. Museo Franz Mayer

58. Unknown author
Jar
China, 18th century
Porcelain with underglaze enamel
30 x 20 cm
Col. Museo Franz Mayer

59. Unknown author
Glass
Mexico, 19th century
Glass with golden motifs
15 x 12 cm in diameter
Col. Museo Franz Mayer

60. Unknown author
Virgin of Guadalupe
Mexico, 17th century
Enconchado (shell inlay) on wood
190 x 139 cm
Col. Museo Franz Mayer

61. Unknown author
Our Lady of the Rosary with Saint Dominic and Saint Catherine
Mexico, 18th century
Bas-relief carved in alabaster, *estofado* and polychrome
28 x 23 x 4 cm
Col. Museo Franz Mayer

62. Unknown author
Vísperas de las fiestas de la Expectación de Nuestra Señora [Eve of the feast of the Expectation of Our Lady]
Mexico, 1800
Leather-bound parchment
66 x 45 x 10 cm
Col. Museo Franz Mayer

63. Unknown author
Vase with handles
Tonalá, Jalisco
Ca. 1675-1699
Polished white-slipped ceramic decorated with slip and gold leaf; 18th century ormolu mounts
Col. The Hispanic Society of America, NY

64. Unknown author
Two-handled vase
Tonalá, Jalisco
Ca. 1675-1725
Polished white-slipped ceramic decorated with polychrome slip
Col. The Hispanic Society of America, NY

65. Unknown author
Glass
Tonalá, Jalisco
Ca. 1675-1725
Polished red-slipped ceramic
Col. The Hispanic Society of America, NY

66. Unknown author
Nun's shield with the image of the Virgin of Balvanera
20th century
Embroidered with silk and silver threads with frame
Col. Museo Franz Mayer

67. Unknow author
The battle of Zempoala
s.d.
Polychrome wood inlaid with shell
Col. Museo Franz Mayer

68. Unknown author
The battle of Cholula
s.d.
Polychrome wood inlaid with shell
Col. Museo Franz Mayer

69. Ávila
Retrato de Doña Sebastiana Inés Josefa de San Agustin, india cacique [Portrait of Doña Sebastiana Inés Josefa de San Agustín, cacique Indian]
Mexico, 1757
Oil on canvas
62 x 51 x 2 cm (without frame)
100 x 78 x 6 cm (with frame)
Col. Museo Franz Mayer

70. Baltasar de Medina
Vida, martyrio y beatificacion del proto-martyr del Japon san Felipe de Jesús [Life, martyrdom and beatification of the proto-martyr of Japan saint Philip of Jesus]
Mexico: Juan de Ribera, 1683
Col. The Hispanic Society of America, NY

71. Unknown author
Trunk
Choapan, Oaxaca, 18th century
Cedar wood inlaid with geometric shapes, sgraffited bone and tortoiseshell.
Wrought iron engraved keyhole
48 x 95 x 51 cm
Col. Museo Franz Mayer

72. Bernal Díaz del Castillo
Historia verdadera de la conquista de la Nueva España [The True History of the Conquest of New Spain]
Madrid: Imprenta del Reyno, 1632
Col. The Hispanic Society of America, NY

73. *Bosquejo ligerísimo de la revolución de Megico desde el grito de Iguala hasta la proclamación imperial de Iturbide* [Very slight sketch of the revolution of Mexico since the Grito in Iguala to the imperial proclamation of Iturbide]
1822
Philadelphia, Teracrouef and Naroajeb Print
Ricardo B. Salinas Pliego/Fomento Cultural
Col. Grupo Salinas

74. Br. J. Miguel Díaz Sáenz
Plan of the jurisdiction of the parish of Orizaba
1766
Oil on parchment
Ricardo B. Salinas Pliego/Fomento Cultural
Col. Grupo Salinas

75. Br. José Mendoza
Plan of the city of Zacatecas
1609
Oil and watercolor on parchment
Ricardo B. Salinas Pliego/Fomento Cultural
Col. Grupo Salinas

76. Carlos de Sigüenza y Góngora
Oriental planeta evangelico epopeya sacro-panegyrica al apostol grande de las Indias s. Francisco Xavier, diolo a la estampa Gabriel Lopez de Sigüenza [Eastern evangelical world. Sacred-panegyric epic devoted to the grand apostle of Indies saint Francis Xavier, given to the press by Gabriel López de Sigüenza]
Mexico: María de Benavides, 1700
Col. The Hispanic Society of America, NY

77. Carlos de Sigüenza y Góngora
Parayso occidental plantado y cultivado en el convento de Jesus Maria de Mexico [Western Paradise planted and cultivated in the convent of Jesus Maria de Mexico]
Mexico, Juan de Ribera, 1684
Col. The Hispanic Society of America, NY

78. Carlos de Sigüenza y Góngora
Libra astronomica y philosophica contra los cometas opuso el r.p. Eusebio Francisco Kino, sacala a la luz Sebastian de Guzman y Cordova [Astronomical and philosophical scales against the comets opposed by reverend father Eusebio Francsco Kino, brought to light by Sebastián de Guzmán y Córdova]
Mexico, Herederos de la Viuda de Bernardo Calderón, 1690
Col. The Hispanic Society of America, NY

79. Carlos de Sigüenza y Góngora
Infortunios que Alonso Ramirez padecio assi en poder de ingleses piratas que lo apresaron en las Islas Philipinas como navegando por si solo y sin derrota hasta varar en la costa de Yucatán [Misfortunes suffered by Alonso Ramírez both held by English pirates who seized him in the Philippine Islands as sailing alone and without course until beaching on the coast of Yucatan]
Mexico: Herederos de la Viuda de Bernardo Calderón, 1690
Col. The Hispanic Society of America, NY

80. Carlos de Sigüenza y Góngora
Theatro de virtudes politicas [Theatre of political virtues]
Mexico: Viuda de Bernardo Calderón, 1680
Col. The Hispanic Society of America, NY

81. Carlos de Sigüenza y Góngora
Glorias de Querétaro en la nueva congregacion eclesiastica de Maria de Guadalupe [Glories of Querétaro in the new ecclesiastical congregation of Maria de Guadalupe]
Mexico: Viuda de Bernardo Calderón, 1680
Col. The Hispanic Society of America, NY

82. Cayetano Cabrera y Quintero
Escudo de armas de Mexico: Celestial proteccion de esta nobilissima ciudad, de la Nueva-España y de casi todo el Nuevo Mundo, María Santissima, en su portentosa imagen del mexicano Guadalupe [Coat of arms of Mexico: Celestial protection of this most noble city, the New Spain and most of the New World, Most Holy Mary, in her prodigious image of Mexican Guadalupe]
Mexico, Viuda de D. José Bernardo de Hogal, 1746
Col. The Hispanic Society of America, NY

83. Mexico City
Representacion humilde que hace la... ciudad de Mexico a favor de sus Naturales a su amado Soberano el Sr. Don Carlos III [Humble representation made by... Mexico City in favor of its natives to their beloved Sovereign Charles III]
Mexico, May 1773
Col. The Hispanic Society of America, NY

84. *Derrotero general del Mar del Sur. Con las distancias de legs. y grads. Que ay de unas ptes. aotras. Sacado de los mas experimentados pilotos* [General route map of the South Sea with the distances in leagues and grades that are from one part to another, derived from the most experienced pilots]
Panama, 1684
Col. The Hispanic Society of America

85. Diego de Ribera
Defectuoso epilogo diminuto compendio de las heroycas obras que ilustran esta ciudad de Mexico [Defective epilogue and minute compendium of the heroic works that illustrate this city of Mexico]
Mexico: Viuda de Bernardo Calderón, 1676
Col. The Hispanic Society of America, NY

86. Diego de San Francisco
Relacion verdadera y breve de la persecucion y martirios que padecieron en Iapon desde 1613 hasta 1624 [True and brief account of the persecution and martyrdom they endured in Japan from 1613 to 1624]
Manila, Tomás Pimpín, 1625
Col. The Hispanic Society of America, NY

87. Diego López
Del comercio de la ciudad de México [About trade in Mexico City]
Mexico, May 6, 1587
Col. The Hispanic Society of America, NY

88. Dionisio de Ribera Florez
Relacion historiada de las exeqvias fvnerales de la magestad el Rey D. Philippo II [Historical account of the funeral obsequies of His Majesty King Philip II]
Mexico, Pedro Balli, 1600
Col. The Hispanic Society of America, NY

89. *Ejecutoria de hidalguía otorgada a Alonso de Marquina* [Patent of nobility granted to Alonso de Marquina]
1574
Tempera and gold on parchment
35 x 24 x 2 cm
Col. Museo Franz Mayer

90. Enrico Martínez
Repertorio de los tiempos y historia natural desta Nueva España [Index of times and natural history of this New Spain]
Mexico, Enrique Martínez, 1606
Col. The Hispanic Society of America, NY

91. Eusebio Francisco Kino
Paso por tierra a la California [Land passage to California]
Mexico, *ca.* 1701
Manuscript on paper
Col. The Hispanic Society of America, NY

92. Fernando de Cepeda and Fernando Alfonso Carrillo
Relacion universal legitima y verdadera del sitio en que esta fundada la ciudad de Mexico [Legitimate and true universal account of the site where the city of Mexico was founded]
Mexico, Francisco Salvago, 1637
Col. The Hispanic Society of America, NY

93. Francisco Álvarez Barreiro
Plano corographico é hydrographico de las provincias de el Nuevo Mexico, Sonora, Ostimuri, Sinaloa, Nueba Vizcaya, Nayarit, Nuevo Reyno de Leon, Nueba Extremadura o Coaguila, y la de el Nuevo Pro. de Phipinas, Provincia de los thesas, todas de el numero de las de la Nueva Espana... [Chorographic and hydrographic map of the provinces of New Mexico, Sonora, Ostimuri, Sinaloa, New Vizcaya, New Kingdom of Leon, New Extremadura or Coahuila, and of the new province of Philippines or Province of the Texas, all belonging to New Spain...]
Mexico, 1728
Col. The Hispanic Society of America, NY

94. Francisco de Celís
Diario derrotero de la entrada que hizo á la baia del Espiritu Santo, y provincia de los Texas, el General Don Martin de Alarcon... que comiença oy dia nueve de Abril, de el año de 1718... [Journal of the entry route into the bay of Espíritu Santo, and province of the Texas, by General Don Martín de Alarcón... starting today, April 9, in the year 1718...]
Mexico: Herederos de Juan Joseph Guillena Carrascoso, 1721
Col. The Hispanic Society of America, NY

95. Francisco de Florencia
Menologio de los varones más señalados en perfección religiosa de la Provincia de la Compañía de Jesús de Nueva España [Menology of the most perfectly religious men of the Province of the Society of Jesus in New Spain]
Mexico, 1747
Col. The Hispanic Society of America, NY

96. Francisco de Florencia
La milagrosa invencion de un tesoro escondido en un campo que hallo un cacique [The miraculous invention of a treasure hidden in a field that a cacique found]
Mexico, María de Benavides, 1685
Col. The Hispanic Society of America, NY

97. Francisco de Seixas y Lovera
Piratas y contrabandistas de ambas Indias, y estado presente de ellas. Dirixido al Exmo. Sr. Conde de Galve Virrey y Cappn Genl. Del Reyno de la Nueva España Por D. Francisco de Seyxas y Lovera Cappn de Mar y Guerra en la Armada Rl. Del Mar Occeano por su Magd. Y assi mesmo Alcalde Mayor de la villa de Tacuba y su jurisdiccion & Tacaba [Pirates and smugglers of both Indies, and their actual state. Addressed to His Excellency the Conde de Galve, Viceroy and General Captain of the Kingdom of New Spain, by Don Francisco de Seyxas and Lovera, Captain and Commander in the Royal Navy of the Ocean Sea for His Majesty and also mayor of the town of Tacuba and its jurisdiction]
1693
Col. The Hispanic Society of America, NY

98. Francisco del Castillo
Our Lady of the Rosary
Mexico, 18th century
Oil on canvas
69 x 58 x 4.5 cm
Col. Museo Franz Mayer

99. Francisco Hernández
La naturaleza y virtudes de las plantas y animales que estan receuidos en el uso de medicina en la Nueva España [The nature and virtues of plants and animals that are accepted in the use of medicine in New Spain], books 1-4.
Mexico, Viuda de Diego López Dávalos, 1615
Col. The Hispanic Society of America, NY

100. Francisco López de Gómara
Historia general de las Indias [con] *La conquista de México* [General history of Indies (and) The conquest of Mexico], 1st and 2nd parts
Medina del Campo, Guillermo de Millis, 1553
Col. The Hispanic Society of America, NY

101. Francisco Xavier Clavijero
Storia antica del Messico, 4 vols.
Cesena: Gregorio Biasini, 1780-1781
Col. The Hispanic Society of America, NY

102. Gaspar de Villagrá
Historia de la Nueva Mexico [History of New Mexico]
Alcalá, Luis Martínez Grande, 1610
Col. The Hispanic Society of America, NY

103. Gastón de Peralta, marqués de Falces
Carta a Felipe II [Letter to Philip II]
1568
Manuscript on paper
Col. The Hispanic Society of America, NY

104. *Gazeta de México* [Mexico's gazette]
Mexico, José Bernardo de Hogal, 1730
Col. The Hispanic Society of America, NY

105. Gregorius Bruin and Franz Hohenberg
Civitates Orbis Terrarum
Coloniae Agrippinae [Cologne], Pedro Brachel, 1612
Col. The Hispanic Society of America, NY

106. Ignacio Castera and Anselmo López (painted)
Plano Ignográfico de la Nobilissima Ciudad de Mexico, hecho en el año de 1776 por D. Ignacio Castera, Mro. De Architectura y Agrimensor de tierras, aguas y minas por S.M. y aumentado en el de 1778 [Trace map of the noblest city of Mexico, made in the year 1776 by Don Ignacio Castera, Master of Architecture and Surveyor of land, water and mines for His Majesty, and increased in 1778]
Mexico, 1778
Oil on canvas
Col. The Hispanic Society of America, NY

107. Ignacio López Aguado
Vista de la Plaza y Catedral de Mejico Como Estaba al Año de 1796 / Copiada de Estampa por Ignacio Lopez Aguado Mejico Octubre 7 de 1810 [View of the Plaza and the Cathedral of Mexico as of the Year 1796 / Copied from a print by Ignacio López Aguado, Mexico City, October 7, 1810]
Mexico, 1810
Perforated paper
Col. The Hispanic Society of America, NY

108. Isidoro Félix de Espinosa (1679-1755)
Chronica de la provincia por antonomesia apostólica de los apostoles S. Pedro i S. Pablo de Michoacán... [Chronicle of the par excellence apostolic province of the apostles San Pedro y San Pablo de Michoacán...]
Mexico, 18th century
Col. The Hispanic Society of America, NY

109. Isidro de Sariñana y Cuenca
Llanto de Occidente en las exequias del rey Felipe IIII [Crying of the West at the funeral of King Philip IV]
Mexico, Viuda de Bernardo Calderón, 1666
Col. The Hispanic Society of America, NY

110. J. B. Poirson
Mapa de Mejico y de los paises limitrofes situados al norte y al este, trazado conforme al gran mapa de la Nueva España del señor A. de Humboldt [Map of Mexico and adjacent countries to the north and east, design according to the large map of New Spain by Mr. A. von Humboldt]
London, 1826
Ricardo B. Salinas Pliego/Fomento Cultural
Col. Grupo Salinas

111. Joanni Nepom
Xalapa, pueblo mixto de españoles e indios [Xalapa, mixed village of Spaniards and Indians]
1769
Ink and watercolor on paper
Ricardo B. Salinas Pliego/Fomento Cultural
Col. Grupo Salinas

112. Joaquín Antonio Basarás
Origen, costumbres y estado presente de mexicanos y philipinos (vol. II). *Diseños en los cuales, puntual mente se demuestran indios de los commarcaneos de Mexico* [Origin, customs and present state of Mexicans and Filipinos (vol. II). Designs that punctually show the Indians of Mexico's regions]
Mexico, 1763
Col. The Hispanic Society of America, NY

113. Joaquín Fabre
Plano general de la ciudad de México, levantado por el Teniente Coronel de Dragones don Diego García Conde en el año de 1793 y grabado en 1807, de orden de la misma Nobilissima Ciudad [General map of Mexico City, made by Lieutenant Colonel of Dragoons Don Diego García Conde in the year 1793 and engraved in 1807, depicting the order of the same noblest City]
Mexico, 1807
Print on paper
Ricardo B. Salinas Pliego/Fomento Cultural
Col. Grupo Salinas

114. José Antonio Alzate y Ramírez
Gazeta de literatura de México
[Mexico's literature gazette]
Mexico: Felipe de Zúñiga y Ontiveros, 1790–1795
Col. The Hispanic Society of America, NY

115. José de los Santos
Relacion de estado de la Provincia de S. Hipolito Martir del órden de Predicadores en el Obispado de Antequera del Valle de Oaxaca de la educacion y crianza de los Indios naturales y predicacion del Evangelio [Account of the state of the Province of San Hipólito Mártir of the Order of Preachers in the Diocese of Antequera, Oaxaca Valley, of the education and upbringing of native Indians and preaching of the Gospel]
Oaxaca, 1753
Col. The Hispanic Society of America, NY

116. José de Páez (Mexico, 1720-after 1790)
La Virgen de la Anunciación y santos
[Annunciation and saints]
Mexico
18th century
Oil on copper plate
Signed
Col. The Hispanic Society of America, NY

117. José Longinus Martínez
Extracto de las noticias y observaciones... [Excerpt from the news and comments...]
Ca. 1803
Col. The Hispanic Society of America, NY

118. José Sáenz de Escobar
Ordenanzas y modo de medir tierras, y aguas, vista de ojos, fechas por el Mro. D. Joseph Saenz de Escobar, abogado de la Rl Audiencia de esta ciudad de México [Ordinances and how to measure land and water, eyesight and dates by master Don Joseph Saenz de Escobar, an attorney for the Real Audiencia in this city of Mexico]
Mexico, 18th century
Col. The Hispanic Society of America, NY

119. José Sixto Verduzco
City of Morelia
1813
Sepia ink on paper
Ricardo B. Salinas Pliego/Fomento Cultural
Col. Grupo Salinas

120. José Sixto Verduzco
Plan of the city of Zamora, Michoacán
1813
Ink on paper
Ricardo B. Salinas Pliego/Fomento Cultural
Col. Grupo Salinas

121. José Sixto Verduzco
Sketch of the city of Celaya (unfinished)
1813
Ink on paper
Ricardo B. Salinas Pliego/Fomento Cultural
Col. Grupo Salinas

122. José Sixto Verduzco
Croquis de una región no identificada que parece ser un itinerario de campaña, en el cual se indican ríos, lagunas y caminos [Sketch of an unidentified region, which appears to be a campaign schedule and lists rivers, lakes and roads]
1813
Ink on paper
Ricardo B. Salinas Pliego/Fomento Cultural
Col. Grupo Salinas

123. Joseph Nava
Mapa y tabla geográfica de lenguas comunes que ai de unos a otros lugares, y ciudades principales de la América Septentrional [Map and geographical table of common languages in some to other places, and major cities of North America]
Puebla, 1755
Print on paper
Ricardo B. Salinas Pliego/Fomento Cultural
Col. Grupo Salinas

124. Juan de Bonilla Godínez
Arco triumphal disceno politico consagrado a la feliz entrada del señor d. Joseph Sarmiento de Valladares [Triumphal arch: Political design dedicated to the successful entry of Don Joseph Sarmiento de Valladares]
Puebla, Herederos de Juan de Villarreal, 1697
Col. The Hispanic Society of America, NY

125. Juan de Martos y Aguilar
Historia de los reyes de la Nueba España y conquista de Hernán Cortés [History of the Kings of New Spain and the conquest by Hernán Cortés]
Mexico, 18th century
Col. The Hispanic Society of America, NY

126. Juan de Palafox y Mendoza
Varon de desseos en que se declaran las tres vias de la vida espiritual... [Man of desire who states the three ways of spiritual life...]
Mexico, Francisco Robledo, 1642
Col. The Hispanic Society of America, NY

127. Juan Francisco de la Bodega y Cuadra
Carta reducida de las costas y mares septentrionales de Californias [Reduced chart of the coasts and northern seas of both Californias]
Port of San Blas, February 22, 1779
Col. The Hispanic Society of America, NY

128. Juan José de Eguiara y Eguren
Bibliotheca Mexicana, Mexici, Exnovâ Typographiâ in Aedibus Authoris editioni ejusdem Bibliothecae destinatâ
Mexico, 1755
Col. The Hispanic Society of America, NY

129. Juan Manuel Gyon
Descripción geográfica al estado y obispado de Oaxaca apoyado en planos antiguos [Geographical description of the State and Bishopric of Oaxaca relied on old maps]
1822
Print on paper
Ricardo B. Salinas Pliego/Fomento Cultural
Col. Grupo Salinas

130. Juan Rodríguez Juárez
Retrato del Virrey Alencastre Noroña y Silva, Duque de Linares [Portrait of the Viceroy Alencastre Noroña y Silva, Duque de Linares]
Mexico, *ca.* 1723
Oil on canvas
200 x 106 x 5 cm
Col. Museo Franz Mayer

131. Juan Rodríguez Juárez (attributed) (Mexico City, 1675–1728)
De Mestizo y de India produce Coyote [Crossbreed and Indian produces Coyote]
Oil on canvas
103.8 x 146.4 cm
Col. The Hispanic Society of America, NY

132. Juana Inés de la Cruz
Carta athenagorica que imprime Phylotea de la Cruz [Athenianwise letter by Phylotea de la Cruz]
Puebla: Diego Fernández de León, 1690
Col. The Hispanic Society of America, NY

133. Juana Inés de la Cruz
Invndacion castalida de la vnica poetisa [Castalian flooding of the only poetess...]
Madrid, Juan García Infanzón, 1689
Col. The Hispanic Society of America, NY

134. Juana Inés de la Cruz
Avto sacramental del Divino Narciso, por alegorias [Sacramental act of the Divine Narcissus, through allegories]
Mexico, Viuda de Bernardo Calderón, 1690
Col. The Hispanic Society of America, NY

135. Juana Inés de la Cruz
Villancicos que se cantaron en la santa iglesia catedral de México, á los maytines del gloriosissimo principe de la iglesia, el señor, San Pedro [Carols that were sung at the holy cathedral church of Mexico, at the matins of the most glorious prince of the church, Saint Peter]
Mexico, Viuda de Bernardo Calderón, 1671
Col. The Hispanic Society of America, NY

136. Juana Inés de la Cruz
Villancicos que se cantaron en la metropolitana de Mexico en honor de Maria, en su assumpcion triumphante [Carols that were sung at the Metropolitan Cathedral in Mexico in honor of Mary, in her triumphant Assumption]
Mexico: Herederos de la viuda de Bernardo Calderón, 1685
Col. The Hispanic Society of America, NY

137. Legajos de pleitos civiles, titulos... pertenecientes a la familia de Mendoza [Documents of civil actions, titles... belonging to the family of Mendoza]
Col. The Hispanic Society of America, NY

138. Lorenzo Boturini Benaducci
Idea de una general historia nueva de la septentrional América fundada sobre material copioso de figuras, caracteres y geroglíphicos, cantares y manuscriptos de autores indios nuevamente descubierto. Dedicala al Rey Nuestro Señor en su real Supremo Consejo de Indias. El caballero Lorenzo Botturini Benaducci, señor de la Torre y de Hono [Idea of a general new history of Northern America based on newly discovered material of copious figures, characters and hieroglyphs, songs and manuscripts by Indian authors. dedicated to the King Our Lord, en his Supreme Council of the Indies, by the gentleman Lorenzo Botturini Benaducci, señor de la Torre y de Hono]
Madrid, 1745
Col. The Hispanic Society of America, NY

139. Luis Becerra Tanco
Felicidad de México en el principio y milagroso origen que tuvo el santuario de la virgen María de Guadalupe [Happiness of Mexico in the foremost and miraculous origin of the shrine of Virgin Mary of Guadalupe]
Sevilla, Tomás López de Haro, 1685
Col. The Hispanic Society of America, NY

140. Manuel Serna
Nun's shield with the Immaculate Conception and saints
Mexico, 18th century
Oil on copper plate
Signed
Col. The Hispanic Society of America, NY

141. Miguel Cabrera
Archangel Raphael
Mexico, 1768
Oil on canvas
98 x 78 x 5 cm
Col. Museo Franz Mayer

142. Miguel de Herrera
Portrait of a lady
Mexico, 1782
Oil on canvas
125 x 101 x 9 cm
Col. Museo Franz Mayer

143. Miguel de Zendejas y José Nava
Mapa de la Biblioteca del Seminario Palafoxiana [Map of the Palafox Seminary Library]
Puebla, 1773
Col. The Hispanic Society of America, NY

144. Hieronymite nuns
Ordo ad induendum novitiam monialem
Mexico, *ca.* 1650
Col. The Hispanic Society of America, NY

145. Pedro Gendrón
La América dispuesta según el sistema de M. Hasius (Dedicado al Exmo. Sr. Conde de Povolide, Gentil Hombre de Cámara del Infante Don Antonio de Portugal) [America displayed according to the system of Hasius (Dedicated to His Excellency Conde de Povolide, gentleman of the bedchamber of Infante Don Antonio de Portugal)
1754
Print on paper
Ricardo B. Salinas Pliego/Fomento Cultural
Col. Grupo Salinas

146. Map of Mexico City from the Letter of Account by Cortés with plain brown frame
Inscription: POVTRAICT ET ICRIPTION DE LA GRAN CITÉ DE TEMIFTAN
Ricardo B. Salinas Pliego/Fomento Cultural
Col. Grupo Salinas

147. *Real Fábrica de Loza del Alcora*
Mancerina
Ca. 1735-1760
Alcora, Castellón de la Plana, Spain
Glazed earthen ware
Col. The Hispanic Society of America, NY

148. *Regla dada por n.p.s. Avgvstin a sus monjas. Constituciones que han de guardar las religiosas augustinas recoletas de Santa Monica de la ciudad de Puebla* [Rule given by Our Father Saint Augustine to his nuns. Constitutions to be followed by the Recollect Augustines Nuns of Santa Monica in the city of Puebla]
Puebla, Diego Fernández de León, 1691
Col. The Hispanic Society of America, NY

149. *Relacion del festejo que á los Exmos. Sres. D. Auguston de Aumada Villalon y su Esposa D. Luisa Maria del Rosario y Vera: Marqueses de las Amarillas, Vireyes de esta Nueva España & se les hizo en la tarde que vicitaron a las Señoras Religiosas del máximo Dr. P. S. Geronimo de Mexico dia 19 de Agosto de 1756* [Account of the celebration for their Excellencies D. Agustín de Ahumada Villalón and his wife D. Luisa María del Rosario y Vera, Marquises de las Amarillas, Viceroys of this New Spain, done in the afternoon they visited the Religious Ladies of the maximum Doctor of the Church Father Saint Jerome of Mexico, August 19, 1756]
Mexico, 1756
Col. The Hispanic Society of America, NY

150. Salvador Meléndez Bruna
Diario del viage al Puerto del Realexo para reconocer y levantar planos del Troso de Costa comprehendido entre el Puerto de Acapulco y el Surgidero de Sonsonante. Amas las exploracion del Golfo de Conchagua con el Bergantin de S.N. el Activo. Ano de 1794 [Journal of the voyage to the Port of Realexo for recognizing and mapping the section of coast comprehended between the port of Acapulco and the anchorage of Sonsonate. Besides the exploration of the Gulf of Conchagua with the brigantine of H.M el Activo. Year of 1794]
Mexico, May 3, 1795
Col. The Hispanic Society of America, NY

151. Salvador Rodríguez de la Fuente
Descripción succinta de la fundacion de la venerable union y congregacion eclesiástica de clérigos presbíteros del Oratorio de N.P. S. Phelippe Neri, de esta ciudad de México y breve relacion de las solmenes honras que celebró en obsequio y memoria de su amantísimo padre e insigne protector, el Ill.mo y r. mo Sr. D. Francisco de Aguiar Seixas y Ulloa, arzobispo de esta ciudad y arzobispado de México, del consejo de su Mag. etc... [Brief description of the foundation of the venerable ecclesiastical union and congregation of clergy priests of the Oratory of Our Father Saint Felipe Neri, in this city of Mexico, and brief account of the solemn funeral rites held in memory of his most loving father and distinguished protector, the illustrious and Reverend Don Francisco de Aguiar Seixas y Ulloa, archbishop of this city and archbishopric of Mexico, of the council of His Majesty, etc...]
Mexico, 1698
Col. The Hispanic Society of America, NY

152. *Vevidas de Nueva España. Explicación del modo de veneficiar cada u[na] de las diversas bevidas que se usan en el Reyno de la Nueva España* [Beverages of New Spain. Explanation of how to benefit each of the various beverages that are used in the Kingdom of New Spain]
Mexico, 18th century
Col. The Hispanic Society of America, NY

Exhibition Credits

Mercedes García Ocejo
Original Concept

Miguel Fernández Félix
Advisor

Salvador Rueda Smithers
Mitchell A. Codding
Curators

Sara Gabriela Baz
Curatorial Liaison and Operative Coordination

Ricardo Pérez Álvarez
Collection

Nina Shor Fastag
Hot Pixel
Luis Lledías
Interpretation Program

Juan Manuel Garibay
Fernando Castro
Museography

Gustavo García
Quadrante Plástico
Design

Emma Hernández Tena
Cultural Management Support

Flor Gutiérrez Flores
Lorena Zárate
Comunication Support

FOMENTO CULTURAL
GRUPO SALINAS

Ricardo B. Salinas Pliego
President and Founder
Grupo Salinas

Mercedes García Ocejo
Executive Director
Fomento Cultural Grupo Salinas

Emma Hernández Tena
Proyects Management

Flor Gutiérrez Flores
Difusion

Rosa Aurora Pérez Alemán
Susana Rodríguez Ramírez
Assistants of the Direction

Jorge Nikaido Bernal
José Luis Anaya Ávila
Office of the Presidency of Grupo Salinas

Alejandro González Galván
Ismael Tovar Ferreira
Administration Office of the Presidency of Grupo Salinas

Edith Salgado Ocampo
David Ramírez Pérez
Guadalupe Castillo Barbosa
Administration Support the Presidency of Grupo Salinas

HISPANIC SOCIETY
OF AMERICA, NY

Mitchell A. Codding
Executive Director

Margaret Connors McQuade
Subdirector

John O'Neill
Manuscript Librarian and Rare Books

Vanessa Pintado
Librarian Assistant of Manuscripts and Rare Books

Monica Katz
Restorer

Daniel Silva
Works Management

MUSEO FRANZ MAYER

Héctor Rivero Borrell M.
General Director

Ricardo Pérez Álvarez
Collection and Restoration Director

Lorena Zárate
Comunication Director

Victor Calafell
Silvia Sentíes
Restoration

Agustín García Real
Collection Control

Juan Bautista Castro
Efigenia Castañeda Ramírez
Andrés Domínguez Santiago
Cristian Raúl González Balderas
Ángel Rodolfo Lastra Huerta
Technical Production

The Criollo in the Mirror. Celebration and Identity, 1521-1821,
was printed in January 2011—when it is celebrated the 330 anniversary
of the *Philosophical manifest against comets* by Carlos de Sigüenza y Góngora,
who tried to fight against the end of the world superstition,
in the New Spain—in Asia Printing Co., Seoul, Korea.
The print run was 1,000 copies.